D1173287

The Great Instrumental Works

Unlocking the Masters Series, No. 7

The Great
Instrumental Works

M. Owen Lee

AMADEUS
PRESS

Copyright © 2005 by M. Owen Lee

Published in 2005 by

Amadeus Press, LLC
512 Newark Pompton Turnpike
Pompton Plains, New Jersey 07444, USA

For sales, please contact

NORTH AMERICA

AMADEUS PRESS, LLC
c/o Hal Leonard Corp.
7777 West Bluemound Road
Milwaukee, Wisconsin 53213, USA
Phone: 800-637-2852
Fax: 414-774-3259

E-mail: orders@amadeuspress.com
Website: www.amadeuspress.com

UNITED KINGDOM AND EUROPE

ROUNDHOUSE PUBLISHING LTD.
Millstone, Limers Lane
Northam, North Devon EX39 2RG, UK
Phone: 01237-474474
Fax: 01237-474774
E-mail: roundhouse.group@ukgateway.net

Printed in the United States of America

Library of Congress Cataloging-in-Publication Data is available upon request.

for

William A. Dresden

Contents

Preface   xi

Instrumental Music   1
   Instruments   1
   Keys   5
   Forms   7
   The Symphony   12
   The Concerto   18
   Chamber Music   25

Italians   31
   Antonio Vivaldi (1678–1741)   31
   Domenico Scarlatti (1685–1757)   35

The Germanic Canon   39
   Johann Sebastian Bach (1685–1750)   39
   George Frideric Handel (1685–1759) 44
   Franz Joseph Haydn (1732–1809)   49
   Wolfgang Amadeus Mozart (1756–1791) 53
   Ludwig Van Beethoven (1770–1827)   67
   Franz Schubert (1797–1828)   84
   Robert Schumann (1810–1856)   95
   Johannes Brahms (1833–1897)   103

More Germans   115
   Carl Maria von Weber (1786–1826)   115
   Felix Mendelssohn (1809–1847)   117

Parisians   121
    Hector Berlioz (1803–1869)   121
    Franz Liszt (1811–1886)   125
    Frédéric Chopin (1810–1849)   130

Masters of Opera   135
    Giuseppe Verdi (1813–1901)   135
    Richard Wagner (1813–1883)   137

Slavs   141
    Alexander Borodin (1833–1887)   141
    Modest Mussorgsky (1839–1881)   144
    Nicolai Rimsky-Korsakov (1844–1908)   147
    Peter Ilyich Tchaikovsky (1840–1893)   150
    Bed ich Smetana (1824–1884)   155
    Antonín Dvo ák (1841–1904)   157

Late Romantics   163
    César Franck (1822–1890)   163
    Edvard Grieg (1843–1907)   166
    Max Bruch (1838–1920)   168
    Anton Bruckner (1824–1896)   169
    Gustav Mahler (1860–1911)   173

More Parisians   177
    Camille Saint-Saëns (1835–1921)   177
    Claude Achille Debussy (1862–1918)   181
    Maurice Ravel (1875–1937)   186

The Twentieth Century   189
    Leoš Janá ek (1854–1928)   189
    Richard Strauss (1864–1949)   193
    Jean Sibelius (1865–1957)   197
    Sergei Rachmaninoff (1873–1943)   200
    Igor Stravinsky (1882–1971)   203

Sergei Prokofiev (1891–1953)   208

Dmitri Shostakovich (1906–1975)   216

Béla Bartók (1881–1945)   220

Arnold Schoenberg (1874–1951)   223

Alban Berg (1885–1935)   227

Ernest Bloch (1880–1959)   230

Edward Elgar (1857–1934)   232

Ralph Vaughan Williams (1872–1958)   237

Gustav Holst (1874–1934)   238

Benjamin Britten (1913–1976)   240

George Gershwin (1898–1937)   242

Samuel Barber (1910–1981)   244

Olivier Messiaen (1908–1992)   246

Arvo Pärt (1935–)   251

Glossary   255

CD Track Listing   265

Preface

The redoubtable twentieth-century music critic B. H. Haggin once wrote a book, and a very good one, called *Music for the Man Who Enjoys Hamlet*. The volume you have in your hand is a book on music for the man, or woman, who enjoys *Hamlet* or Handel, Hammerstein or Hitchcock, and wants to enjoy as well—and to find out what is going on in—the symphonies of Schubert and Shostakovich.

It is also, perhaps paradoxically, a book on instrumental music written by someone best known for his books and broadcasts on vocal music. Opera—the enduring works of Mozart, Verdi, and Wagner—and "the great American songbook"—the perennial melodies of Kern, Porter, and Rodgers—have been a great part of my life, and writing about them has been a joy. But I have often had occasion to notice that many fans of popular song, of jazz, and of the several varieties of rock regard the music of the concert hall as impenetrable and forbidding. And that operagoers familiar with all twenty-eight of the operas of Verdi may have no idea that he ever wrote a string quartet. To some music lovers, the very idea of listening to something as austere, undramatic, and off-putting as a string quartet, or to something as senseless as an overture without an opera or a Broadway musical to follow, is anomalous. Or worse.

I hope in this book to convince those people, and lovers of literature and the lively arts as well, that what is usually called "classical music" can provide them in abundance with the depth and delight they find in their other enthusiasms. I hope that I can assure those who love popular song—including the twenty-first-century varieties—that "classical music" also sings. I hope that I can persuade operagoers that listening to the strictly instrumental works of their favorite composers will enrich them, not only with hours on hours of great music, but with a new understanding of the scores they already know from their evenings at the opera house.

During the twenty-three years of my appearances as quiz panelist and, occasionally, quizmaster during the intermissions of the Saturday afternoon radio broadcasts from the Metropolitan Opera, I limited most of my listening to opera, filling my head with its facts and fictions, plots and peripheries, learning and lore. Through those years I heard well over a thousand different operas—close to thirteen hundred if such quasi-operatic works as *Die Fledermaus* and *Carmina Burana* can be counted. (Leporello-like, I kept a catalogue.) When at last I called it quits on the quiz and opted exclusively for intermission commentaries on the Met broadcasts, I turned my attention, after too long a period when the field lay fallow, to strictly instrumental works. For the first time in decades I actually settled down to hear again, with the concentration they deserved, the symphonies of Haydn, the string quartets of Beethoven, the piano sonatas of Schubert, the orchestral pieces of Debussy and Ravel. It was an exhilarating experience, like being in college again, meeting anew the great musical works of the Western tradition that had excited me in my teens and twenties. That set me to writing this book.

It is a book in which there are no musical examples. Some music lovers can read music. Many more cannot. So instead of quoting from scores I have fallen back, to some extent, on the "first-theme second-theme" analysis, replete with adjectives, that is common in other books of this kind. I will be the first to admit that this is an inadequate and potentially exasperating approach, but I have tried to avoid its pitfalls and to keep the discussions clear, engaging, and non-technical.

There are, in the main, two ways that one can come to enjoy classical music. One is to analyze a few individual works in detail. The other is simply to listen to as many works as possible until the general idea behind them—the structures and the various other means the composer has of conveying his personal feelings—becomes clear. I would suggest that if you are relatively new to instrumental music you might begin with the first chapter of this book, reading with some care, listening, via the provided CD recordings, to the three works—one each by Beethoven, Mozart, and Schubert—discussed in the chapter, and using the glossary at the back of the book for terms that may be unfamiliar to you. Then, fortified with some notion of classical form, you might select a composer from the subsequent chapters to explore in detail. The composers are discussed more or less in chronological order, and grouped according to the various traditions in which they wrote, so that your reading and listening may give you some sense of how classical music has developed over the past three centuries. Pieces by several of these composers are included on the second CD accompanying this book. I have also suggested, for each work discussed at some length, the single recorded performance that, for me, stands out among the many currently available.

I make no apology for what, in the pages that follow, contemporary deconstructionists will call my "hegemonic" attitudes—grouping a few chosen composers into a canon and suggesting that some works are intrinsically more important than others. The readers I am writing for are, I trust, not afraid of canons, quick to choose favorites, and not necessarily convinced that dead white European males bear the guilt for all the evils in the world.

I have not discussed such early figures as Palestrina, Gesualdo, Monteverdi, Purcell, Rameau, Alessandro Scarlatti, and Gluck—

all composers of extraordinary accomplishment but generally known for vocal, not instrumental, music. I ought, perhaps, to have found room for orchestral works by such later composers as Fauré, Wolf, Dukas, Delius, de Falla, Nielsen, Respighi, Poulenc, Ives, Copland, and many more—including our American minimalists. Even in the case of composers who are considered in this book, I have not discussed the orchestral works that occur in their operas: so seven Mozart overtures and any number of Wagnerian excerpts that the operagoer will already know thoroughly go virtually unmentioned here. A medium-sized book has to stop somewhere, however regretfully.

I owe a debt of thanks to my predecessors in this sort of musical analysis—to Edward Downes, B. H. Haggin, Joseph Machlis, Ethan Mordden, and to the various writers in the Penguin series of handbooks on music. I wish also to thank Doug Hilmer for expert computer guidance, and, for help given in various ways, Donald Finlay, Thomas Mailloux, Emmet Robbins, and the good people at Amadeus Press—John Cerullo, Gail Siragusa, and Caroline Howell.

Finally, I would like to thank the friend of more than sixty years to whom this book is dedicated. He taught me to love—and to some extent even to play—the piano pieces of Debussy and Ravel and the songs of Jerome Kern and Richard Rodgers. He will, I expect, find much to disagree with in these pages, and if he does I am still ready to learn from him. Gratefully.

Instrumental Music

Welcome to the world of instrumental classical music. And if your interest in music has heretofore been largely vocal, where better to start than with the various voices of the orchestra? I shall provide examples of them from their use in opera and in popular music.

Instruments

The Strings

The violin, the highest-pitched member of the string section, is the most expressive of instruments. Only a human voice can equal the emotional intensity of the sound a sensitive hand produces on a vibrating string. Operagoers will know the violin's unique effect from the long solo given it in the baptism scene in Verdi's *I Lombardi*, or from the ethereal sound of the massed violins in the opening measures of his *Aida*, or from the first and second violin sections divided, as it were, into choirs in the prelude to Wagner's *Lohengrin*.

The viola, similar in shape to the violin but larger in size, lower in range, and darker in sound, is often used to give harmonic support to the first and second violins—though the reader will, I hope, discover in these pages that it has an expressiveness, often a sadness, of its own. You may remember its special sound from the viola solo in Britten's *Peter Grimes*—the solo that accompanies Captain Balstrode's search of the desperate fisherman's abandoned quarters.

The cello, much larger in size and lower in range than either the violin or the viola, is the ideal instrument for meditative, melancholy statements. Massed cellos intone the famous opening phrase of Wagner's *Tristan und Isolde*, and a solo cello searches the mind of King Philip in his "Ella giammai m'amo" in Verdi's *Don Carlo*.

The double bass, or bass viol, or simply bass, is a massive violin, taller than the average man, with a range that reaches several octaves below middle C on a piano. Verdi uses massed double basses to signal Otello's stealthy entrance into Desdemona's bedchamber. Wagner uses them to suggest the darkness that gives way to sunrise in the interlude that follows the Norn Scene in *Götterdämmerung*. And of course the "bass fiddle," its strings plucked rather than bowed, provides a beat, and an occasional lively solo, in many jazz combos.

The Woodwinds

The piccolo, a small flute, is the highest-pitched of the orchestra's instruments, instantly identifiable for its a bright, piercing sound. It rarely has a solo to play, but in opera it sparkles through the "Magic Fire Music" in Wagner's *Ring* and depicts lightning flashes in the storm in the last act of Verdi's *Rigoletto*.

The flute, pitched an octave lower than the shrill piccolo, has a unique, silvery sound. There are famous flute solos in Gluck's *Orfeo*, in Mozart's *The Magic Flute*, and in the introduction to the third act of Bizet's *Carmen*. Three flutes accompany the dance of the priestesses in the first act of Verdi's *Aida*.

The clarinet, an instrument loved by Mozart, Weber, and Tchaikovsky long before it was appropriated by jazz and swing bands, can be mournful, as in the long solo that accompanies the silent Andromache approaching Hector's tomb in Berlioz's *Les Troyens*, or passionately lyrical, as in the introduction to "E lucevan le stelle" in Puccini's *Tosca*, or light and lightsome, as in the entrance of young Siébel in the Garden Scene in Gounod's *Faust*.

The oboe, a reed with a more limited range than the clarinet (and much more difficult to play), has a plaintive sound that is very effective in solo passages. Verdi uses it memorably to sing the phrases that the dying Violetta cannot manage in the last act in *La Traviata*, and to suggest the nostalgic pain Aida feels when, in the Nile Scene, she remembers her "Patria Mia."

The English horn is an alto oboe that, strangely, is neither English nor a horn. Wagner wanted its haunting quality for the shepherds piping in both *Tannhäuser* and *Tristan und Isolde*.

The bassoon, lowest of the woodwinds and by far the largest in size, has an inimitable hooty sound that can be dreamily reflective, as in the introduction to Donizetti's "Una Furtiva Lagrima," or—much more often—witty, even buffoonish, tootling away at the very start of the overture to Mozart's *Le Nozze di Figaro*.

The Brass

The trumpet has an unmistakable bright sound, wonderful for fanfares, as in the introductory measures of Verdi's "Celeste Aida." A solo trumpet has a virtual monopoly on the "sword" motif in Wagner's *Ring*. Several trumpeters led big bands in the swing era, and jazz musicians often got delicious doo-wah effects by deft muting of the trumpet's brassy tone.

The trombone, once reserved almost exclusively for massed effects in religious music, provides the solemn background for

Neptune's oracular statements in Mozart's *Idomeneo* and has (again) a virtual monopoly on the motif of Wotan's spear in Wagner's *Ring*. In the big band era, trombone players specialized in soft romantic ballads.

The French horn, still shaped like the curved ram's horn it once was, is perhaps the most difficult of all brass instruments to play and has the mellowest and most romantic of tones. It is, of course, ideal for Siegfried's "horn call" in the *Ring*. It whoops orgasmically at the climax of the prelude to Strauss's *Der Rosenkavalier*. But most of the time its beautiful sound sets moonlit scenes, as in the same composer's final *Capriccio*. The Germans have always favored it more than the French have, but Gounod, a Parisian, uses it memorably in the Garden Scene in *Faust*.

The tuba, lowest-pitched of the brasses, was relegated mostly to march music until Wagner felt a need for it, and for kindred instruments, to support sonorous brass chords in the *Ring*. Hunding's entrance in *Die Walküre* is a famous instance.

The Percussion

The timpani, or kettledrums, can actually be tuned at certain pitch levels, and can add a quiet but ominous touch to suspenseful passages, as in the scene in Puccini's *Tosca* where the heroine assures herself that Scarpia is dead. They can also thunder forth impressively, as when Thor strikes up the storm in *Das Rheingold*.

The snare drum, familiar from marching bands, has a soldierly sound that adds to the horror of the torture scene in *Tosca* and the imminence of execution at the end of *Faust*. When equipped with various percussive paraphernalia, it provides the rhythmic support for many jazz groups.

There are any number of other percussion instruments used

for special effects. And, lest we forget, the piano is a percussion instrument. But nothing need be said about it here except that, for the music this book will concern itself with, it is the most important instrument of all.

Keys

Songs have titles. Operas have titles. Rock albums have titles. But most pieces of instrumental classical music are titleless, identified only by their numerical position in the composer's output (hence, "Beethoven's Fifth Symphony, Opus 67") and the key in which they begin (hence, "in C Minor"). Uninitiates can find this off-puttingly pedantic, and tend to like best pieces of instrumental music that are known not by their numerical designations or key signatures but by the titles they have acquired over the years—the "Surprise" symphony, the "Appassionata" sonata, the "Raindrop" prelude. (Conversely, *The Magic Flute* might be called "Mozart's Opera No. 20 in E-Flat Major," and *Lohengrin* "Wagner's Opera No. 6 in A Major." But of course they never are.)

To a listener who has never learned to read music there is no more mystifying and potentially off-putting term than "key." But a key is merely the basic tonality of a piece of music. After the first few measures of any piece a listener can sense that the music is affiliated with, bound in a kind of allegiance to, a "home note" that is designated by a letter of the musical scale and can be sounded on a piano—a tonality or "home base" to which, in Western music, the piece, however long it lasts or however much it seems to change, will eventually return. Even in the simplest of our popular songs, the music will change, for variety or contrast, into another key for a time—only to return eventually to its initial key.

The key relationships in a piece of instrumental music can be as important as its melodies or "themes." An alert ear will detect, and feel, the effect when the first theme in a symphony is replaced by a second theme in a different key, higher in pitch than the first, or darker (in what is called a minor key), or different in sound because it is stated by a new combination of instruments. And even an untrained ear will feel a sense of returning—after several minutes of exploration in which the two themes are varied, expanded, or condensed—to the tonality where everything started. It might take a more practiced ear—acquired in time—to detect, once that home point is returned to, how the first theme will draw the second into its own tonality. And often that is the point where the composer achieves his finest effects. As Cole Porter once exclaimed in a memorable lyric, "How strange the change from major to minor!"

Mozart's choice of keys, to some extent determined by the instruments he is writing for, is remarkably consistent. He seems to imbue each key with its own emotive quality. D Minor is his tragic key. G Minor is for pain. C Minor in Mozart anticipates the seriousness and tragic power of Beethoven; it is also the key in which Mozart composed much of his Masonic music. Among the major keys, G is, for Mozart, cheerful, almost carefree—it is Papageno's key in much of *The Magic Flute*. A is pastoral. E Flat is imposing. B Flat is spacious (Brahms would agree with that), and C Major, the fundament of tonality, is grandly affirmative. (Mozart uses it for his "Jupiter" symphony, and Wagner uses it to begin and end his magisterial comedy *Die Meistersinger*.)

Some composers in the twentieth century attempted to evolve new systems not dependent on keys. But audiences found it difficult to follow the logic of their music, and "atonality" and "serial composition" are systems that have now been largely abandoned—though I have no doubt that new systems will be attempted in this new millennium.

Forms

Now we reach the heart of the instrumental matter. And here an opera lover may have an advantage over other listeners because he or she will already have a well-developed sense of musical drama. Most of the great instrumental music written in the West is dramatic in nature. Any symphony, concerto, sonata, or string quartet is a drama whose characters are the musical themes, whose three or four acts are the three or four movements, whose action follows a well-defined structure in which a composer of genius can introduce surprising developments, thrilling climaxes, and inspiring final curtains. And by far the most important of these structures is . . .

Sonata Form

The sonata form is the most ingenious structure ever devised in Western instrumental music, and for the better part of three centuries composers have used it as the preferred means of expression. Ask a musician to compile a list of the hundred essential pieces of classical instrumental music, and chances are that more than seventy percent of those pieces will be composed, in whole or in part, in sonata form. The form is at once remarkably simple and compellingly dramatic. It allows a composer full scope for expression while tensing his musical ideas with the inevitability of a Greek or Shakespearean drama, through climax after climax, toward a moving, sometimes surprising, and always emotionally satisfying conclusion.

The drama in a sonata-form movement is played out in contrasting keys. The beginning of a movement establishes a certain key as its fundament—so much so that listeners versed in instrumental music often refer to, say, Mozart's twenty-third piano concerto not as No. 23 (its position among the composer's

twenty-seven piano concertos), not as K.488 (its catalogue designation), but as his piano concerto in A Major. And yet we are
certain that, once Mozart has grounded us in this key, the music
will eventually move into one or more contrasting keys—hence
the plot of the drama—before it returns, eventually, to its home
base in A Major.

Shaping the current of the movement and riding the crest of
it are the themes. They can be fairly long—there are sixteen
notes in the opening theme of Mozart's A-Major piano concerto—but the most useful themes in a sonata-form drama are
brief, incisive, and memorable. Even the longer themes can be,
and usually are, broken up into smaller musical phrases, capable
of development. In more complicated sonata-form movements,
the themes gather in clusters. But generally the drama turns on
just two contrasting themes that convey built-in tensions. The
themes in a classical work are not so much beautiful melodies as
pithy musical ideas that can be subjected to changes in texture,
tempo, and tension.

In the opening section of a sonata-form movement, usually
called the *exposition*, the first theme (and perhaps a group of satellite themes) is clearly stated and grounds the listener in the basic
key of the movement. A transitional passage leads to the second
theme (and perhaps a group of satellite themes) in a higher key.
The second theme is composed in contrast to the first—major
where the first theme was minor, or languid where the first was
militant, or simply harmonized where the first was harmonically
rich, or sounded in the woodwinds where the first was sounded
in the strings, or—in still common parlance—"feminine" where
the first theme was "masculine."

There follows what is often the most interesting and dramatic
section of a sonata-form movement—the *development*. Here
some, perhaps all, of the musical ideas stated in the exposition
are taken up one-by-one or in combination, propelled through a

number of different keys, shifted in tonality from major to minor, broken into components, recombined, expanded, contrasted, tossed from instrument to instrument, and finally tensed toward a return to the home key.

We feel the tension lifting as we return to that home key and the final section of the sonata-form movement, the *recapitulation.* The first theme (and its satellite musical ideas) returns pretty much as we first heard it. But, with the changes it has undergone since its first appearance, it seems to mean much more now than it did before. Then—and many composers achieve their subtlest effects here—the second theme, with its satellite ideas, is drawn into the tonality of the home key. And often, when we feel that at last the struggle is over and the drama is done, a classical composer will add a short final section, a coda, to drive home the tonality of the home key.

Such is the basic structure on which Haydn, Mozart, Beethoven, Schubert, Brahms, and indeed most composers of the eighteenth, nineteenth, and early twentieth centuries based their most famous compositions. Needless to say, they took liberties with it—affixing an introduction before the first theme makes its appearance, introducing third and fourth themes to add richness, conflict, or tension. Every symphony, concerto, sonata, or work of chamber music is, in fact, a different solution to the sonata-form "problem." But all the geniuses of the Classic and Romantic eras thought in sonata-form terms for their most important musical statements. They respected its concentration, its dynamism, its potential for drama, the struggle it makes to reach its conclusion.

A final note: the sonata form, almost invariably used in the opening movement of a classical work, may be used in the later movements as well. But there are other structures a listener ought to be alerted to.

Theme and Variations

This is the form sometimes used for the second and often for the final movement of a classical work. An operagoer will be familiar with it—or at least with one model of it—from the quartet "Mir ist so wunderbar" in Beethoven's *Fidelio*. There, four characters—Marzelline, Fidelio, Rocco, and Jacquino—stand motionless on the stage, caught, as it were, in a moment of time. Marzelline intones a simple melody that will serve as the theme for the quartet. Then Fidelio takes up the melody while Marzelline does a variation on it, singing a different musical line but keeping the tempo and the harmonic outline of the initial melody. Then it is Rocco's turn to take up the melody while Marzelline and Fidelio do their separate variations. Finally Jacquino joins the quartet, and his plain statement of the melody is almost submerged in the variations the other three are embroidering around it—all of them giving us intimations of their quite separate emotions. It is a magical moment in a great, heroic opera, simple in structure but marvelous in its effect.

A jazz combo will often use the same structure, except that, after the initial straightforward playing of a thirty-two-bar song like Gershwin's "Oh, Lady Be Good," the song only hovers over the variations. The clarinetist will have a thirty-two-bar solo in which he keeps in mind the melodic, harmonic, and rhythmic outline of the song but does "his own thing" with it. Then the trumpeter, and the sax player, and the bass player will each get his own thirty-two bars to inprovise a solo that is a variation on the song. An attentive listener will be able to hum "Oh, Lady Be Good" throughout each solo, even though the melody itself is not explicitly sounded. And finally the members of the combo will join forces for a fairly straightforward statement of the song.

Similarly, a classical composer using theme and variations will state his melody as clearly as possible at the start, and then, in successive variations, he may change the tonality (from major to minor), the rhythm (from four-quarter to three-quarter time), the tempo (from a stately pace to a quickened one), the harmony (from simple to complex), and the texture (introducing different instrumental colors). And a good musician, a jazz enthusiast, or possibly just an attentive listener should be able to hum the original tune through most, and sometimes all, of the variations. Finally a point is reached, after four or five or more variations, when the composer returns to restate his melody in its original tonality, tempo, and texture. But, as in sonata form, the melody will by this time have gone through so many transformations— the theme will have gone through so many variations—that it seems at the close to have revealed more potential than we ever thought it had. Even if it is restated exactly as we first heard it, it seems utterly transformed.

It should be said, finally, that theme-and-variations structure is not nearly as complicated as this description has perforce made it seem. Try a couple of listenings to the wonderful fourth movement of Schubert's "Trout" quintet, and you'll have the idea.

Scherzo

In the eighteenth century, the third movement of a classical work was a minuet, a courtly dance in three-quarter time in simple A-B-A form—A for the minuet proper and B for a contrasting section, the trio. The minuet and trio provided a quiet six or seven minutes before the work surged forward to its more complicated final movement. When Romanticism came storming in, the elegant third-movement minuet was displaced by the more impulsive and vigorous scherzo (the Italian word for "joke"), which kept the simple A-B-A structure but, especially in the hands of Beethoven, provided humor, irony, and rhythmic drive.

Rondo Form

This is the form most often used for the fourth movement of a classical work. It generally follows the pattern A-B-A-C-A-B-A— that is to say, an instantly memorable musical idea (A) is succeeded by a contrasting idea (B), then A returns, only to be succeeded by the center of the movement (C), after which A returns, to be succeeded by B once again, and then A makes its final appearance. In the eighteenth century a rondo rounded off a musical work with vivacity and cheerfulness. Later, with Romantic composers, it could be used to make more complex and passionate statements.

We are now ready to do some concentrated listening to three full-length works that, in their several movements, use these forms. We shall discuss a symphony (a four-movement work composed for full orchestra), a concerto (a three-movement work for orchestra and solo instrument), and a piece of chamber music (in this case, a four-movement work for five string instruments only). You might want to have the music playing, with your hand on the stop button on your CD player, as you make your way through the paragraphs that follow.

The Symphony

To know the symphony, the most exalted of all forms of instrumental music, is to know, above all others, Beethoven. All nine of his symphonies are still, after some two hundred years, in the repertory of every major orchestra in the world. And the number nine has remained, after Beethoven, the great, forbidding boundary in symphonic composition. Schubert, Dvo ák, and Bruckner never went beyond their ninth symphonies. Schumann and Brahms stopped at four, Tchaikovsky at six, Sibelius at seven.

Mahler hesitated, tried a tenth, and never completed it. After Beethoven, no major composer until the doughty Shostakovich thought he could or should surpass the master. Let us look at the most familiar of his nine symphonies.

Beethoven, Symphony No. 5 in C Minor, Op. 67 (1807)

The first movement of Beethoven's Fifth is perhaps the most powerfully concentrated musical structure ever written, built as it is almost entirely from one thunderous four-note theme. More than a hundred years ago, George Grove—he of the music dictionary—wrote that those four opening notes were "probably the most famous theme in the world," and during World War II their claim to that position became even stronger. The four notes became the battle cry of the Allied Forces when, written in Morse code as ···— (the signal for the letter *V*), they came to symbolize "V for Victory" as much as the two fingers stubbornly raised to form a V by Winston Churchill in his wartime appearances.

Beethoven's biographer Anton Schindler recorded that the composer said of the four-note theme, "Thus Fate knocks at the door." Many commentators wish that the composer had never used the phrase. Some insist that he never did. (Schindler was a naïve man, and more than once Beethoven seems to have had fun impressing him.) And yet only a forceful image can do the theme justice. Schumann, Berlioz, and other Romantics described music—their own and others'—in terms that seem equally extravagant today. Wagner even imagined Beethoven insisting from his grave that conductors had to observe the pause mark he placed over the last of the four notes in the theme: "The life-blood of the note," quoth Beethoven's spirit in Wagner's imagination, "must be squeezed out of it to the last drop."

In any case, the theme (CD 1, track 1) is forcefully stated, rages with an almost frightening insistence throughout the first movement—and figures in all three subsequent movements. It first appears in C Minor, the key Beethoven favored for passionate and vehement utterances. But when, less than a minute into the first movement, the horns sound the theme almost as a summons (0:44), we find that we have entered a major and mellower key, E Flat, where the violins and woodwinds introduce a second theme—for the movement is in sonata form. Commentators, we have said, almost invariably observe that the second theme in a sonata-form movement is "feminine" to the first theme's "masculine." Certainly Beethoven's gracious second theme seems intent on placating the aggressive opening theme. But an attentive listener will be able to detect, beneath its pleading, the quiet but insistent repetition, in the cellos and basses, of the opening theme's ··· — rhythm.

In Beethoven's day all of this exposition (which takes less than ninety seconds) would be repeated so that the audience could sort out its various elements in preparation for the development section. Today not every conductor thinks this is necessary, but Béla Drahos, on the enclosed CD, and Carlos Kleiber, in the marvelous recording recommended below, rightly think that it is.

In the development section (2:50) the placating second theme drops out entirely, and the main theme is allowed to rage onward, from instrument to instrument, and through several shifts in tonality.

Then, in sonata-form tradition, we are back in C Minor (4:11), recapitulating the opening material more thunderously than before, but with a remarkable moment (4:27) when everything seems to stop and a solo oboe unexpectedly sings a plaintive phrase. But that is soon swept away by repetitions of the ··· — rhythm, a return to the horn-call summons (4:58), and the "feminine" theme. And then the movement ends, as many sonata-form movements do, with a coda in a quicker tempo (5:43) that carries us onward and upward via the insistent ··· — theme to an almost savagely triumphant ending.

There is plenty of drama in that first movement, but listeners who are used to having their dramas set to a text may want at least some sort of context, of subtext, for what is happening in the music. George Grove has not hesitated to suggest one: At the time of the symphony's composition, Beethoven, a tempestuous and, to some, physically repellent man who hoped in vain for marriage and a domestic life, became engaged to the Countess Theresa Brunswick. The three unsent love letters found in his desk after his death were, in Grove's opinion, intended for her. But Beethoven had serious doubts about the marriage surviving his uncontrollable emotions. ("Oh God," he prayed in one of the letters, "let me at last find her who is destined to be mine, and who shall strengthen me in virtue.") Years before, when Theresa was only fifteen, Beethoven had, in the course of giving her a piano lesson, struck her forcibly and fled the house without his hat and coat. She, in forgiveness, took them and ran after him in the snow. Grove asks, "Are not these two characters exactly expressed" in the two themes of this movement? He raging, she attempting to placate. First-time listeners may find that incident helpful in feeling their way into this tumultuous movement—though the music itself seems at every measure much larger than life. And in the end the music will be text enough for a good listener.

The second movement is, as with the great majority of symphonies, the slow movement. The tempo is andante (i.e., at a walking pace), and the key, A Flat, is one of the mellowest of keys. Beethoven uses here the structure we have called theme and variations, though his "theme" is actually two quite distinct "songs" and his variations on them are considerably freer than is the case with theme-and-variations structure in other pieces we shall discuss in this book. So some readers may prefer to postpone any structural analysis of this movement till later and simply to listen for the two "songs"—they are easily remembered—as they recur in various guises. For others, let me offer a kind of analysis—though hardly a technical one.

Beethoven begins (track 2) with a smooth-flowing song stated by the violas and cellos. When it has been rounded off by a few chords, the woodwinds and plucked strings quietly introduce the second song (0:51)—built on an upward-moving, six-note phrase and cresting in a remarkable shift to a higher, brighter tonality—C Major. (Operagoers will spot this stunning moment [1:07] as a phrase Gounod used—not consciously, I rather think—in his *Faust*, at the moment when the imprisoned Marguerite recognizes Mephistophélès as a satanic force and cries, "Chasse-le du saint lieu!") At this point Beethoven's initially quiet second song becomes confidently brassy.

There follows (at 1:26) a mysterious little bridge, and suddenly we are into the first variation (1:51) on our two songs. The first song now flows along even more agreeably than when we heard it before, for its once-uneven quarter-note rhythms have been smoothed away in rippling sixteenth notes (your music teacher might have called them semiquavers). And after this quickening impulse the second song (2:41) seems eventually to take on a more martial quality than before.

We cross another mysterious bridge (at 3:14), and find ourselves in the next variation (3:41). The first song flows along more volubly still, its rhythm now smoothed into undulating thirty-second notes (yes, demisemiquavers). Then (at 4:41) Beethoven breaks both of his songs into fragments, toying affectionately with the first, rendering the second (at 5:35) in its most stirring form, and indulging in a little duet for clarinet and bassoon.

Then suddenly the tempo changes, and (at 7:44) we are into the movement's coda. Here Beethoven is particularly tender with his first song, as if unable to let it go. Finally, perhaps for fear of lapsing into sentimentality, the two-fisted composer ends the movement with determinedly manly chords. On repeated hearings of this beautiful movement you will notice that, if you lop off the two introductory notes of the six-note second song, you have the ··· — rhythm, and that that basic rhythm often sounds insistently here and there in the accompaniment of the movement. It simply pervades the entire symphony.

The third movement, a scherzo (track 3), turns the tonality from major back to minor. It opens very quietly with a mysterious theme that, we can tell from Beethoven's sketchbooks, owes something to the theme with which Mozart ended his Symphony No. 40. Then (at 0:20) the horns sound the ··· — motif, no longer defiant now but rather a call to action, and the music builds steadily on its impetus. But the trio of this scherzo movement (1:48) is all Beethoven-bluster: the lower strings begin it with a fugal theme in which the composer seems ready to take a lighter view of his uncontrollable nature. There is a repetition (at 3:22) of all of this material—the initial "mysterious theme" and the blustery trio—and eventually some of the details are treated with almost Hitchcockian playfulness. This leads without a break into . . .

. . . a far more mysterious and dramatic passage (7:58) in which, for some forty seconds, the whole orchestra seems suspended in hushed expectation, weaving a fragment of the scherzo while the timpani tap out what seems the beating of a great heart, pulsing with the rhythm of our ··· — motif. Nothing like it had been heard in music before, and nothing quite like it has been heard since. The tension is almost unbearable until, in an orchestral sunburst, we find ourselves without a pause in the fourth movement. The C-Minor "storm and stress" is over, and everything now is blazing C-Major affirmation, as radiant and joyous as it is unsubtle.

This last movement is in sonata form and has four contrasting themes, not unlike the ending of Mozart's "Jupiter" symphony. The first theme (track 4, 0:00), for full orchestra, is built on the basic C-Major chord. The second (0:35) is a fanfare sounded by horns in harmony. The third (1:01), on the strings again, is a leaping, vigorous theme in G Major, sprung from our ···— rhythm. The fourth (1:29) is a six-note fragment that Beethoven will use now as a building block.

In the glorious development of these four themes, there comes an unexpected lull when (at 5:38) the ···— theme returns falteringly—only to be swept away, vanquished forever, by the recapitulation of the movement's four great themes and their concluding coda. Everything ends in a torrent of sound as the basic C-Major chord is hammered home by the full orchestra.

"Unsubtle" is the word I have used for this ending. Others might call it "naïve." But Beethoven, you will learn, often made unsubtle and (perhaps) naïve statements serve larger purposes. The finale is not so much naïve as unashamed and full of joy—the almost cosmic joy of a great hearted-man determined at all costs to triumph over the deafness that was closing in on him.

Recording

C. Kleiber, Vienna Philharmonic (DG)

The Concerto

To know the concerto is to know, above all, Mozart, and above all in Mozart, the piano concertos. He gave us twenty-seven of them, far more than any other great composer—compare Beethoven with five, Brahms with two, Tchaikovsky with three, Rachmaninoff with four, and many composers of the first rank with none at all. Of Mozart's prodigious output in this genre,

I think I can say that at least ten rank among the greatest piano concertos ever written. And even the others, spread across the whole of his career, are valuable because in them we can see how, in Mozart's thirty-five short years on this planet, the Classical style evolved from the Baroque and anticipated the Romantic. The piano concertos of Mozart are a virtual history of the music of their period and, especially in their slow movements, point beyond that period to the future.

They also trace the early history of the piano as an instrument. In Mozart's youth, the harpsichord was the instrument of choice. But the new pianoforte was, it was soon clear, capable of much greater resonance and expressiveness, and Mozart, a master at the keyboard and a man fascinated with what the piano could do, wrote concerto after concerto, sometimes for himself, sometimes for his students, to play in concert. And he revealed himself in these pieces as much as he ever did in the more intimate chamber works.

Mozart, Piano Concerto No. 17 in G Major, K.453 (1784)

The seventeenth piano concerto was one of four that Mozart wrote in a two-month period when he was twenty-eight years of age. The soloist at the Vienna premiere was Mozart's student Barbara (Babette) von Ployer, and she and the composer joined forces afterward to perform, at the same concert, his sonata for two pianos. Mozart arranged for a carriage to bring the then preeminent composer Giovanni Paisiello to hear his student—and of course to hear his music as well. At subsequent performances, we may easily presume, Mozart himself took over the keyboard for this very charming work.

The piano concertos of Mozart are built like little dramas. Often in his first-movement sonata form he would use, not just a first and a second theme as was generally the case with earlier composers, but a whole cluster of themes as a kind of first subject, and a whole cluster of themes, in a different but related key, as a second subject. Then he would set his themes interacting in the development section, and finally he would reconcile them, restoring everything to the original key, in the recapitulation. So why should we not, in our perusal of the first movement of this Mozart piano concerto, think of Mozart's themes as characters in an opera? Let's make a sonata-form drama out of the first movement of this concerto. A kind of *Marriage of Figaro*. The movement was composed some two years before *Figaro*, and its dominant key, G Major, is the key of the opera's wedding march for Figaro and Susanna in that opera. Let's see what we can do.

In the opera, Figaro announces, "Ecco la marcia!" when he summons all the characters in the palace to his wedding—and in the concerto the first theme is not only in the same key (G Major) but also sports the same dotted rhythm as the opera's march. Let's think of the concerto's march-like opening theme, then, as *Figaro* himself (CD 1, track 5), striding confidently and cheerfully through the palace at Aguas Frescas, peering this way and that, without (he thinks) a care in the world. This jaunty "Figaro march" goes on for sixteen bars; then the orchestra shifts for a brief eight bars to a slightly chromatic section, and we hear Figaro laughing a merry "AH-ha-ha"—twice (0:27).

But before we know it the orchestra has swirled us into a cluster of themes that I, for one, think of as a musical characterization of Figaro's saucy bride-to-be, *Susanna*: four bars (0:44) of a bright tune sharply struck on the strings, and then six bars (0:50) of an almost conspiratorial figure in the woodwinds, with the bassoon, that most comical of instruments, tootling away briefly but prominently.

Susanna's quick themes introduce us, as they often will in this movement, to our second main theme, that of the *Countess*— characterized by a plaintive melody (1:00) that hovers between minor and major for fourteen bars, sung first by the strings and then by the winds. This is the first indication we have had that serious feelings may be involved in this little drama. The Countess, opera lovers will know, has lost her husband's love. Her theme is in a key (D Major) distinct from but related to the opening key—as the second ("feminine") theme of a sonata-form movement must be. But we know that in the recapitulation this theme will be drawn into the key of the opening (G Major), and all through the movement we look forward to that happening—that sonata-form happy ending for the Countess.

But just now her wistful melody is interrupted by a totally unexpected change of key (1:25)—and the imperious *Count* makes an appearance in the very *un*related key of E Flat. Then, with a few wary transitional bars (1:40), we are back to the original G Major—the tonality, shall we say, of the palace—and something of the Count's true nature, the nature we know from the first of Beaumarchais's dramas, is expressed in an aristocratic new theme (1:52) and a series of laughing flourishes (1:59).

After the orchestra has presented us with this wealth of musical ideas, the piano enters (2:08). At this point an inferior composer would repeat all of the material we have just heard, and assign the piano the task of embellishing it. Mozart starts as if he were going to do no more than that: he has the piano embellish the opening sixteen-plus-eight-bar *Figaro* section—including the AH-ha-ha—with some fast finger-work. But then (2:53) he deftly modulates into a new tonality . . .

. . . and gives us a cluster of new themes—to represent, in our analysis, *Cherubino* (3:10). The page boy gets a generous sixteen bars for a passage adorned with turns, trills, and staccato notes.

Then there is a lovely modulation (3:37) to the key of B Flat, as if now the scene were changing from the G-Major palace to the pine-tree garden of the opera's last act. We have moved into the sonata form's development section. Mozart doesn't feel he has to develop all of the six, seven, eight, or more themes he has generously given to his characters. He chooses *Susanna* (3:44) as his catalyst. Her theme—the bassoon tootle—introduces, as before, the *Countess* (4:00). The piano gets another chance to indulge in virtuoso runs, and the orchestra gives us just a hint of a new melody for the Countess (4:36) that Mozart will eventually use in the first-act finale of his Figaro opera. (It's not something the listener is likely to pick up on the first hearing—all the more reason to delight in this concerto over and over.)

Now, in the darkness of the garden, we hear two laughs— *Figaro's* (4:56) and then the *Count's* (5:06)—before the piano takes off on an exhilarating series of running triplets (5:17) in a kaleidoscopic series of key changes, as shadows seem to close in on the scene. We also hear the *Count* (his former E-Flat dignity diminished into C Minor) pursuing the disguised *Susanna* (6:03) and being befuddled by her (6:17): her sly bassoon tootle is now disguised as a piano tidbit.

The orchestra then takes us back to the palace—that is to say, to our home key, G major (6:31). It is time for the recapitulation. How reassuring it is to hear *Figaro's* theme striding confidently again, and *Susanna's* theme (7:13), and, for a full sixteen bars, *Cherubino's* cluster of tunes (7:29)! Then, after a short but beautiful transition—the one we had been waiting for, the one needed to bring the betrayed lady at last into the palace key, G Major—Susanna (8:08) brings the *Countess* onstage again (8:19), her themes now fully developed. The *Count* disrupts things for a moment, appearing in the wrong key (his lordly E Flat, at 9:09), but the orchestra takes us back to where we want to be—G Major (9:26). And there we wonder, "Who is going to solve this problem?"

The piano, of course! Mozart wrote these concertos for himself to play, and it is Mozart at the piano who will determine how the instrumental drama is going to work out. Actually, for this crucial dramatic moment, he left us two separate cadenzas (long solo passages) for the pianist to play while the orchestra is silent. Perhaps one was for young Mlle. Ployer at the work's premiere, and the other, more difficult, for himself at later performances. In any case, the cadenza we usually hear uses two of our characters—*Figaro* (9:28), to effect the reconciliation, and the *Countess* (9:58), after several passages of virtuoso piano work, to forgive. And that is what happens.

When the cadenza is over, the orchestra hurries through a few more bars to show the *Count* (10:40) gallantly accepting his humiliation, even laughing (11:00). And, as is only fitting, the last six measures (11:07) pay tribute to the comedy's subtle catalyst, *Susanna*.

If you haven't followed any of this, simply listen to the movement, attending to each theme as it enters, as it confronts, as it challenges, as it adjusts to and affects the brisk little drama presented for you by the all-but-unstoppable orchestra and the wittily perceptive composer/soloist at the piano.

The second movement, profoundly introspective, is also cast in sonata form. Its main melody is developed from the theme we associated with the Countess in the first movement. Moreover, it is stated in the key of C Major—the key in which the opera's Countess sings her plaintive "Dove sono."

In fact, the whole of the second movement may be thought a kind of reverie in which Mozart's Countess remembers her past and wonders about her future. And here it *is* best, especially for a first-time listener, simply to let the succession of themes pass by one-by-one, yielding to the special quality of each, and always thinking of Mozart at the piano, saying to the orchestra, in effect: "Yes, I agree that the Countess feels her loss in the way you have expressed it. But let me go even deeper here at the piano."

The music passes from major to minor, from key to key, and the piano is given a long cadenza before the movement resumes its original, heartbroken measures and the last shadows close in. It is a harbinger of the Romantic slow movements to come in the piano concertos of such very different composers as Beethoven, Tchaikovsky, and Rachmaninoff.

The final movement takes us back to G Major and to another Mozart opera. Here virtually every listener thinks of *The Magic Flute* and its most loveable character Papageno, the bird catcher. G Major is the key both of his opening aria and of his joyous final duet with Papagena.

The movement, in an easy-to-follow theme and variations, begins with the orchestra playing what we might call Papageno's song—all thirty-two bars of it.

Then we get the first variation. The piano enters and plays the song, with a few embellishments, for another thirty-two bars. See if, while listening to this variation, you can hum the tune as you first heard it.

In the second variation the woodwinds chatter away at the tune, and the piano responds with virtuoso runs. For a real treat, try humming the tune along with this slightly more advanced variation. If you can make your way with it throughout the thirty-two bars, bravo! If not, at least you now have some idea of how the formal device known as "theme and variations" works.

In the third variation, things slow down a bit, and the oboe and the bassoon use the first half of the tune for a duet, commented on by the piano—and then the flute and the oboe use the last half of it for another duet. Try humming along. By now you may feel that *you* are Papageno!

The fourth variation shifts the whole tune from major to minor. You may need a special musical sensitivity to hum the tune through this variation. If you can't make it, be content with listening, for the variation shows how Mozart can find unsuspected depths of feeling in even the most cheerful tune.

Then comes the crown of the movement—not a variation but a vigorous, hilarious coda using the outlines of the theme. It is one of the most joyous passages in all of Mozart. For a few bars it slips into the minor, and the effect is like a passing cloud. But the last page is all sunlight and promise. It is as if Papageno were leaping into a nest with his Papagena in a hurry to make more Papagenos and Papagenas!

There is one last point to be made about the Piano Concerto No. 17 in G Major. Mozart had a pet starling, and he taught it to sing part of the tune that is the subject of the variations in the last movement. Actually, the chirpy little fellow couldn't get one of the notes right and held another too long, but Mozart—who has supplied us with these details—loved him all the same and, when he died, buried him in the garden with a piece of verse as a grave marker. Some commentators are so carried away with all of this that they have improved on it: it wasn't Mozart who taught the bird the tune, it was the bird that taught the tune to Mozart! In any case, we weren't far from wrong in sensing something of Papageno in the tune—or rather, something of the tune in Papageno.

Recording
Pires, Abbado, Chamber Orchestra of Europe (DG)

Chamber Music

The chamber music literature is as vast and rewarding as the symphonic, but it is almost invariably the last musical genre that the average listener approaches. Even as German lieder come last, and yet with great rewards, to the music lover with a special interest in the voice, so with instrumental music massively orchestrated symphonies, concertos, tone poems, overtures, ballet suites, and even spare-sounding sonatas for solo instruments capture the attention of the listener before he or she becomes attuned to the glories of string quartets and other "chamber music" written for small combinations of instruments. And yet, in the days of Haydn and Mozart, chamber music was the most performed of all classical forms. And from Beethoven and Schubert to Bartók and Shostakovich, it is in the chamber works that the composer reveals his most intimate and profound feelings. It is true that, to reap the rewards of most chamber music, a listener must accustom his or her ear to following four (or occasionally a few more) luminous strands of sound simultaneously. But for a connoisseur of the more complex rock music, or for an operagoer accustomed to hearing vocal quartets and quintets by Verdi and Wagner, this is not an insurmountable challenge.

Sometimes, with a chamber work, it may seem to a novice listener that the performers are the only ones really involved in the music—and, in fact, no musical experience is more rewarding than playing in concert with other skilled musicians, and nowhere else is a concert musician likely to feel more at one with the composer he or she serves than in playing his chamber works. But a really attentive listener is soon drawn into the charmed circle—and will feel that the composer is, in an admittedly small-scaled but nonetheless full-length work, speaking to him, or to her, more personally and more profoundly than ever before. So I do not hesitate to introduce you, gentle reader, to chamber music by way of one of the great masterpieces of the form.

Schubert, String Quintet in C Major D.956 (1828)

This extraordinary composition, written by the thirty-one-year-old composer in the last year of his life, is, I think, the best introduction to the realm of chamber music—for the good reason that, to the usual combination of two violins, viola, and cello, Schubert has added a second cello and thereby given a darker, almost symphonic depth and dimension to his intimate musical statements. Mozart, in *his* two string quintets, had added a second viola, an instrument of which he was very fond, to the usual foursome, and produced wholly new sonorities. But Schubert, adding a deeper-voiced cello, proceeds as far as chamber music can go in the direction of orchestral resonance while still retaining its own special intimacy.

The work that converted me to chamber works was Beethoven's "Archduke" trio for violin, cello, and piano, partly, of course, because I found it simply wonderful music, but partly as well because the piano part gave it the feel of a concerto rather than what had seemed to me (quite wrongly) the scratchy, irritating sound of the typical string quartet. But my most overwhelming experience in this remarkable genre was my first hearing, at a live concert, this rich-sounding, highly charged, intensely personal work by Schubert. At the time I had been listening to music for more than forty years, and had long since thought that I had heard all the masterpieces of the past. But I felt in my very soul, when I heard this quintet, that I had never heard any music so moving. And I still think so.

The work begins with all five instruments playing a unison C and then swelling into a C-Major chord. C Major, as we have already remarked, is the most affirmative of keys—the key of the joyous finales of Beethoven's *Fidelio* and Wagner's *Die Meistersinger*. But once Schubert's instrumentalists have sounded their affirmative chord, three of them change the inner contours of the C-Major chord till they have formed what is, technically, a diminished seventh, casting a shadow of doubt, or a suggestion of ambiguity, over the C-Major context, and the first violin, for just a brief measure, enters C Minor. Thereafter, the C-Major

tonality in the quintet is never quite the same, never as affirmative as in other works.

The movement that follows is conceived on a grand scale—
longer, at some twenty minutes, than any movement we have
yet considered here—and there are commentators who say that
any analysis of it along the usual sonata-form lines is bound to be
inadequate. All the same, readers of this book may find it helpful
to note that out of the ambiguous opening a first subject emerges
that seems to hover between major and minor. Then a second
subject—the two cellos singing in parallel thirds and then in
sixths—seems strangely to evoke, for anyone who has been to
Vienna, the city that Schubert knew.

The exposition, which is repeated in its entirety, ends with a
quizzical eight-bar march, introduced almost as an afterthought.
And yet it is this enigmatic bit that is given most attention in the
development section: Schubert uses it to take us dramatically
through eight different keys on our way to the recapitulation.
And there, in the recapitulation, the "Viennese" duet for two
cellos sounds more hauntingly than before, as we feel ourselves
drawn back toward the initial C Major. By the time we reach the
movement's quiet closing measures, C Major seems to be a tonality wholly different from that announced by the unison note that
opened the work. It has now been imbued with human feelings
beyond description.

The wonderfully moving second-movement adagio (CD 1,
track 6) is cast in the key of E Major, which Schubert often
reserved for contemplative statements. Its main section is a par-
tial reworking of a piece, called simply "Notturno," that Schubert
had composed earlier for an uncompleted piano trio. He seems
to have known then that it could serve a greater end, and here,
radiantly voiced by the five string instruments, it comes closer
than any other music I know to describing a state of rapt, almost
stilled, contemplation. The theme, little more than a series of

shifting, almost becalmed chords floated by the three middle instruments of the quintet, is punctuated by what seem like little shafts of light from the first violin and propelled by the gentlest possible pulsation of the cello. The violinist Nathan Milstein was moved by this passage to say that only God could give a man the capacity to sing in such a way.

But this state of contemplation is suddenly disrupted by a troubled middle section (5:17) that seems burdened with all the woes humanity has known and been unable to escape from or even understand. The movement shudders to a halt (8:22), gathers itself together, and turns again to contemplation. The opening music returns (9:12), poignantly charged now with reminiscences—from the same violin and cello that once enlightened and comforted—of the shattering experience we have just gone through. By the movement's end (11:29), the wondrous peace of the opening measures is restored—except for one momentary, cautionary chord in the minor (14:15). And this listener at least finds himself in agreement with the Schubert scholar John Reed, who confessed, "If one was obliged to choose one movement as evidence of Schubert's greatness it would have to be this one."

The third-movement scherzo has about it the excitement and even the sound of the hunt. But there is something disquieting, almost daemonic, about its C-Major ferocity. And these anxious feelings are deepened by an extraordinarily slow, somber, and sorrowing trio in a wholly new key, D-Flat Major. For some, this trio is the center and ultimate meaning—if, indeed, we can find any meaning—not only of the movement, not only of the whole quintet, but of everything Schubert wrote in his last few months. For John Reed, "it is as though, choosing the key of D-Flat Major in opposition to the assured certainties of the Scherzo's C Major, he is questioning . . . the very essence of the tonal system on which his own work, and that of his great predecessors, had been based." For a moment the music seems to die before our very ears—until the sounds of the daemonic hunt come crashing back.

The finale has disappointed some, just as has the finale of the closest thing Mozart ever wrote to this work—his Quintet in G Minor—has disappointed. We hear, first, a cheerfully rhythmic opening tune, almost Hungarian in its styling, and then a second subject that might serve as music for a Viennese wine garden. Both themes seem inadequate to what has gone before. But harmonic shadows begin to cross even this sunny music. And soon we reach a muted section reminiscent of the second movement's contemplation. Then the opening tune returns, unable now to foot it lightly as before—and the other melodies are similarly subdued. Finally the music begins to race with, again, an almost daemonic energy toward a conclusion that is strangely abrupt, even chilling. The movement is by no means an anticlimax, and a great performance will reveal the desperation in it.

But when the performance is over, it is the second moment that stays with the listener. That intimate revelation is the crown of this quintet, and perhaps of all the chamber music ever written.

Recording

Stern, Schneider, Katims, Casals, Tortellier (Sony)

Italians

Antonio Vivaldi
1678–1741

Vivaldi, the composer of much choral music and of some twenty surviving operas (and possibly thirty more that are now lost to us), has nonetheless been regarded primarily as an instrumentalist—as a virtuoso on the violin and a writer of concertos. He may even be thought the inventor of the concerto as it existed in his time—a musical piece in three movements for an instrumental soloist and orchestra of strings and harpsichord. He was also an ordained cleric, known in his native Venice as "the red priest" for his fiery hair and his sometimes combustible personality. For two centuries his fame was moderate at best, but in the last few decades it has increased to a degree where he is often mentioned in the same breath as his younger contemporaries Bach and Handel. This unpredictable state of things came to be largely because, with the recent increase of interest in Baroque music of all kinds, one set of four picturesque Vivaldi "concertos," rediscovered in 1950, captured the fancy of millions of record buyers:

The Four Seasons (Le Quattro Stagioni) (ca. 1725)

Vivaldi may properly be said to have invented the concerto when, in his three-movement pieces for string orchestra, he gave a prominent role to a solo violin. His method of procedure in the first and third movements of the best known of these "concertos," *The Four Seasons*, is to set his string orchestra playing a generalized description of the season in question, then to provide the solo violinist with a series of episodes to depict that season's individual sights and sounds. Between each episode, the orchestra returns to repeat its initial music—which is called, suitably enough, a ritornello.

For many listeners, however, it is the slow second movement of each of the *Four Seasons* that lingers longest in the memory— a five-minute piece that captures a single moment's seasonal experience.

Vivaldi provided four sonnets, perhaps of his own composition, to explain his four seasonal "concertos." The following commentary uses quotations from those sonnets to describe the music we hear.

Spring

Vivaldi's first sonnet begins with the words "Giunt'è la Primavera" ("Spring is upon us"), and his first "season" begins with the whole string orchestra imitating those words via a jolly, jostling tune that will return—as a ritornello—between each of the four episodes sung by the solo violin. Those episodes describe in succession how, in the words of the sonnet, "the birds joyfully welcome Spring with happy songs," how "the streams race murmuring along, propelled by zephyrs," how "thunderstorms fill the sky with darkness," and how, "when the storm is over, the birds return again to their wondrous singing." It doesn't take long to get the idea: the movement is built of descriptive violin solos alternating with the orchestra's generalizing ritornello.

In the slower second movement, which is like a painting come to life in music, the violin soloist depicts "a goatherd sleeping in a flowery meadow," while the orchestra imitates "the murmur of the leaves," and the violas, with forceful single utterances, suggest the arf-arfing of the goatherd's "faithful dog." (Vivaldi himself has attested to that last detail.)

The last movement reverts to the structure of the first. The swaying ritornello depicts a dance of "nymphs and shepherds under spring's bright canopy," and in the episodes, while the orchestra drones, the soloist imitates different varieties of "sylvan pipes."

Summer

This time the orchestra's ritornello suggests the "languishing of man, herd, and pine tree under the blazing sun." And in the episodes the soloist imitates the calls of the cuckoo, the turtle dove, and the goldfinch, and finally sings the plaintive lament of "a shepherd who fears the onset of a summer storm and what fate might bring to him."

In the brief second movement, the melancholy soloist/shepherd is unable to rest because of impending "lightning and thunder"—and besides, as the shuddering orchestra assures us, he is beset by "a swarm of gnats and flies."

Finally, in the last movement, the storm breaks in the orchestra, and the soloist is given several opportunities for virtuoso scene-painting as "hailstones flatten the crops and fields."

Autumn

In the first movement, soloist and orchestra vie in depicting villagers heartily dancing, singing, and drinking at harvest time— till sleep falls on them all.

In the hushed second movement, the mellow season invites us to join the harvesters in enjoying "the sweetest of all sleeps."

In the third movement, "at the crack of dawn, hunters set out for the chase, with horns, shotguns, and hounds." The soloist, galloping along between the ritornellos, finally depicts the death of the hunters' quarry—to tremolos in the string orchestra.

Winter

This is the most remarkable of these four "concertos." In the first movement, the orchestral ritornello shivers in dissonant chords, "frozen in the wintry frost," and in the episodes for solo violin, we hear the "biting breath of the fierce wind," "the stomping of feet" and "the chattering of teeth."

In the slow movement, the soloist blissfully conveys in sound the contentedness of "passing the days quietly at the fireside" while the orchestral accompaniment depicts the raindrops plip-plopping outside the window.

The episodes of the last movement tell us what it is like "to walk on the ice, to take slow steps for fear of falling, to tumble, to pick yourself up, to continue on your way, careful lest the ice should break." In the final measures, a wintry storm blusters in, and the music is inspired by lines from the first book of Virgil's *Aeneid*: "The North Wind and South and all the winds break through their bolted gates to do battle."

While all of this may well represent the birth of the violin concerto, it is hardly the earliest instance of what has been called, sometimes condescendingly, "program music." Narrative descriptions in music go back at least as far as pre-Classic Greece, when a solo aulos player depicted in sound the battle of Apollo and the Python at Delphi and won a prize for his effort—in the sixth century B.C.!

Interestingly enough, *The Four Seasons* was all but forgotten in the century and a half when "concerto" meant a large-scale three-movement showpiece for solo instrument and full symphony orchestra. But in recent decades, with interest in Baroque music rising steeply, recordings of these four seasonal "concertos" have outsold even the classic violin concertos of Beethoven, Brahms, and Tchaikovsky.

Recording

Carmignola, Marcon, Venice Baroque Orchestra (Sony)

You may also want to hear...

...any one or all twelve of the concertos for string instruments and continuo in the collection called *L'Estro Harmonico* (Harmonic Inspiration). These are less descriptive than *The Four Seasons* but equally joyous and sometimes even more beautiful. *L'Estro Harmonico* may in fact be the most influential collection of instrumental music in the whole of the eighteenth century: Bach himself transcribed six of the pieces for other instruments, and countless other composers learned from them.

...among the other Vivaldi concertos for various instruments (he wrote almost four hundred!), the bright, blazing Concerto in C Major for Two Trumpets and Orchestra, one of the works that sparked the new interest in Baroque music in the 1950s.

Domenico Scarlatti
1685–1757

Opera lovers are likely to know Alessandro Scarlatti, composer of Mitridate, Tigrane, Griselda, *and thirty-six other operas (plus many more that have not survived intact), better than his son Domenico, whose five surviving operas and other fragments are hardly known at all. Domenico's claim to fame, equal in its way to that of his father, is an astonishing collection of over six hundred short pieces for harpsichord. He called them merely* esercisi *(exercises), but in recent times, when the greatest pianists have found them eminently worthy of concert performance, they have come to be called sonatas.*

Keyboard Sonatas (1738)

Each of Domenico Scarlatti's sonatas demonstrates, and affords an opportunity of acquiring, some feature of harpsichordal performance—flexibility, fingering techniques, hand-crossing, and so on. But in the process of educating they often introduce rhythms, harmonies, and combinations of sounds that previously we had thought originated later, with Bach and Mozart, and even much later, with Chopin and Wagner.

Most of the sonatas are quick in tempo and best heard on the harpsichord for which they were written. But modern concert pianists, with pedaling Scarlatti never had at his disposal, have favored the slower ones and turned them into Chopinesque etudes and even nocturnes. Chopin himself used the *esercisi*, both the quick ones and the slow, in teaching his pupils, and he predicted, "There will come a time when Scarlatti will often be played in concerts, and people will appreciate and enjoy him." Brittle and biting or dulcet and dreamy—almost any style seems possible with the prolific and amazingly prescient Domenico Scarlatti.

There are two numbering systems currently in use—*L* for the pioneering edition of Alessandro Longo and *Kk* for the authoritative study of Ralph Kirkpatrick, whose recordings are among the best.

Perhaps the easiest way to discuss this massive collection is to single out the sonatas chosen by Vladimir Horowitz in his best-selling album *Horowitz at the Met*. This, of course, is just a start. And be forewarned: in recordings made over the decades there has been little overlap in the choices made by pianists Robert Casadesus, Myra Hess, Guiomar Novaes, by harpsichordists Ralph Kirkpatrick and Valda Aveling, and by guitarist John Williams. There is simply too much to choose from for any unanimity in the matter—and we should be grateful for that. For his memorable Met concert, recorded live, Horowitz made six choices:

Sonata in A-Flat Major (L.186, Kk.127): An allegro—in effect a five-minute drama—in which the musical configurations change as often and as kaleidoscopically as in the sonatas of Mozart.

Sonata in F Minor (L.118, Kk.466): An andante moderato that begins as an exercise in passing a musical figure from hand to hand and soon becomes a poignant, obsessive reverie, with dissonances à la Liszt.

Sonata in F Minor (L.189, Kk.184): An allegro that anticipates Bach in both harmony and counterpoint, with a repeated passage that might have come out of a Mozart fantasia.

Sonata in A Major (L.494, Kk.101): A sparkling allegro that, even in a performance marked by liberal use of pedal and very sensitive playing, magically preserves its harpsichordal quality.

Sonata in B Minor (L.33, Kk.87): An andante that, at least under the fingers of Horowitz, becomes a languorously beautiful, almost Chopinesque nocturne.

Sonata in E Major (L.225, Kk.135): An allegro molto, the quickest of Horowitz's choices—and the great pianist, using rallentando and accelerando, makes one long to hear it played with consistent quickness on a harpsichord, where it is likely to sound like a completely different piece. Such is the chameleon effect of Scarlatti's amazing keyboard sonatas.

Recording
Horowitz: *Horowitz at the Met* (RCA)

The Germanic Canon

Johann Sebastian Bach
1685–1750

The most prominent member of a German family that produced musical artists for some two centuries, and one of the unquestioned greats of music, Johann Sebastian Bach established the well-tempered scale still in use today, brought the art of counterpoint to its highest estate, and influenced virtually every important composer for the next two centuries—especially after the "Bach revival" in the early 1800s. Prolific in life (twenty children) and in art (hundreds on hundreds of compositions), he maintained that any pious man could do what he had done (in music, that is) if he worked hard enough. His legacy, sacred and secular, is the summation of late Baroque art and at the same time astonishingly modern. He made important contributions to every form of music available to him except opera. So the opera lover with any claim to musical literacy must know at least the following instrumental pieces, which he or she will certainly come to love.

Toccata and Fugue in D Minor (ca. 1703)

"The most dramatic and awe-inspiring piece of music that has ever been written." So said Arthur C. Clarke, the novelist who co-authored, with Stanley Kubrick, the script of *2001: A Space*

Odyssey, and who selected this Toccata and Fugue as one of the Seven Wonders of the World. To the average listener, it makes little difference that we cannot always establish a precise date for many of Bach's earlier works, and that there is even some doubt as to whether this piece, one of the great works in the organ literature, was originally composed for the organ. In fact, for more than three centuries it has been performed in various instrumental transcriptions. (You may remember it as the opening number in Walt Disney's 1940 *Fantasia,* where it is played by Leopold Stokowski and the Philadelphia Symphony Orchestra—and it was Stokowski's orchestral arrangement that so impressed Clarke.)

In the last century it was customary to sniff at such arrangements, even though, to suit different occasions, Bach himself did many transcriptions of his own work. But there is no question that to modern ears this Toccata and Fugue sounds best as a powerful, even frighteningly powerful, demonstration of what the organ can do when a man of prodigious powers writes passionately for it.

If the terms "toccata" and "fugue" are new to you, see the entries for them in the glossary at the end of this book. But concentrate mainly on surrendering to the wonder of this ten minutes of music.

Recording
Koopman: *Great Organ Works* (Teldec)

Passacaglia and Fugue in C Minor (ca. 1712)

This is another great, awe-inspiring work for organ that is, again, often transcribed for full orchestra. Bach starts with a solemn fifteen-note theme (the "passacaglia") in the pedals and, through a series of variations, builds from this foundation a cathedral in sound. Those who find Bach passionless will be amazed at the emotion that pulses through this work and resonates in the listener. The formidable critic B. H. Haggin rightly remarked, "The emotion is religious; the organ was Bach's most immediately personal medium, through which he expressed what was strongest in him—his religious feeling and his feeling for musical architechtonics."

Recording

Koopman: *Great Organ Works* (Teldec)

The Goldberg Variations (1742)

This half-hour of rapt wonder comprises thirty variations on a sixteen-measure sarabande (a slow dance in three-quarter time with a stress on the second beat). The separate movements were written to be played on the clavier (an ancestor of the piano) by one Johann Gottlieb Goldberg for an insomniac Russian ambassador who had asked for something soporific. The last half-century has, on the other hand, found the Variations something to get very excited about. Popularized in the 1940s by the fiery harpsichordist Wanda Landowska, they became a chart topper in the 1960s when they were recorded, on the piano, by the eccentric but brilliant Glenn Gould. Since that recording they have deservedly become one of the most familiar and best-loved large-scale pieces of music in the world.

Recording

Gould: *The Historic 1955 Recording* (Sony)

Concerto in D Minor for two violins and orchestra (ca. 1720)

This is the Bach "Double Concerto" that symphony orchestras unwilling to play transcriptions of the above toccata and passacaglia will feature proudly when two virtuoso violinists are available. Don't look for sonata form this early in the development of the concerto. What you will find is a great composer demonstrating his contrapuntal skills in music as stirring, as sensitive, and—in the marvelous slow movement—as spiritual as any music ever written by anyone. (This work is sometimes played in a transcription for two pianos, in the key of C Minor.)

Recording

Perlman, Zuckerman, Barenboim (EMI)

The Brandenburg Concertos (1711–1721)

These six joyous works are not concertos in the familiar sense of solo instrument with large orchestra. They are scored for various solo instruments playing with small instrumental combinations. Bach assembled them hastily from movements in his best recent work and hurried them off on demand to the Margrave of Brandenburg—who, the story goes, didn't bother to listen to them! Rediscovered in the twentieth century and popularized by period-instrument enthusiasts, they became so much a part of contemporary consciousness that a movement from the second concerto was selected for enclosure in the module that, to preserve the best our planet could do, was rocketed into space in 1977.

The second of the six concertos is, then, the one to begin with, especially if you can hear it performed with the piercingly bright solo trumpet of Bach's day. But no one on the planet should be unaware of the first concerto, with its happily thumping horns; the third and the sixth, scored for strings only; the sonorous fifth that, with its extended harpsichord cadenza, might lay claim to being the first piano concerto in the modern sense; and the irresistible fourth, with two flutes vying with a solo violin—and a last movement that Glenn Gould arranged poignantly for the scene in the film *Slaughterhouse Five* in which American soldiers gaze in amazement at the baroque beauty of Dresden just days before the fire-bombing. All but the third of these concertos have profound slow movements that, Paul Henry Lang has written, "are Passion music, and belong to the greatest poetic achievements of the German spirit."

Recording
Karajan, Berlin Philharmonic (DG)

You may also want to hear . . .

. . . the popular Italian Concerto and the charming Partita No. 1 in B-Flat Major for solo clavier (or, more recently, for piano); the familiar Concertos in D Minor and F Minor for clavier (or piano) and orchestra; and that exciting keyboard showpiece, the Chromatic Fantasy and Fugue in D Minor.

Proceed then to the forty-eight preludes and fugues from *The Well-Tempered Clavier*; the Suite No. 3 in D Major for chamber orchestra (which contains the familiar movement that has come to be called "Air for the G String"); the six eloquent suites for unaccompanied cello popularized by Pablo Casals; the violin concertos in E Major and A Minor (which were transcribed by the composer into piano concertos in, respectively, D Major and G Minor); the electrifying prelude to the Violin Partita in E Major (which has been transcribed for violin and piano by Schumann, for piano solo by Rachmaninoff, for guitar by Andrés Segovia, and for orchestra by Leopold Stokowski); and the awesome Chaconne from the Violin Partita in D Minor (which has been transcribed for piano by Busoni, for piano left hand alone by Brahms, for guitar by Segovia, and for orchestra by Stokowski). And there is much more of value even before you explore the magnificent choral and vocal music that lies outside the scope of this book. Get pleasantly lost! Bach is a whole world!

George Frideric Handel
1685–1759

Georg Friedrich Händel, the German composer of forty-five operas and twenty-one oratorios (at least half of which have been staged as operas), is beyond any question one of the greatest composers—and was also one of the busiest musical craftsmen—of all time. Born the same year as Bach, he became an international figure, the acknowledged master of eighteenth-century Italian opera and an honorary Englishman whose name was officially Anglicized—the surname unumlauted and the given name spelled George, like the king's. Meanwhile, his contemporary Bach remained a lowly German laboring largely unknown in German traditions. Now, more than two centuries later, it is, of the two, Bach who is recognized as the true innovator, the genius who may be said to have explored the very nature of music. All the same, Handel, newly emergent today as an opera composer, is still a force to be reckoned with, even if the purely instrumental works in his vast output are comparatively few.

Water Music (ca. 1717)

This is the famous music Handel wrote for George I's elaborate nightly fêtes on the Thames—with the king and his courtiers on the royal barge, the orchestra on another vessel alongside, and, if we are to believe the reports, a fleet of boats of various sizes in attendance, filled with people eager to hear the new music. As we have three suites composed for three slightly different instrumental groups, it is possible that Handel wrote "water music" for floating orchestra on three different occasions.

No complete autograph of the *Water Music* survives, nor do any of the earliest scores. The following description is based on the 1962 reconstruction by Hans Redlich for Bärenreiter's *Hallische Handel-Ausgabe.* The numbers given here may or may not be helpful, because the order of the pieces varies both in the different editions and in performance. The titles given the numbers, some of them only indications of tempo, also vary. Until fairly recently the *Water Music* as performed both on records and in concert consisted of only six of the pieces, selected and arranged by Hamilton Hardy. Today audiences rightly demand to hear every piece that has come down to us. Here they are:

Suite No. 1: Ten pieces in F Major or in its related key, D Minor, scored for two oboes, bassoon, two horns, two solo violins, and massed strings. To these a keyboard instrument is added in the score, probably for concert performance.

1. *Overture:* A suitably grand opening replete with trills and flourishes and cast in the familiar form of a "French overture": a slow section followed by a faster one. In this case, an ostentatious processional is followed by a lively fugal movement.
2. *Adagio and staccato:* An oboe solo accompanied by gently plucked chords on the strings.
3. *Allegro:* One of the really famous movements. Two putt-putting horns frolic in the orchestra. The effect of them sounding over the water must have been sensational.
4. *Andante:* Two oboes and a bassoon sing a slow air in a minor tonality, in concert with the strings. This fourth movement is often played immediately after the third, which is then reprised—and rightly so, for any repetition of those frolicking horns is welcome.

5. *Untitled:* The two horns get a different melody to harmonize with, in a movement that bears no tempo marking in early editions but is always played briskly.

6. *Air:* One of Handel's loveliest and best-known melodies—a gently swaying air in the massed strings with sustained support from the two horns.

7. *Minuet:* The usual courtly dance is here rendered outdoorsy by the two discreetly blasting horns, which observe a respectful silence during the trio (middle section).

8. *Bourée:* A sprightly dance played by strings, then oboes, then strings once again.

9. *Hornpipe:* A nautical bit, played, as was the Bourée, by strings, then oboes, then strings. One would have thought horns more suited to a hornpipe, but this movement is a rather delicate thing, not likely to have been danced by any of the sailors attending the royal barge.

10. *Untitled:* We are not sure where Handel wanted this almost Bachian D-Minor movement placed. Most concert performances use it to end the first suite. In any case, it is a wonderful piece of contrapuntal writing.

Suite No 2: Five pieces in the key of D Major for the same instruments as before, but with the addition of two trumpets. This suite was composed some two years after the first, presumably for another evening of music on the Thames.

11. *Allegro:* An overture cast in the form of a festive march. Trumpets are now a welcome addition to the orchestral mix, and their brilliant fanfares are imitated by the whooping horns.

12. *Alla Hornpipe:* This best-known number in the second suite (and this time there *are* horns for the hornpipe, and trumpets, too) is so engaging that in many concert performances it is

moved to the end of the three suites to make an exhilarating nautical finale to the whole of the *Water Music*.

13. *Minuet:* Now that trumpets have been introduced to this music on the water, Handel seems incapable of keeping them down. Imagine, a minuet scored for horns and trumpets!

14. *Lentement:* This placid interlude for strings alone might have come from any of Handel's operas.

15. *Bourée:* This lively movement, like the former one, is for strings alone. Perhaps the trumpeters have disembarked.

Suite No 3: Now the trumpets, horns, and oboe are all, lamentably, gone, but flute and piccolo add a new, softer dimension. Only four movements, in the keys of G Major and G Minor, survive. There may well have been others.

16. *Untitled:* The flute adds its silvery tone to the massed strings in this sarabande (a slow dance in three-quarter time, with the accent on the second beat).

17. *Presto:* This movement is a rigaudon (a lively seventeenth-century dance), here played as quickly as possible, with unexpected rhythmic turns. The middle section turns from major to minor.

18. *Minuet:* This swift-moving dance is more courtly than the minuets in the other suites. This time the middle section turns from minor to major.

19. *Untitled:* This movement is a gigue, a more refined French version of the countrified Irish jig, often used to end Baroque concerts.

Finally the *Water Music* ends, in performance today, with a repetition of the famous "Alla Hornpipe" from the second suite.

Recording

Gardner, English Baroque Soloists (Philips)

The Concerti Grossi for Strings, Op. 6 (1739)

These "grand concertos" for string orchestra, twelve in number, were quickly composed—or assembled from previous work—in a matter of weeks in the autumn of 1739, and though they were intended as pieces suitable for any occasion (some of them were fitted with optional parts for other instruments), together they constitute Handel's greatest contribution to instrumental music, worthy to stand beside the Brandenburg concertos of Bach. Handel was in poor health and financial straits at the time. His long and successful career as an opera composer/manager had ground to a halt, and he was turning to oratorio when pressing circumstances all but forced him to write smaller-scaled instrumental works of general appeal.

"Concerto" here, as with Bach's Brandenburgs, means a collection of movements—four, five, or six, in related keys but with contrasting moods and rhythms. Handel uses a small group of string instruments in concert with a larger string orchestra, with harpsichord accompaniment. Everything the instrumental Handel is famous for is in these Concerti Grossi—brisk allegros, meltingly beautiful largos, minuets, fugues, and seventeenth-century adaptations of national dances. There is a polonaise in No. 3, a hornpipe in No. 7, an allemande and a siciliana in No. 8, a gigue in No. 9. It's a glorious outpouring of genius. I've listened through all twelve concertos in a single sitting and still wanted more.

Recording

Manze, Academy of Ancient Music (Harmonia Mundi)

You may also want to hear...

...*The Royal Fireworks Music.* Splendid music for another of King George's royal fêtes, commissioned to celebrate the end of the Wars of Austrian Succession that—operagoers may know—drew Don Alvaro and Don Carlos to Spain (in *La Forza del Destino*) and enabled Faninal (in *Der Rosenkavalier*) to make his profiteering millions and put in a bid for aristocratic standing.

. . . the Concerti Grossi for Wind and String Instruments, Op. 3, six in number, earlier than the twelve concerti grossi mentioned above, but almost equally impressive.

Franz Joseph Haydn
1732–1809

Often called "the father of the symphony" and "the father of the string quartet," Haydn was at the very least responsible for the coming of age of those two great musical genres, as well as for the development of the sonata form. For those reasons alone he belongs in the canon. But over and above that, "Papa" Haydn, as Mozart often called him, wrote thirteen operas and an abundance of life-affirming, inexhaustibly inventive music in other forms as well. (You will certainly have heard his joyous trumpet concerto.) Some lovers of nineteenth-century Romantic music find him shallow. They couldn't be more wrong. Haydn's achievement, leading the symphony from its origins as a fast-slow-fast Italian overture to an art form ready to serve the titanic genius of Beethoven, looms larger than anything most Romantics ever dreamed of. And in his kindly, unsentimental, gently knowing way, Haydn remains, for those who have come to know him, a friend for life.

Symphony No. 102 in B-Flat Major (1795)

Faced with the impossible task of choosing just one of Haydn's 104 (now officially 108) symphonies, I have simply opted for my favorite—the delicious, innovative, proto-Romantic symphony that lies untitled between the more famous 101 (the "Clock") and 103 (the "Drum Roll") and, like them, is overshadowed in popularity and critical esteem by the final 104 (the "London").

Composed, like its sister symphonies, during Haydn's second trip to London, the "hundred and second" begins with a slow introduction—one of Haydn's more influential innovations—but here, every instrument in the orchestra sounds the same note in unison and holds it like a laser beam for several seconds. This unison note recurs once again in the introduction and several times throughout the first movement. (Not even Wagner attempted a one-note leitmotif.) The slow introduction gathers into something like a devotional statement and finally bursts into its main theme—an almost Romantic vivace that might have been penned, a half-century in the future, by Schumann or Weber. The second theme, almost opera buffa in character, turns the sonata-form movement into a little drama in the style of Mozart's mature instrumental works. The music dips dramatically, now into a minor mode, now into fugato (fugue-like) sections, and almost comes to a comic-opera halt just before its end.

The main melody of the second movement is surely one of the subtlest and loveliest anyone ever wrote—so subtle that Sir Donald Tovey used it to begin his extensive entry on rhythm in the eleventh and in subsequent editions of the *Encyclopedia Brittanica*, and so lovely that it seems to me to surpass even the slow-movement melodies in Mozart's symphonies, for, even more than they, it expands from a lyric beginning into a dramatic, almost tragic statement. The aura of Romanticism seems to hover over every changing mood of this all-too-brief slow movement.

Some hundred symphonies earlier, Haydn had introduced a third-movement minuet between the slow movement and the rapid finale that were traditional for symphonies, and gradually in his hands the minuet, and its contrasting middle section, the trio, became less courtly and more bumptious—ready to be turned, in Beethoven's hands, into a scherzo. Here the minuet manages somehow to be courtly and bumptious at the same time, and there are chromatic turns in the relaxed middle section that anticipate Romanticism.

The last movement is a rondo that might have come out of *The Barber of Seville*, had Rossini ever thought of turning out a rondo. This finale is more fun than a barrel of other rondos. And the main melody, like the main melodies in every movement of the "hundred and second," stays deliciously in the memory long after the sound of it has died away.

Recording

Davis, Concertgebouw Orchestra (Philips)

String Quartet in C Major, Op. 76, No. 3 ("Emperor")(1797)

This formidable quartet was one of six Haydn wrote in the fullness of his powers after his second visit to England, where he had been impressed by the emotions stirred in the people there by the playing of "God Save the King." Franz Joseph Haydn thought it was high time for him to pay homage to the emperor whose name he bore, and, as we might expect, he did so in innovative ways.

First we get a sonata-form movement without a second theme. Its whole structure is built from the confident opening statement and from material derived from it. The theme is passed from instrument to instrument, transmuted into varying moods, recast with exhilarating ease in different styles—including a rustic dance complete with bagpipe-like drone—and finally stated almost affectionately in a quiet coda.

There follows the movement that gives the quartet its name. It is a heartfelt statement, with four variations, of "Gott erhalte Franz den Kaiser," the anthem Haydn had written for the emperor's birthday, which was later adopted as Austria's national anthem. (Before and during the Second World War it was obscenely appropriated by the Nazis and fitted with jingoistic words. Now younger generations of many countries sing it, with yet another set of words, as a hymn.) Haydn does not subject the noble melody to the usual variation treatment, but, after the ensemble has played it in its simplest form, he gives each of the four instrumentalists—second violin, cello, viola, and first violin—an opportunity to play it as a solo, accompanied by the other three players. Each repetition is, however, more closely woven, more harmonically interesting, and more poignant than the last, and the fourth variation is supremely beautiful.

After approaching sonata and theme-and-variation forms in new ways in the first two movements, Haydn seems to be settling for the usual, enjoyably bumptious, minuet for the third, and this one is a real clodhopper. But then we get a lovely surprise: the movement's trio is a lyrical, introspective interlude that passes almost Romantically from minor to major.

The dramatic fourth movement also moves back and forth between C Minor (which was to become, with Mozart and Beethoven, the tonality best suited to tragic statements) and a relatively sunny C Major. But most of the movement is thunder and lightning, requiring tremendous versatility from the four instrumentalists.

Some listeners have been tempted to construct a "program" for this quartet: the four movements may be thought to be, first, a celebration of Austria's confident role in European history; then of its beloved emperor; then of its happy peasantry; and finally of its prowess in war. But, it must be said, Haydn would have been the last one to think of his quartet that way.

Recording
Kodály Quartet (Naxos)

You may also want to hear...

...among the symphonies, to cite only the rest of the top ten, No. 45 in F-Sharp Minor (the "Farewell"); No. 88 in G Major; No. 92 in G Major (the "Oxford"); No. 94 in G Major (the "Surprise"); No. 97 in C Major; No. 100 in G Major (the "Military"); and the aforementioned "Clock," "Drum Roll," and "London" symphonies—by which time you may well have discovered your own favorites.

...among the string quartets, to cite only the rest of the top ten, Opus 20, No. 1 (the quartet come to its full estate) and No. 5 (the quartet now capable of making profound statements); Opus 50, No. 3 (with its wonderful set of variations); Opus 64, No. 5 (the "Lark"); Opus 74, No. 1 (almost symphonic in texture); Opus 76, No. 4 (the "Sunrise"), No. 5 (with its superb largo), and No. 6 (with its unusual fantasia); and the final Op. 77, No. 2—by which time you will be happily embarked on making further discoveries of your own in one of the great treasure troves of music.

Wolfgang Amadeus Mozart
1756–1791

The most gifted human being that has ever been born (so said Sacheverell Sitwell, and many have agreed with him) left us four supreme operas, three more that have in recent years become repertory fixtures, and over six hundred other works in every musical form available to him in his thirty-five years on the planet. Almost any form of instrumental music you select as your starting point with Mozart will guarantee you a masterpiece right off. Here are my choices of two symphonies, two concertos, and two chamber works that every operagoer must know for full appreciation of Don Giovanni *and* The Magic Flute, *and any member of the human race will likely find himself more human for the listening to. (The K numbers are named for Ludwig Köchel, who catalogued Mozart's voluminous output.)*

Symphony No. 40 in G Minor, K.550 (1788)

Mozart's "fortieth" is a classical symphony in which powerful emotions are expressed in the most formal structures—and, almost paradoxically, it affects many of us as powerfully as any symphony written in the free-spirited Romantic period. The fortieth has often been called the single musical work that establishes a link between Classic and Romantic. Composed in one midsummer's inspiration with the thirty-ninth symphony (in which twinges of pain interrupt moods of Watteauesque repose) and the forty-first (the crowning "Jupiter"), it forms the central piece of what Mozart lovers have come to call "Mozart's symphonic trilogy." Yet the fortieth is distinct from the other two, more often chosen for performance than they, and much deeper in feeling. Sadly, none of the three symphonies was, as far as we know, ever performed in the composer's lifetime, let alone in his presence.

There is no formal introduction to this work, no proud instrumental flourish to catch an eighteenth-century listener's attention. Instead, over a quiet, quivering accompaniment, Mozart's plaintive violins thrust themselves immediately on our consciousness with a restless, anapestic, insistently questioning theme in G Minor. It is an opening many Romantic composers learned from.

G Minor is a special key for Mozart—a key associated in his work with pain and unexplainable loss. In the operas, it is the key of Konstanze's "Traurigkeit" ("Sadness") as she remembers the loss of her Belmonte, and the key of Pamina's "Ach! Ich fuhl's" ("Ah, I feel it") when all of a sudden her Tamino seems not to love her anymore. It is also the key of Mozart's greatest chamber work, the String Quintet K.516 (see below). But above all it is the key of this first movement.

The exposition continues with a gentler second theme, shared by oboe and clarinet, in B-Flat Major. Then, in a development section that seems almost to have left the Classical period entirely (the feeling is like Schubert, almost like Beethoven), the first theme is tossed from one key to another—expanded, shortened, inverted, and fragmented. There is a breathtaking transition back to the initial G-Minor tonality, and, when we come to the recapitulation, the B-Flat second theme is poignantly drawn into the G-Minor context.

The andante melody of the second movement is broken, after four measures, into pulsing, sighing eighth- and sixteenth-note phrases. The mood is not tragic—but it is, for a slow movement, unusually disconcerting.

The third movement is a minuet—but again, it is a driven, disconcertingly harsh and insistent minuet. Only the middle section, somewhat pastoral in feeling, brings some of the relief that a third movement, whether minuet or scherzo, was expected to give.

The fourth movement, an energetic rondo with an upward-leaping theme, returns the work finally to its original, dark tonality—G Minor. Some conductors will shape this allegro music into something hopeful; others keep it balanced in a no man's land between determination and despair.

Recording

Walter, Columbia Symphony Orchestra (Sony)

Symphony No. 41 in C Major, K.551 ("Jupiter") (1788)

The "Jupiter," the longest of all symphonies until Beethoven's "Eroica," was given its Olympian title by Johann Peter Salomon, the London violinist for whom Haydn's last symphonies were named. The title may refer to the rumbling effects in Mozart's opening C-Major theme—the thunder familiar from the father god's appearances in literature as far back as the first book of the *Iliad*. Thereafter the movement rolls on in eighteenth-century grandeur, with what journalist Alan Rich called "one dazzling melodic idea after another," with occasional outbursts of divine thunder, all in classic sonata form that keeps the music traveling through different tonalities.

The second movement begins with a brief, sorrowing theme in the violins, to which the full orchestra affixes a brusque chord like a single questioning word: "Why?" This unusual theme, not much more than a fragment, is developed with other musical ideas, some of them consoling, some almost despairing, some punctuated by that recurrent "Why?" The opening section ends tentatively. Then there comes, as a part of the second subject, an anguished cry in a minor key from the full orchestra. The development section takes this material through ever-changing regions till we return to a recapitulation of the sorrowing statement and its brusque questioning chord. Beethoven was to write the words "Must it be? It must be!" over the score of his last string quartet. And that is the kind of questioning I hear in this movement, a longer slow movement than is usual with Mozart, and a Romantic one despite its eighteenth-century stylization.

The third-movement minuet, too, is built on a larger scale than any minuet Mozart had written before, though only in the trio does the questioning mood of the second movement assert itself.

But it is the last movement of the "Jupiter" that is the seal on the work and, indeed, on all of Mozart's symphonic output. It is a dazzling structure built from five separate themes that are stated singly, in combination, in contrapuntal relationships with one another, and finally, in one of the most amazing moments in all of music, simultaneously. Everything is superbly confident (the first of the five themes is one that Mozart and many others had used, and many would continue to use, in their church music) and supremely joyous (another of the five themes is played backward, and yet another is stood on its head). And yet the import of the movement is essentially serious. Mozart, at the end of those few intensely creative weeks in the summer of 1788, seems to have decided at this point that the skittish, lighthearted rondo that till then was traditional for the end of a symphony was inadequate. He had used it in his thirty-ninth, where it seemed unworthy of what had gone before. He had used it, more weightily, at the close of his fortieth. Here he transcends it. Yes, there are lighthearted, even skittish, elements in this last movement, but its essential mood is triumph.

After Mozart's "Jupiter," the symphony was a different musical form, one that could make statements as profound in its final movement as in its first and the second. Beethoven, Schubert, Schumann, and Brahms were to end their large-scale symphonies with triumphant finales that gave answers to their questioning and sorrowing earlier movements. After the "Jupiter" the symphony was ready to become what Mahler said it should be—a whole world.

Recording

Walter, Columbia Symphony Orchestra (Sony)

Piano Concerto No. 23 in A Major, K.488 (1786)

Mozart's three greatest symphonies were written in six weeks, and his two greatest piano concertos were composed in a single month. These are the A Major, discussed here, and the near-tragic C Minor. Mozart himself was the soloist for the first performance of the A Major, and, as one of those in attendance, Ambrose Rieder, recalled, "I had never heard anything so great and so wonderful. Such bold flights of fancy, flights that seem to reach to the highest heavens, alike a marvel and a delight, even to the most experienced musicians present."

Features of Mozart's concerto writing that were only tendencies before—the close interaction of pianist and orchestra, the wider and deeper emotional range—become the norm here and for the remaining four piano concertos. But none of those four surpasses what we have in this radiant piece. A Major is Mozart's pastoral key, the key in which the aristocratic Don Giovanni all but seduces Zerlina the peasant girl, and also the key of his last, sometimes ineffably sad, instrumental statement, the clarinet concerto. So the tone of this concerto is, like the best of Mozart's work, like any of his four great operas, partly comic and partly tragic, and sometimes a marvelous fusion of the two.

The work is scored modestly for flute, two clarinets, two bassoons, two horns, and strings. There are no trumpets, trombones, or percussion. This is Arcadia, the quiet but subtly allusive land of the Virgilian eclogue. First, the strings introduce two leisurely themes, each of them long-lined (eight measures apiece). The piano develops both with exquisite feeling, then introduces the movement's second subject in the brighter key of E Major. This is given an unusual amount of development, some of it contrapuntal, some of it forecasting the second movement's F-Sharp-Minor sadness, all of it of extraordinary beauty.

The second movement, in that melancholy tonality, F-Sharp Minor, is one of Mozart's most poignant statements, a page of music to suggest to any art lover those eighteenth-century landscape paintings that bear the legend "Et in Arcadia ego." It is as if two shepherds, Mozart's two clarinets, have pulled the branches away from an Arcadian tomb, read the inscription there ("I too am in Arcadia"), and wondered who might have inscribed the words. Could it have been—as many read the Latin phrase to mean—Death? Does the phrase mean that, even in pastoral Arcadia, Death is present?

The last movement, a fleet-footed rondo filled to overflowing with A-Major and D-Major melodies, effectively banishes all sorrowing reflections. The exhilarating writing for piano in this movement has made the twenty-third perhaps the favored choice of all Mozart's concertos for the virtuoso pianist.

Recording

Brendel, Marriner, Academy of St. Martin in the Fields (Penguin Classics)

Clarinet Concerto in A Major, K.622 (1791)

Mozart had used clarinets prominently in his A-Major piano concerto. He returned to the same radiant key for his clarinet quintet and, in the last days of his life, for this heart-wrenching concerto. He was writing the *Requiem* at the same time (morbidly, he began to think he was writing it for himself). And his last opera, *The Magic Flute*, was playing nightly at Vienna's popular Freihaustheater outside the walls (happily, he could follow its progress every evening with his pocket watch). The only other composing that occupied him once this concerto was completed was music for a little cantata commissioned by his Masonic friends. As it turned out, they were the ones who would look after his burial.

Meanwhile Mozart was dealing with disappointment, rejection, poverty, and the thought that he would die before attaining the fullness of his powers. Eric Blom, a noted Mozartian, wrote that "his precarious state seems to be reflected in the hectic beauty" of the clarinet concerto. But much of the piece is not hectic at all but unusually placid and serene. Abraham Veinus, countering the statement of Blom, rightly says, "Nearly everything one can find in [Mozart's] instrumental music seems condensed into this unassuming work . . . Mozart knew, even in his early concertos, that elegance of phraseology was not incompatible with eloquence of feeling. This knowledge he imparts again here, more quietly and more firmly than ever."

In fact, the concerto opens with a theme so limpid and relaxed that one can hardly forgive Blom for that word "hectic," and it proceeds quietly, simply, quite without the stream of musical ideas we might have expected after hearing Mozart's piano concertos. Everything, from second subject to development section to recapitulation, is lucidly laid out, and the music passes through wondrous changes of mood and color.

Then, as so often occurs with the other concertos, it is the second movement that crowns the work. First, the clarinet sings a plaintive melody over a swaying accompaniment of strings. Then the melody is taken up by the strings themselves. Then the clarinet returns with a five-note figure that descends stepwise, and is repeated three times. Nothing could be simpler than those opening measures. Yet they are almost unbearably moving. For some listeners, just the thought of that descending phrase can be enough to bring tears. No concerto movement of Mozart is so straightforward. Yet we can sense depths beneath the surface, and the clarinet, which Mozart thought of almost as a human voice, was never before or since given such eloquent music to sing.

The third movement is the expected rondo, full of flourishes for the soloist and felicitous touches for the orchestra. But there is a strain of sorrow in it that becomes increasingly clearer on repeated hearings. As H. C. Robbins Landon, the chronicler of Mozart's last year, has put it, "The heart dances, but not for joy." As with the A Major piano concerto, Mozart has dispensed here with the heavier brasses and all percussion, and scored for two flutes, two bassoons, two horns, and strings as a counterpart for the solo instrument he had loved since his early twenties. "Oh, if we only had clarinets!" he once wrote to his father from Mannheim. "You cannot imagine the glorious effect a symphony has with flutes, oboes, and clarinets." Then in his thirties he met a virtuoso on the instrument, Anton Stadler, who had designed a special clarinet, the basset horn, that was capable of playing two notes lower than the instrument's usual range. Mozart wrote extended obbligatos in two arias in his opera *La Clemenza di Tito* for Stadler, as well as the earlier clarinet trio and clarinet quintet. But it is this concerto, a valedictory, that shows the full range and expressiveness of what had become, in Mozart's last year, his favorite instrument of all.

Recording

Goodman, Munch, Boston Symphony Orchestra (RCA)

String Quartet in D Minor, K.421 (1783)

This is the second of the six quartets that Mozart, in an rare act of homage from one great composer to another, dedicated to Joseph Haydn. The master from Esterhaz, the father of the string quartet, visited Vienna in 1785 and heard the twenty-nine-year-old Mozart performing three of his own quartets in concert with his father and two friends. Mozart had been studying the polyphonic works of Bach and Handel and had learned to treat the four strands of sound in his quartets with a new complexity without sacrificing any of the elegance and apparent ease for which he was already noted. The quartets were not commissioned, as so much of his work was; Mozart had written them simply because he wanted, with all deference to Haydn, to expand the expressive range of the most popular musical form of the day.

Mozart's father wrote that Haydn, on first hearing the three new quartets, confided to him, "I tell you before God and as an honest man that your son is the greatest composer known to me either in person or by reputation."

Mozart published the three quartets Haydn heard on that occasion, along with three composed a few years earlier, and sent them to the elder composer with this dedication:

> To my dear friend Haydn: A father who had decided to send his children into the world at large thought it best to entrust them to the protection and guidance of a famous man who fortunately happened to be his best friend as well. Behold here my six children. They are the fruit of long and arduous work, but . . . you yourself, dearest friend, have shown me your approval of them during your last sojourn in this capital. Your praise, above all, encourages me to recommend them to you, and makes me hope that they shall not be entirely unworthy of your good will. May it please you, therefore, to receive them kindly and to be their father, their guide, and their friend.

The "second Haydn quartet," as it is often called, is cast in the dramatic (some critics have said daemonic) D-Minor tonality that Mozart, a few years later, would give to the avenging statue of the Commendatore in *Don Giovanni* and eventually to the Queen of the Night in her vengeance aria, "Der Hölle Rache," in *The Magic Flute*. Here he begins with a disquieting theme—the first violin dropping a full octave from its initial emphatic D—and repeats it insistently. He moves to a major tonality for his second theme, sung by the first violin accompanied by pulsing triplets in the other instruments. The serious mood is, however, not dispelled. And there is an abrupt key change in the development section that, even after repeated hearings, registers strongly. Though twenty-first century ears have grown accustomed to taking in stride such "dissonances" as appear in this and other Mozart quartets, it was not so in the composer's own day. When the six quartets dedicated to Haydn were sent to Italy, they were returned to the publisher with the complaint that the engraving was full of mistakes. And a Hungarian prince, convinced that his musicians were playing incorrectly, and shown in the score that what he heard was what was written, tore the pages up in fury. A good performance will make it clear, even two centuries later, why that reaction was prompted.

The second movement, in the related key of F Major, is a strangely halting, haunting andante that suggests deeper feelings beneath its placid surface. When the mood shifts to minor, the music seems to express thoughts "too deep for tears."

Even the minuet that follows runs deep. The tonality returns to an almost painful D Minor, and it comes as a relief when, in the middle section, cello and violin change the general mood to major in a naïve Ländler (country dance). But it is the last movement that makes the deepest impression. It is a set of variations, mostly minor, on a haunting siciliana (a rhythmic eighteenth-century dance). The melody, with its ringing four-bar refrain on a repeated high note, is turned, almost savagely, into a succession of mysterious, ghostly airs. (I always feel, on hearing it, as if I were being led in a lantern-lit procession down a dark eighteenth-century Sicilian street.) Nineteenth-century critics referred to the "daimonische Klang" in Mozart's music. Here, D Minor is firmly established as Mozart's daemonic key.

Recording
Cleveland Quartet (Telarc)

String Quintet in G Minor, K.516 (1787)

With this work we are back in the tonality where we began our consideration of these representative works of Mozart—in the key of G Minor. And like the "fortieth" symphony we spoke of first, this string quintet is an intensely personal and very moving statement. The addition of a second viola—rather than, say, a piano or clarinet—to the four string voices gives the work a darker color and weightier feeling than most other chamber pieces have, and the piece is regarded, by critical consensus, as the finest of Mozart's works in this genre.

Mozart was in financial straits in 1787. He was being paid only a pittance by the emperor, Joseph II. He was, in addition, losing his public. His music was increasingly regarded by critics, musicians, and the public as too difficult. Some of it went unperformed. He thought he was facing failure. And his father was dying. W. H. Turner suggests that Mozart decided from that year on to write mainly for himself and the few musicians who were capable of understanding his music.

The G-Minor quintet's first movement, which seems to reflect all of this, is a relentlessly forward-moving, slightly panicky, utterly poignant expression, in sonata form, of something close to despair. The mood established by the rapid, chromatic, unforgettable opening phrase is not changed, only furthered, by subsequent themes. The G-Minor tonality prevails throughout the movement.

The tense minuet that follows, savagely punctuated by off-beat chords, is similarly despairing, though its trio moves for a few dozen bars from minor to major.

The slow movement, played with mutes on all five instruments, is in the related key of E-Flat Major, and promises to throw the tragic tone of the work into some relief. Its main theme is a hymn-like melody—but one that finds its attempt at prayer constantly interrupted. Other themes come and go, among them a ravishing exchange in a higher key for the first violin and the first viola. When this second theme returns in the recapitulation, drawn into the lower tonality of the movement's beginning, the effect is, like much in this adagio, almost unbearably sad.

There follows another, slower adagio, as sorrowing as anything Mozart ever wrote. We wait breathlessly to hear what will happen—and can only be disappointed when the movement breaks unconvincingly into a rondo. This finale is beautifully wrought, of course, and with a poignancy of its own, but it seems inadequate after all that has gone before. Mozart had yet to make the important decision to change the last movements of his extended works from the traditional happy ending to monumental triumph, as in the "Jupiter" symphony, or to resignation, as in the clarinet concerto. All the same, that "all that has gone before" is music no one who has heard it will ever want to do without.

Mozart's father, with whom he had a difficult relationship, especially in the later years, died within a few days after Mozart entered the G-Minor quintet in his catalogue. Meanwhile, in this six-month period of extraordinary stress, Mozart wrote not only the G-Minor quintet but a quintet of comparable stature in C Major, two piano sonatas, two rondos, two concert arias, two songs, the *Musikalischer Spass*, the serenade *Eine Kleine Nachtmusik*, and—incredibly—most of *Don Giovanni*.

Not all of these works show signs of abnormal stress, but it is hard to think of any period in any artist's life that was so compulsively creative, and H. C. Robbins Landon, wondering especially about the unusual "combination of tragedy and tenderness" in the G-Minor quintet, cites the research of an Australian doctor, Peter J. Davies, into Mozart's late compositions in minor keys, into events in the last seven years of his life, and into his letters and observations made by his friends: "There is convincing evidence for the insidious onset during Mozart's early adult life of a chronic mood disturbance, which persisted until his death, and which was associated with pathological mood swings of hypomania and depression."

Whatever the cause of the audible suffering in Mozart's minor-key music, and especially in this quintet, we know that all too soon, in his thirty-fifth year, the voice of "the most gifted human being that has ever been born" was stilled.

Recording

Heifetz, Baker, Primrose, Majewski, Piatigorsky (RCA)

You may also want to hear...

...the Symphony No. 39 in E-Flat Major, K.543, the almost Romantic work composed in the same midsummer's inspiration that gave us the sorrowing G Minor and the triumphant "Jupiter." Among the earlier symphonies, don't neglect No. 29 in A Major, K.201, a radiant work from start to finish, with a brief but magical coda at the end of its first movement that seems, like Pygmalion, to bring a Galatea to life. Other enjoyable symphonies are No. 34 in C Major, K.338; No. 35 in D Major, K.385 (the "Haffner"); No. 36 in C Major, K.425 (the "Linz"); and No. 38 in D Major, K.504 (the "Prague"). Once you've met them, each of Mozart's symphonies takes on an identity all its own and remains a companion for life.

...the other piano concertos that Mozart, in the midst of writing his greatest operas, composed almost as little dramas wherein he, at the keyboard, could interact with the instruments of the orchestra, engaging in any number of encounters in each movement. The pantheon of superb Mozart piano concertos is crowded to overflowing, so it may be helpful to characterize the best of them, as the "Jupiter" symphony is characterized, by assigning each a suitable god from Roman antiquity. Thus, No. 20 in D Minor, K.466, serious and impassioned for most of its length, might be named the "Pluto," for the implacable Lord of Hades. No. 21 in C Major, K.467, a virginal work with an idyllic slow movement, might be the "Diana"; then we would no longer need to refer to it by the name of the insignificant film, *Elvira Madigan*, that popularized it in the mid-twentieth century. The gracefully ambling No. 22 in E-Flat Major, K.482, might be the "Venus"; one critic remembered Virgil's goddess of love when he heard it, and quoted "vera incessu patuit dea" ("by her step the goddess revealed herself"). If No. 23 in A Major, K.488 (discussed in our first chapter), is the "Mercury," then that powerful concerto of many contrasting moods, No. 24 in C Minor, K.491, could rightly be named, also from his appearance in Virgil, the "Neptune." The stately and imperious No. 25 in C Major, K.503, is as surely the "Juno" as the harmoniously proportioned No. 27 in B-Flat Major, K.595, is the "Apollo." All of these planetary concertos are works of astonishing wit, grace, and lightly borne wisdom. Alongside them, Mozart's violin concertos, also composed to demonstrate his virtuosic skill, seem to me to be works of lesser stature.

. . . at least six more chamber works—the five other quartets dedicated to Haydn and the Sinfonia Concertante for violin and viola in E-Flat Major, K.364, with its superb slow movement.

. . . among the works for solo piano, the charming and ever-popular Sonata in A Major, K.331, and that treasure for the young pianist, the Sonata in C Major, K.545. From there I would move on to the late Sonata in B-Flat Major, K.570, and the powerful Fantasie and Sonata in C Minor, K.457/475.

But be assured that there is much, much more.

Ludwig Van Beethoven
1770–1827

Beethoven bestrides the ages of Classicism and Romanticism like a colossus. He enlarged the scope of the symphony, the concerto, the sonata, and—perhaps especially—the string quartet, and in the process he transformed them from delicate musical structures into new, powerful ways of expressing both his personal feelings and the revolutionary ideas of his time. His only opera, Fidelio, is a testament to the resilience of the human sprit. No other composer is so elemental, idealistic, and—increasingly in the late compositions—sublime.

Symphony No. 3 in E-Flat Major, Op. 55 ("Eroica") (1804)

The "Eroica," as Beethoven's third symphony is invariably called, is the kind of monumental work that is easier to respect than to love. In 1804 it was by far the largest-scaled symphony anyone had ever heard. Each of its four movements is as long as any number of whole symphonies by Mozart or Haydn. Its sounds and rhythms have an intensity, an insistence, that in 1804 was wholly new to audiences. And it was, at least partly, autobiographical.

Two years before its completion, Beethoven knew without a doubt that he was going deaf. It was a crushing blow to a young man of thirty-two who gave every indication of having a brilliant future in music. We can read of his almost suicidal despair in the moving "Heiligenstadt Testament" he wrote in 1802 to his brothers. The struggle to survive released in him creative energies such as few men have ever known, and there issued from his pen not just *Fidelio*, but symphonies, sonatas, string quartets, and concertos that are still mainstays of the concert repertory. These works were not the neatly structured "abstract music" that Europe, and Vienna in particular, held dear. They were often chaotic and disturbing, and seemed always to be communicating some extra-musical significance. William Mann observed that, while earlier composers wrote for a small public, suddenly "Beethoven was speaking, sometimes shouting at the top of his voice, to the whole of humanity and to posterity after him."

The "Eroica" symphony was among the first of these revolutionary compositions. Initially it was dedicated to Napoleon, whom Beethoven regarded as the heroic champion of Liberty,

Equality, and Fraternity. Then he heard that his ideal hero had had himself crowned emperor. He flew into a rage and, in the presence of several friends, ripped the title page off his score and threw it on the floor. Thereafter the symphony was named, as if for "the unknown soldier," "Sinfonia Eroica, composed to celebrate the memory of a great man."

The first movement begins with two brutally abrupt E-Flat chords—two sabre slashes that, Ethan Mordden says, constitute "perhaps the great moment in the history of the symphony." And immediately Beethoven's orchestra sails into a ten-note "hero" theme as uncomplicated as a military fanfare, except that it ends with an unsettling, unresolved "wrong note," a C Sharp that is utterly foreign to the E-Flat tonality so heavily imposed by the two chords just a few measures before. Dissonance and struggle will fill the twenty-minute sonata-form movement to follow, as the theme strives to escape that C Sharp, fighting to free itself from its own built-in tension even after a mass of second-subject material attempts to soften and domesticate it. Something new was happening in this music, and the brutal shock and the tension—even of the exposition, let alone what follows—must have bewildered every listener at the start of the nineteenth century.

But the development section is even more stupendous. As the "hero" theme is transformed by passion, by obstinacy, by fury, we hear veritable explosions of dissonance and the wildest of rhythmic patterns. We also hear, by way of another innovation, a new melody (something unusual in a development section), a chromatic phrase played first in octaves by oboes and cellos. Then, when the orchestral sound has been reduced to a whisper and we feel that we are returning at last to the terra firma of a recapitulation, Beethoven has a solo horn introduce the "hero" theme before the harmony has progressed into the required E Flat. (Even professional musicians were certain, at the first run-through, that the horn player must have made a premature entrance, four measures too early. But when the poor man was called to account for his "mistake," Beethoven was furious with the traditionalists; the horn player had followed the score exactly.)

Then comes the most amazing moment of all: at the end of the onwardly pulsing recapitulation, the tonality shifts and shifts and shifts away from the harmonic implications of that unsettling C Sharp to a radiant C Major before finding its way firmly to the E-Flat tonality we have been waiting for. The technical aspects of this are beyond the scope of this book, but any listener will sense that something of importance is happening here to the sonata-form structure, just as any opera lover feels the awesome power of the similarly shifting tonalities at the very end of Wagner's *Ring*. And at the close of the movement, when Haydn or Mozart might have added a satisfying little coda, Beethoven makes his crowning statement: the "hero" theme is sounded triumphantly with the discord in it resolved.

The second movement bears the title "Marcia funebre." It is as if the struggling, conquering hero of the first movement has been killed in battle and is being given a state funeral with full military honors. Needless to say, the question has often been asked, "If this symphony was originally dedicated to Napoleon, why does it contain a funeral march when, at the time of its composition, Napoleon was still very much alive?" There is no one answer to that question. But, since the symphony was eventually dedicated to an *ideal* hero, we can rightly consider the march—a powerful and extremely moving lament—an expression of tragic grief for the heroes slain in defense of freedom at all times and places.

There are several sections to the march—an inexorable, slow-moving, ever-recurring processional in the minor; a rising, comforting melody in the major; a quasi-religious fugato; a brief but heroic blast of trumpets; and a hopeful strain introduced by a figure on the strings that sounds for all the world like the relentless ticking of the second hand on a giant clock. But always, between the sections, the processional music returns, ineffably sad. Wagner, who conducted the "Eroica" many times throughout his life (and without a score, which was unheard of in his day), wrote for his hero Siegfried the only funeral march comparable with this one, a march that travels through some of the same keys and many of the same moods of triumph and tragedy.

With his third movement, Beethoven, writing near the beginning of a new century, makes a change that was to affect symphonic composition for at least a hundred years to come. He had planned the movement traditionally, as a minuet. But eventually he substituted—as he had, rather tentatively, in his second symphony—a scherzo, a "joke." And this time he wrote an immense, laughing scherzo, with a jubilant trio built on horn calls. Henceforth it would be a scherzo, not a minuet, that would stand in contrast to the slow movement in virtually every symphony written by subsequent composers.

Some conductors, mostly Germans, have problems with this scherzo. Thinking they ought not to contradict the seriousness of the previous movement with too much merriment, they take this liveliest of pieces at a lugubriously slow pace, ignoring the marking given it—allegro vivace. And thereby another question has arisen: "Why does this laughing celebration of the hero follow on his funeral march?" Berlioz, with his usual erudition, provided one answer to that question: in the *Iliad,* Achilles followed the elaborate funeral obsequies given his friend Patroclus with lively funeral games in his honor. But there is a more profound answer. J. W. N. Sullivan, one of the most perceptive commentators on Beethoven, writes, "Beethoven was here speaking of what was perhaps the cardinal experience of his life, that when, with all his strength and courage, he had been reduced to despair . . . there came this turbulent, irrepressible, deathless creative energy surging up from depths he had not suspected." For Sullivan, the whole "Eroica" is "a most close-knit psychologic unit"—four movements in which Beethoven struggles with the threat of deafness, then grieves for his loss and even contemplates suicide, then feels new creative energy stirring within him, and, finally and gloriously, *creates*. Ultimately, for Sullivan and many others, it is not Napoleon's heroism that is being depicted in the "Eroica." It is Beethoven's.

Whether the hero in question is Napoleon or some idealized warrior or the composer himself, the next and final movement seems to this listener to audaciously attempt a cosmic apotheosis of him—the kind of welcome into Valhalla that Wagner first envisioned for his Siegfried. The movement is essentially a set of twelve variations on a theme Beethoven had used three times before—in an unimposing set of country dances, in the piano variations that came to be called "the Eroica Variations," and in the ballet suite *The Creatures of Prometheus*, which celebrated the mythical figure who stole fire from heaven and bestowed it on mankind—and who in some accounts actually created the human race.

The Promethean theme of this last movement is primer-simple, and Beethoven, in his Promethean role as creator, sometimes plays with it in ways that have been thought simple-minded. But with hindsight we can see that both the "hero" theme of the first movement and the horn calls of the third have been derived from it: Sullivan was right in calling the symphony "close-knit." And by its closing pages, the "Prometheus" theme—which is, after all, no simpler in outline than the first theme used by Mozart for the finale of his "Jupiter" symphony—has gone through several extraordinary mutations, some of them contrapuntal, one of them wild with gypsy abandon, the greatest of them gloriously triumphant. An opera lover will also remark that the movement opens and closes with excited rushing passages for the strings that conjure up the whole heroic world of *Fidelio*.

In any case, with Beethoven's "Eroica" the symphony was henceforth forever changed into a vehicle for expressing, in four successive movements, striving, sorrow, reawakening, and ultimate triumph. Romanticism had, beyond any doubt, finally arrived in music.

Recording
Karajan, Berlin Philharmonic (DG)

Symphony No. 6 in F Major, Op. 68 ("Pastoral") (1808)

Not all of Beethoven's major works are the statements of a passionate man defying fate. Some are filled from start to finish with the joy that was finally to emerge triumphantly in the Ninth Symphony. And one of those works, the symphony that Beethoven himself dubbed the "Pastoral," gives expression to his almost pantheistic love of nature. "No man on earth," he wrote, "loves the country more than I." He conceived some of his best musical ideas on his daily walks in the countryside around Vienna, sketchbook in hand, in awe of what he saw. "Every tree," he said, "seems to say Holy, Holy."

The first movement of this beautiful work, titled "Awakening of cheerful feelings on arriving in the country," observes the niceties of sonata form but is not constrained by them. Virtually everything develops out of the charming introductory melody. Beethoven extracts a five-note figure out of its second bar and repeats it some eighty times throughout the movement. And a dozen other short phrases, joyously repeated, insist, in the words of an American lyricist, that "all the sounds of the earth are like music."

In the second movement, "By the Brook," muted cellos gently imitate of the murmur of the water; massed violins introduce a melody of truly idyllic calm; and other instruments provide trills and grace notes—the songs of birds and the whispers of the wind—reminiscent of the imitative effects that Gluck used for his Orpheus entering the Elysian fields. Once again, though the movement is cast in the most correct sonata form, there is none of that structure's built-in tension. The listener is lulled away from all such concerns by the irresistible onward flow of the music.

Beethoven insisted that this symphony was "more an expression of feeling than a painting." All the same, there is some tone-painting at the movement's end: we hear the trilling of a nightingale (flute), a quail (oboe), and a cuckoo (clarinet). Beethoven said that he told his impressionable—and perhaps gullible—biographer Anton Schindler that he wrote the passage while those very birds were calling from the trees around him, and that he intended it "only as a joke." If so, it is a charming one.

In the brief third movement, Beethoven introduces human figures. He titled it "Merry gathering of country folk" and seems to have used it to caricature, playfully, seven village musicians from the inn, "The Three Ravens," where he used to stop on his trips to the country. Those rustic instrumentalists seem, in this movement, to have come out-of-doors to accompany some light trippers and tipplers. Happiest of the bunch are the two "horn players," whose whooping is one of the most joyous effects in all the music I know. The "oboist" in the group can play seven notes on his instrument while the poor "bassoonist," it seems, can only play three—though he puts them to solid, comically stolid use. The "clarinetist" and horn player use the oboist's tune for their own purposes. Then suddenly it seems as if, in a kind of trio introduced by thumping bass viols, a fight breaks out between these instrumentalists and the dancers, till the "trumpeter" issues a warning and the playful stomping starts as before. Just when we come again to the whooping horns, we suddenly we find ourselves thrust without a break into . . .

. . . the fourth movement: "Thunderstorm." First, in an orchestral hush, we hear the swaying of the forest leaves and the first plops of the raindrops. Then the storm breaks in all its fury, with very realistic thunder and lightning and with some impressive high-pitched shrilling from the piccolo. But the finest of the effects is the subtly Beethovenesque growling of the lower strings that underlies much of this. Eventually the storm subsides—to a marvelous passage in which we seem to hear the thunder and rain receding into the distance—and a rising octave run on the flute leads us directly into . . .

. . . the fifth movement, which Beethoven titled "Shepherds' Song. Happy, thankful feelings after the storm." A clarinet intones a mountaineer's "Jodel"; a horn happily answers it; and from these phrases emerges one of the composer's most felicitous inspirations—a "Shepherds' Song" that is at once an evocation of a pastoral landscape and a prayer of thanksgiving. At this moment I can't help but remember, with poignancy, that by the time Beethoven composed this music deafness was closing in on him. "How humbling it was," he remembered, "when someone stood beside me and heard a flute in the distance and I heard nothing, or someone heard a shepherd singing and I heard nothing. Such incidents brought me to the verge of despair."

And yet only thankfulness and quiet joy pervade the music that closes the "Pastoral" symphony, as the orchestra plays variation after variation on the "Shepherds' Song," climaxing in a sunlit organ-like passage for upper strings that, on its second appearance just before the close, always brings tears to my eyes. Edward Downes, the beloved critic best known from his appearances on the Metropolitan Opera broadcasts, has written, rightly, "It is as if the whole world were exulting in the miracle of the fresh-washed sky and air and the return of the sun." And he adds, "That a man of sorrows and self-erected miseries like Beethoven could glimpse such glory and, by the incomprehensible alchemy of his art, lift us to share his vision—even if only for a few moments—is a miracle that remains as fresh as tomorrow's sunrise."

Recording

Böhm, Vienna Philharmonic Orchestra (DG)

Piano Concerto No. 4 in G Major, Op. 58 (1806)

In the early 1800s Beethoven was better known as a pianist than a composer, and he wrote his piano concertos to be performed by himself. He could command the keyboard with a burly virility that sometimes left the instrument with snapped strings, damaged keys, and a broken frame. He could also woo it with the loveliest and most ingratiating finesse. The most famous of his concertos, the "Emperor," is a commanding, frame-breaking piece. This earlier concerto is by turns ingratiating, meditative, and joyous. It is amazing to think that it was first performed publicly, with Beethoven at the piano, on an evening in 1806 in Vienna when the fifth and sixth symphonies also received their public premieres, along with the C-Minor Fantasy for piano, chorus, and orchestra, the aria "Ah, perfido," and three pieces from the C-Minor Mass. Two hundred years later, when new works appear far more rarely and are soon forgotten, we can only gasp in astonishment at this plethora of new riches crowded into that single evening.

We are told that the concert was poorly attended, the theater freezing cold, and the musicians under-rehearsed. Beethoven, nonetheless, astonished those in attendance; according to one listener, he played his concerto "with astounding cleverness and in the fastest possible tempi," and in the second movement "he sang on [the] instrument with a profound melancholy."

The audience would have expected the concerto to begin with the traditional orchestral flourish and a statement of the principal themes of the first movement. Only then would the soloist enter. But that evening, as a hush fell on the auditorium, the audience first heard Beethoven at the keyboard, unaccompanied, gently playing the quietest of themes. Perhaps some of the listeners might have sensed that that theme actually took its rhythm from the defiant four-note motto—the "V for Victory" theme—that began the fifth symphony that night. But how changed the theme was when played in the silence of the auditorium on the piano alone! Then, after six bars, the orchestra answered—taking the theme to a different key. The effect must have been startling then, and remains so in the concert hall today.

Then, on that evening in Vienna, the first violins, followed by a solo oboe, sang a gracefully leaping phrase, the second of a number of almost Mozartian themes in the movement to follow. Once again the piano entered to join the orchestra in a restatement and then a development of the opening theme and several others. Never had a concerto theme been so quietly insistent, so pervasive, as the transformed "Victory" theme, sounded over and over—its four notes now delicate rather than defiant, romantic rather than resolute. The audience must have been amazed at the arpeggios, the delicate filigree work, the sudden contrasts, the pervasive lyricism of this music. It sounded like Mozart, but had a virility and an introspection all its own—and not even Mozart had crowned his recapitulations with so crystalline a cadenza. The whole first movement of the fourth piano concerto is, like the "Pastoral" symphony, a corrective to the notion that Beethoven's music is always the work of a two-fisted Titan. Here he seems rather the composer who naturally bridges the period between the genial Mozart of the late concertos and the youthful, songful Schubert.

But it is the five-minute second movement that has made this concerto famous. The prominence given the piano soloist and the responsiveness of the orchestra now reach a new level of musical eloquence. The orchestra begins with a harsh statement in almost threatening octaves. Then the piano enters into dialogue with it, in gentle phrases, poignant utterances, and eventually in a slow cadenza-like passage of surprising emotional force—until the orchestra is, in effect, silenced, its relentless octaves finally melting into peaceful harmonies. Franz Liszt compared the movement, memorably and accurately, to the myth of Orpheus taming the beasts. It could as easily be an interior dialogue between Beethoven the defiant hero and Beethoven the man coming to terms—like Florestan in the prison scene in *Fidelio*—with his human condition, resigned and quietly submissive. Certainly it is a movement of sustained drama and sublimity, a movement in which music all but becomes speech.

The third movement follows almost without a break. The strings quietly strike up an animated theme, which the piano immediately embellishes. Soon the whole orchestra enters, and we are swept into a rondo with remarkably varied inner sections, the piano urging the orchestra ever onward through now determined, now reflective moods toward a forceful, glittering cadenza and a full-scaled orchestral presto.

One cannot hear this concerto without remembering that during its gestation no fewer than seven other masterpieces were taking shape in the composer's mind—the "Appassionata" sonata, the three Razumovsky Quartets, the violin concerto, and the fourth and fifth symphonies—music of many moods, and not the least of these works is this remarkably beautiful concerto that Beethoven wrote for himself to perform at the piano.

Recording

Kovacevich, Davis, BBC Symphony Orchestra (Philips)

Piano Sonata No. 32 in C Minor, Op. III (1822)

Many of Beethoven's thirty-two sonatas for solo piano are among his greatest works, so familiar that concertgoers have given them names—the "Pathétique," the "Moonlight," the "Appassionata," the "Waldstein," the "Hammerklavier."

But perhaps the greatest of them is the one simply called "Opus 111" or, less often, "Number 32"—the composer's last piano sonata, in only two movements, written while he was struggling with his titanic Ninth Symphony and Missa Solemnis. It is not a work in which you will hear beautiful melodies. The critic Henry Kreibel said it was "a musician's sonata" that "discourses music rather than the charms of pianoforte tone." But I can guarantee that what Beethoven does with the theme of his last sonata movement will stay with you long after the conventionally beautiful melodies of other composers have faded. This is not beautiful music so much as music itself.

The first movement begins *maestoso*, majestically, with a demanding downward-moving phrase that is answered three times, at rising pitches, with phrases that speak of submission and plead for release from pain. There is some development of this material, and then the main theme of the movement enters, a fugal subject marked "with fire and passion." The second subject is a kind of pianistic chorale, a lull in the musical storm. Both themes are developed with an intensity that struck audiences in its day—and can still strike today's audiences—as eccentric. Finally the music finds its way quietly from its C-Minor fundament to C Major, the key in which the next movement will write *finis* to Beethoven's keyboard works.

Beethoven unassumingly called the second movement's only theme an arietta, a little aria, and marked it "very simple and songlike." It begins without introduction, each of its two eight-bar sections played with the utmost slowness and then calmly repeated. Several variations on that theme follow. Beethoven did not number them. The tempo does not change. The little aria seems at first to amble amiably, then to be rocked by disorienting rhythms, then to explode in cascades of heavily syncopated (modern listeners might even say "jazzy") and almost agonized sound. Finally, in what might be thought the fourth variation, fragments of the theme are quietly transformed, now in a quietly sustained bass, now in a delicate tracery on the highest keys of the keyboard.

Then we hear the first of the trills for which this last pianistic statement is famous. The trill, once a mere decorative device, here becomes the substance of Beethoven's musical thought. The theme, stated in full but without the repeats, returns. For several quiet pages it is as if the composer has had a mystical experience. And so it is with us as we listen. The trills return, and the theme seems to be wafted to the skies, leaving the soloist with only intimations of its first few notes. The rest is silence.

Beethoven's publishers, receiving the manuscript and finding only two movements, wrote to ask if perhaps the copyist had forgotten to send on the last part of the sonata. Beethoven's bumbling biographer Anton Schindler encouraged him to write a rondo to finish off the work. But the composer knew that there was no more that need be, or could be, said.

Recording
Pollini (DG)

String Quartet in C-Sharp Minor, Op. 131 (1826)

The last music Beethoven wrote, his five "late string quartets," were all but incomprehensible to critics and audiences in their day. But they are not as forbidding as you may have heard. Twenty-first-century ears accustomed to the tormented and introspective string quartets of Bartók and Shostakovich will not find Beethoven's final statements overly difficult. Many individual movements in them are immediately accessible. All the same, there are other movements—mainly the slow movements that J. W. N. Sullivan called "unsuspected islands and even continents" in "strange seas of thought"—that are like nothing written before and like very little written since, and they have seemed to Sullivan and to many of us the musical expressions of almost mystical experiences. The "late quartets" are unquestionably great music, and no one who has heard only the Beethoven of the symphonies can really claim to know the composer until he or she has listened through these extraordinary works and pondered them.

Surely there is nothing in operatic music like the nakedness of soul—of a soul in both rapture and torment—at certain moments in the "late quartets." Perhaps, for an opera lover, the recurrence of the "resignation" motif at pivotal points in the last act of Wagner's *Die Meistersinger*, or the compassionate orchestral interlude before the last scene in Berg's *Wozzeck*, compare. But those are less private moments, fully scored, parts of larger dramas upon which they comment. The emotionally naked moments of the "late quartets," in which only four string voices contemplate or suffer or wonder in music that seems to be struggling to express experiences beyond the expressive nature of music, are moments in which we are altogether alone with the great composer. Those moments have long been thought uniquely valuable. Sullivan even calls them "experiences to which the race, in its evolutionary march, aspires."

Beethoven was isolated by total deafness and in constant pain when he wrote the "late quartets." In them he largely abandoned the sonata-form structure and wrote in as many movements as he deemed necessary. The C-Sharp Minor Quartet has seven movements. The first of these, brief but perhaps the most affecting of them all, is a slow, pained, passionless, almost unearthly fugue. I have not seen any commentators remark that its twelve-note theme follows in outline the subject of Bach's "Little Fugue in G Minor." But what is exuberant and spirited in Bach becomes meditative and utterly private here. Wagner thought it the greatest expression of melancholy in music. For others it is not melancholy but submission, or inner peace, or "seeing life steadily and seeing it whole" that is suggested. Sullivan has pointed out, and I in my lectures on *Fidelio* have often remarked, that the earlier Beethoven familiar from the third and fifth symphonies is a man *defiant* in the face of suffering; that, with Florestan's aria in *Fidelio* and with the words of his own "Heiligenstadt Testament," he has become a man who has learned to *accept* suffering with submission; and that in the "last quartets" he is, finally, a man who has learned to *welcome* suffering as a blessing. That is what we have here.

The second movement is a discreet allegro in which Sullivan heard a "virginal purity." But there is a disturbing sadness under its quietly animated surface.

The brief third movement, with its heart-piercing chords, is actually an introduction to the fourth—a theme-and-variations movement in which Beethoven's experience of suffering turns by almost imperceptible degrees to feelings of happiness and peace, especially in the unexpected series of trills that introduce the final variation. (The variations, it should be said, follow not the melody of the theme but its harmonic outline.)

The fifth movement is a scherzo-like outburst of joy, with exhilarating touches of humor. (Verdi, who kept the scores of Beethoven's quartets at his bedside in Sant' Agatha, seems to have remembered a strain from its middle section when he wrote the ballet music for *Aida*.)

The sixth movement is a brief, twenty-eight-measure adagio in which the heavens seem to open for the suffering composer. And the seventh—in an almost defiant sonata form—can be seen as the composer's fierce determination to live the rest of his life as resolutely as he can. But then again, some listeners hear nothing in the swirling music except the Grim Reaper at his work. The quartet remains, to most listeners, disconcerting. And after the journey we have made with Beethoven in its seven movements, there is still the extraordinary experience of the next quartet, the A Minor, to be shared with the suffering composer.

Recording
Végh Quartet (Music and Arts)

You may also want to hear...

...the other symphonies—the Haydnesque No. 1, classical in form but filled with a new, almost aggressive sense of humor; the relatively unclouded Nos. 2 and 4, with their beautiful slow movements; the great, heroically rhythmic No. 7, which Wagner called "the apotheosis of the dance"; and the disarmingly light and consistently underrated No. 8. (The monumental No. 9 is, doubtless, already familiar to most music lovers and, with its last-movement vocal contributions, is, for the purposes of this book, *hors-concours*.) Other indispensable works for orchestra are those stirring overtures, "Egmont" and "Coriolanus."

...the Violin Concerto in D Major, perhaps the classic work in its genre, and all four of the other piano concertos—the first three enjoyably Mozartian, and the fifth, the magnificently imposing "Emperor," all Beethoven.

...among the early and middle-period piano sonatas, the often played "Pathétique" and "Moonlight"; the great "Appassionata" and "Waldstein," in both of which the composer is struggling with the realization that he is going deaf; the almost program-matic "Les Adieux"; and the charmingly lyrical Opus 90, which somehow has never been given a title like the others.

. . . the other four "late piano sonatas"—No. 28 in A, Op. 101; No. 29 in B Flat, Op. 106 (the "Hammerklavier," which Harold C. Schonberg called "the longest, grandest, and most difficult sonata in history"); No. 30 in E, Op. 109; and No. 31 in A Flat, Op. 110. All of these are works in which Beethoven reveals himself as, in Sullivan's phrase, "a man of infinite suffering, of infinite courage and will."

. . . among the other chamber works, the "Archduke" trio for piano, violin, and cello, with its wonderful third-movement variations; two popular violin sonatas, the lovely "Spring" and the lengthy "Kreutzer" (which became the subject of the short story by Tolstoi that inspired a string quartet by Janá ek); and the string quartets that extend the form beyond the horizons seen by Haydn and Mozart—the three confident "Razumovsky" quartets, with their occasional Russian themes, and the "Harp" and "Serioso" quartets, which strike out in new directions.

. . . the other four "late quartets"—the accessible Op. 127 in E Flat; the decidedly less accessible but often very moving Op. 130 in B Flat (which should always be performed with the ter- rifying—to both performers and listeners—"Grosse Fuge" that was its original ending but was rejected by the publisher); Op. 132 in A Minor, which is the most searing expression of human suffering I know; and the short, relatively uncomplicated Op. 135 in F, which Beethoven, writing "Must it be?" and "It must be!" over the music, knew would be his last complete work.

Franz Schubert
1797–1828

In 1815, when he was still in his teens, Franz Schubert produced two symphonies, two Masses, five operas, a great number of smaller instrumental pieces, and a full 146 songs—among them two of the greatest songs ever written, "Der Erlkönig" and "Gretchen am Spinnrade." His productivity scarcely abated thereafter, through the twelve years still left to him on this earth. Only in opera was he unsuccessful. It is said that he had no feeling for the stage. But who can tell what he might have become? There is plenty of drama in the songs and symphonies; there is promise in the operas; and in Schubert's last year his powers were expanding prodigiously. If our best operatic composers had died at thirty-one, we would never have had any of Handel's stage works (or any of his oratorios, for that matter), any of Mozart's four operatic perennials, any of Verdi's works except those from his pre-Rigoletto "years in the galley," anything of much value from either Puccini or Strauss, and of Wagner only The Flying Dutchman *and the lesser works that preceded it. In any case, no lover of vocal music can afford to disregard the instrumental legacy left by the most gifted and prodigal songwriter who ever lived. (The D numbers below are named for Otto Deutsch, who catalogued Schubert's voluminous output.)*

Symphony No. 8 in B Minor ("Unfinished"), D.759 (1822)

Why did the twenty-five-year-old genius leave his most famous composition unfinished? Why, after he died, did it lie gathering dust for more than thirty-five years on the shelf of one Anselm Hüttenbrenner? There are no answers, but there is no shortage of suggestions: Schubert thought the work perfect with only two movements (unlikely, in view of his working procedures). Or Schubert, eager to compete with Beethoven, came to an artistic impasse when he realized that the first two movements were too similar in nature (even less likely, as the first movement is intensely dramatic and the second predominately lyric). Or Schubert came actually to dislike what he had written because it reminded him of several unpleasant experiences at the time of its writing (highly unlikely, as Schubert composed for five more years while struggling with illness and depression). Or Schubert knew that the two movements were the best things he had done so far and hoped to have them performed immediately (rather likely, as individual movements of symphonies were often given at Viennese concerts). Or Schubert actually wrote third and fourth movements, which were lost (possible, as Hüttenbrenner, to whom the score had been entrusted, had to be induced, years later, to relinquish the two movements he had).

What we do know is that Schubert was notoriously careless about his manuscripts, that a hundred or more of his songs lay for periods of time in other hands, that—astonishingly—none of his nine symphonies was performed or even published in his lifetime, that he left other works unfinished, and that some of his music has been lost, seemingly forever.

The "Unfinished" symphony's first movement, at ten minutes one of the marvels of the repertory, is as clear and concise in its sonata-form outline as anything in Haydn or Mozart, instantaneously and unforgettably melodious, and overwhelmingly tragic in its implications. It begins with a powerful, darkly foreboding figure, played pianissimo by the cellos and double basses, that will serve not as a first theme but as a motto for the entire movement. This is hardly stated before an accompaniment of mysterious, shivering semiquavers on the violins—an effect that, once heard, is never forgotten—leads to the first theme proper, a thin, plangent tune sung by the oboe and clarinet. And this has no sooner built to a climax than horns and bassoon modulate quickly from the prevailing minor tonality to G Major and one of the most familiar melodies in the literature, voiced first by the cellos. Suddenly there is a moment of silence and a series of fortissimo chords. Then, with a few variations on the cello melody, the exposition ends.

The development turns to the minor mode again and is concerned entirely with exploring the tragic implications of the motto theme, working steadily to a series of powerful climaxes. It is something of a relief when the recapitulation begins with the return of the mysterious semiquavers and the melancholy oboe tune. The cello theme is now drawn into the relative major, if not the actual key, of the original tonality. The motto theme reinstates itself, and the movement ends with four implacable chords. Every bar of the movement has seemed inevitable; our attention, riveted at the very first, has never been allowed to falter. Even after a hundred hearings, this listener is left profoundly moved and awed.

The second movement, only slightly longer than the first, seems at first to inhabit a more tranquil region, with its quiet main theme on the upper strings and its softly plucked descending accompaniment on the double basses. But this pizzicato accompaniment eventually turns heavy, almost menacing, and the main theme must rise resolutely to counter it. The second subject, first heard on the clarinet and then passed to oboe and flute, is peaceful, almost idyllic, but, once again, the composer soon begins exploring its tragic implications. The two themes pass then through several keys, moods, and changes of texture, with the pizzicato accompaniment urging them onward. The ending, after we have learned not to trust any appearances of serenity, is nonetheless serene.

The third movement scherzo survives only in nine fully scored bars and an incomplete piano sketch. There is no trace of a fourth movement at all. Attempts to complete the scherzo and perform it with an entr'acte from the ballet music to *Rosamunde* for the last movement have long since been discontinued. The best solution, after two completely realized and seemingly deathless movements, is silence.

Recording

C. Kleiber, Vienna Philharmonic (DG)

Symphony No. 9 in C Major ("Great C Major"), D.94 (1828)

This heroic creation, which Schubert called "this, my symphony" and which this author personally regards as his favorite among all symphonies, was returned to its composer as being too long and too difficult for the Vienna Philharmonic Society. In fact, the composer, who at the time had only a few months to live, never heard it performed. Nor, for more than ten years, did the rest of the world—until a venturesome Robert Schumann visited Schubert's brother in Vienna, found it in what he called "a fabulous pile" of unpublished manuscripts, and persuaded Felix Mendelssohn to conduct it at one of his Gewandhaus concerts in Leipzig. The devotion of the two composers to their predecessor was more than justified. Schumann wrote to his wife, Clara, about the symphony's "heavenly length" and claimed, in a review, that it "reveals to us something more than beautiful song, mere joy and sorrow. It leads us into regions that—to our best recollection—we have never before explored."

The work was, nonetheless, slow to take with performers. It was twice more rejected in Vienna, openly laughed at by the players of the London Philharmonic, and in Paris the musicians, exhausted after the first movement, refused to go on with the rehearsal. (After its initial performance there it went unheard for almost fifty years.)

The "Great C Major," as it is often called, begins with a superb theme first intoned by two unaccompanied French horns playing in unison, then by the woodwinds, then by the strings, then by the brass, and eventually, with increasing tension, by all the orchestral choirs. The Schubert scholar John Reed has found "self quotations" in this theme that link it to the song "Die Allmacht," Schubert's "hymn of praise to the Creator." Schubert counted his trips to the mountainous regions of Upper Austria, and his meeting there with Archbishop Pyrker, who wrote the poem

"Die Allmacht," as a uniquely inspiring time in his life. And, indeed, there is something of mountains, and of the almost religious feeling they can inspire, in this symphony's unforgettable opening theme.

Yet that "hymn of praise to the Creator" is not the main theme of the movement to follow; it is, more importantly, the source of almost all of the subsequent themes. The actual main subject fairly bursts out of the "hymn"; it is a brusque rhythmic figure, in distinct contrast to the elfin second theme, which is first played by oboes and bassoon. But the really haunting figure in the movement is given, pianissimo, to the trombones—a three-note fragment clearly derived from the second measure of the "hymn." Eventually the whole orchestra takes it up.

Schubert hoped with this symphony at last to match the heroic forcefulness, the intensity, and the impressive length of Beethoven's great works, and he did so while maintaining, in the expansive development section that now follows, his own characteristic lyricism, sweetness, and subtle harmonic and instrumental coloring. Perhaps the most impressive feature of the first movement is how its propulsive rhythms churn on and on, straight through the development section into the recapitulation, and yet the total effect seems utterly natural, unforced, almost leisurely. The recapitulation ends with an excited, triumphant restatement of eight bars of the introductory "hymn" theme. This is hardly called for by the movement's sonata form, but somehow we have all along been waiting for the superb opening melody's reappearance.

The main theme of the second movement, an unexpectedly eerie march in the key of A Minor, is first sounded simply by a solo oboe, then by a clarinet, and then gradually becomes a passionate statement for the full orchestra. The movement's second subject, lyrical and even devout, leads to a return of the march, which is slowed almost a halt when, as Schumann wrote, "a horn call sounds from a distance, as if it were descended from another world, and every other instrument seems to listen, as if some heavenly visitant were hovering above the orchestra." The march starts up again, softly adorned at first with delicate figures in trumpets and winds, gradually swelling to a climax that comes to a complete halt—and a devastating moment of silence. Then the cellos and oboe take up the lyrical second subject again, and that consoling melody confronts the march rhythm and calls the movement to a close, leaving us to wonder what it all might mean.

The scherzo—no Haydnesque minuet but a big, burly thing worthy of Beethoven—begins with a thumping country dance, continues with a waltz-like melody for the upper strings and a counter-subject in the cellos, and eventually introduces a graceful melody for flute, oboe, and violins. The trio, in a new tonality, sounds as if it has come from some outlying region of the empire (Dvoák's Slavonic Dances seem not far away.) Then it's back to more enthusiastic thumping and waltzing.

The last movement is beyond praise. The whole symphony is often compared, favorably, to Beethoven's seventh, that "apotheosis of the dance." Both works have strangely rhythmic processionals in A Minor for their slow movements; both have explosive scherzos with notably contrasting trios; and both are crowned with finales unsurpassed for their propulsive rhythmic energy. Schubert's has, in fact, been called an "apotheosis of rhythm." He begins it with an excited four-note figure, the first three notes of which form a triplet—and rightly so, for triplets will pervade and propel the entire movement. This first theme is whirled through several pages and eventually called to a halt by a punctuating chord from the full orchestra, and the glorious second theme—beginning with four repeated Cs—takes over. The accompaniment here, which scarcely lets up for a full ten minutes, is made up of hundreds of repeated triplet figures. (This is the accompaniment that so taxed the elbows of the exasperated fiddlers of the London Philharmonic.) Just as we feel we are nearing the end of an unusually long exposition and are poised for the development section, Schubert quiets his orchestra to a whisper, drops the key, and introduces a new melody on the woodwinds that seems, to some ears at least, to be a quotation, more in texture than in actual notation, from the "Ode to Joy" of Beethoven's ninth. (Many Schubertians think it was not intended as a quotation, but certainly any suggestion of joy is right for this context.)

We now have plenty of material for a sonata-form development section, but it is mostly the four repeated notes of the second theme that Schubert uses—over and over as the music builds with impressive power. Finally, the thematic ideas of the exposition are brought back with renewed energy in a thrilling recapitulation. Just when the time comes for reappearance of the "Ode to Joy" theme, Schubert begins instead an absolutely unstoppable coda, reworking the "Joy" theme in combination with other earlier motifs in a vast tympani-thumping celebration of almost cosmic gladness. As the genial Metropolitan Opera broadcast commentator Edward Downes once put it, "Schubert goes on to show us that Beethoven was not the only one who could laugh and exult with the elements."

Recording
Furtwängler, Berlin Philharmonic (DG)

Piano Sonata in B-Flat Major, D.960 (1828)

In the last year of his life the thirty-one-year-old Schubert turned out more masterpieces than any predecessor, even Mozart, had

produced in a similar period of time—the "Great C Major" symphony, his song cycles "Die Winterreise" and "Schwanengesang,"
his superb String Quintet in C Minor (discussed in the first
chapter of this book), and—extraordinary by any standard, even
in this mass of masterpieces—the three final, posthumously
published piano sonatas, a genre at which Schubert, who never
owned a piano, was not thought particular adept. Alfred Brendel
has written that the first two of these, in C Minor and A Minor,
"lead us into Romantic regions of wonderment, terror, and awe."
And Claudio Arrau has called the third, in B-Flat Major, "a work
written in the proximity of death," though its last two movements
are an attempt to face the future optimistically.

The prayer-like melody that begins this final sonata and returns
many times in the first movement is as deeply moving and quietly
poignant as any ever penned, "analogous," says B. H. Haggin,
"to what is communicated by the last sonatas and quartets of
Beethoven—that inner illumination of a great spirit who has
suffered all to know all and understand all." But its initial statement is called to a halt after only a few measures by a mysterious,
ominous trill in the bass. The melody is then completed, and its
full-length span is, for Haggin, "an indication that the movement
itself will be on a time-scale unusual for any sonata." The first
movement is, in fact, more than twenty-five minutes long, as the
melody is interrupted again and again by that rumbling in the bass
and by unexpected and disturbing pauses.

The second theme, sprightly at first and deliberately introduced in an unrelated tonality, F-sharp Minor, is eventually fragmented and subjected to the same—by now tragic—rumblings
and pauses. In the development section, the opening melody
reestablishes itself—now humble, even devout, now with proud
determination, despite pounding ostinatos, rumbling bass trills,
heart-stopping pauses, and unpredictable key changes.

A new six-note theme emerges in the development section and is especially prominent in the passage leading to the recapitulation. The Schubert scholar John Reed has pointed out that it is a variant of a theme Schubert had used for a setting of the cathedral scene in Goethe's *Faust*—a scene in which a soul praying for forgiveness is threatened by the powers of evil. Some of that Goethian feeling may rightly be said to enter now into the midst of this tormented first movement.

The recapitulation itself is straightforward, with the once sprightly second theme brought into the tonality of the main theme. At the close, the quiet manner in which that main theme submits to the last threatening bass trill is, for me and for many others, an overwhelming experience.

Commentators have spoken of the next movement as conveying the sense of time standing still, and have even invoked T. S. Eliot's phrase "the still point of the turning world" to describe it. But to my ears the opening melody in thirds seems rather to be drifting through a surreal landscape bedewed by falling tears as, in measure after measure, the pianist's left hand crosses his right to sound a single plaintive note. The middle section is a contrasting episode in which an ostinato bass supports a second, more urgent song. But the movement is kept from becoming merely picturesque by its often threatening bass line, and kept from falling into sentimentality by its unexpected modulations. Many listeners find it an experience as affecting as the first movement.

The scherzo, in which Haggin hears a "succession of Schubertian miracles of instantaneously achieved loveliness and expressiveness," nonetheless has about it a note of desperation. A brief central trio is unquestionably darker in mood, and the return to the scherzo theme is uneasy.

The finale, a generally lighthearted rondo, is interrupted periodically by sounding octaves that come like warning signals. The second section, with its rippling bass, seems to anticipate Chopin. The third, central section is surprisingly stormy, Beethovenesque in both its heavier and lighter phrases. After all the themes are given their moments in the sun, a brief coda based on the main theme ends the work. Schumann observed: "Thus Schubert ends both happily and cheerfully, as though fully able to face another day's work." Schumann could not have known that this was to be the last instrumental work Schubert would write. But I think Schubert knew.

Recording
Brendel (Philips)

You may also want to hear...

...among the works for solo piano, the two other large-scaled, posthumously published, unquestionably great works that Schubert composed in the last year of his life—the relentlessly driven C-Minor Sonata (D.958) and the A-Major Sonata (D.959), with its heartbreaking slow movement. Scarcely less impressive are the earlier sonatas in A Major (D.664), D Major (D.850), and G Major (D.894). Concert pianists have tended to neglect these in favor of what I think is a lesser piece—the song-based Fantasie in C Major ("The Wanderer"), which has more virtuoso display passages. Many of the smaller pieces for piano are irresistible, perhaps especially the Scherzo in B Flat, the third of the Moments Musicaux, and the first of the Trois Marches Militaires—all of them thrice familiar to young piano students. And, above all, there are two Impromptus from Op. 90, the noble and deeply moving third and the delicately textured fourth.

...among the orchestral works, the lovely incidental music for a now forgotten play called *Rosamunde*. Of the early symphonies, which the teenaged Schubert wrote mainly for private performances with his friends, the best are No. 4 in C Minor (the "Tragic") and the Mozartian No. 5 in B Flat.

. . . among the chamber works, the joyously buoyant Quintet in A Major for piano and string quartet (D.667, the "Trout"), with its fourth-movement variations on one of Schubert's most famous songs. You might follow that with the intense Quartet in D Minor (D.810), which features variations on another famous song, "Death and the Maiden." If these fail to win you over—which is highly unlikely—try the radiantly happy Trio in B Flat for piano, violin, and cello (D.898). After that you will want to move on to the generous six-movement Octet in F Major for strings and winds (D.803); the powerful single-movement Quartettsatz in C Minor (D.703), which seems to anticipate the storms of Wagner; the profoundly disturbing String Quartet in G Major (D.887), which has a long, obsessive first movement that remembers Haydn as it anticipates Bartók; and above all the poignant String Quartet in A Minor (D.804), with its superb first movement and its later echoes of *Rosamunde* and some of the songs.

Then, of course, there are the hundreds upon hundreds of songs themselves, many of them miracles of Romantic feeling. But they—and the operas, cantatas, Masses, and various other vocal works—lie outside the scope of this book.

Robert Schumann
1810–1856

It was Schumann, an impetuous, high-spirited young man, who unearthed Schubert's "Great C Major" symphony, and it was on hearing that "symphony of the heavenly length" performed for the first time in Leipzig that he was encouraged to spread his own poetic wings and move from writing piano miniatures toward full-scale symphonic compositions. Schumann was troubled for much of his life by a manic-depressive condition, and in his journalistic writing, battling for the cause of new music, he signed his articles "Florestan" (for his extraverted side) and "Eusebius" (for his contemplative side). His marriage to Clara Wieck, though much opposed by her father, brought him years of stability, and he fashioned a third name for himself—Raro—by playfully joining the last syllable of her name to the first of his. But eventually he succumbed to his malady and, thinking his life a failure, attempted to end it by throwing himself into the Rhine. He spent the last of his forty-six years on earth in an asylum near Bonn. Clara, one of the great pianists of the nineteenth century, survived him for forty years, raising their six children and keeping her husband's work alive.

Schumann's only opera, Genoveva, *was unsuccessful, but his* Scenes from Faust *is one of the best musical works based on Goethe's drama. And, of course, he was a master of German song; only Schubert was greater. But, above all, it was in his writing for piano that Schumann made his greatest contribution to Romantic music. Hence my choices below.*

Carnaval, Op. 9 (1835)

The best approach to the young Schumann's fantastical imagination, and the best index to the arcane allusions he made in his music, is this set of twenty-one piano pieces—a tantalizing work in which he represents the two sides of his personality lost in the midst of a masked ball populated by *commedia dell'arte* figures, various waltzing couples, his own lady loves, and two famous candidates for the imaginary guild, the Davidsbund, that he envisioned as poised to combat philistinism in music. The unifying principle in *Carnaval* is a kind of musical acrostic: permutations of the letters ASCH (in German notation, A, E Flat, C, and B) that form the name of his fiancée's birthplace and, anagramatically, part of his own surname. The four notes are the starting point for most of the pieces. All of this may make *Carnaval* seem more abstruse and less enjoyable than it is. Schumann gave it the subtitle "Scènes mignonnes sur quatre notes" ("Pretty Little Scenes on Four Notes"). The following description will not, I hope, strike the reader/listener as too mignonnesque:

Préambule: A-Flat fanfares invite us listeners to a masked ball. The chords are stately, but there is a curious mock-seriousness to the total effect, and once we have passed within, there is an even stranger recklessness about the whirling figures we see populating the "carnaval" that is Schumann's imagination.

Pierrot: The sad, white-faced *commedia dell'arte* figure, dressed in his loose white costume, seems to stumble and apologize again and again as he greets us, speaks his piece, and says his adieux. (The notes ASCH figure in the left hand.)

Arlequin: Masked, merry, and—in sharp contrast to the preceding figure—dressed in colorful tights, this second character from the comic troupe cavorts quite unapologetically and seems to pay no attention to us at all. (The notes ASCH figure in the right hand.)

Valse noble: Couples circle about us in a slow waltz (ASHC) with an exaggeratedly Romantic strain.

Eusebius: Schumann himself appears in one of his moods— dreamy, introspective, and utterly sincere. (The notes ASCH are woven into his melody, curling like the smoke from the cigar he always favored.)

Florestan: Schumann appears in another mood—passionately involved (his melody begins with ASCH), carried off on flights of enthusiasm, and quick to exit when he spies . . .

. . . *Coquette*: Temptation herself, fluttering her fan, tapping her foot, intent on Florestan. Could she be Meta Abegg or Agnes Carus or another of Schumann's early loves?

Réplique: Schumann seems now to brush Coquette aside, and she withdraws.

(At this point the pianist is confronted by three "Sphinxes"—the notes ASCH, written out in different positions and in a deliberately obscure notation, but clearly intended as a clue to the musical code that pervades the work. Clara Schumann advised pianists not to play the notes, and I have never heard them sounded in performance.)

Papillons: I wish Clara had told us why these winged creatures are so much less gossamer than those in the collection her Robert issued earlier under the same name. Perhaps the piece depicts not so much actual butterflies as the fanciful images that flit so intriguingly in Robert's brain.

ASCH-SCHA (*Lettres dansantes*): The "dancing letters" of the town (Asch) where one Ernestine von Fricken lived, and of the name of her fiancé, Robert Sch[um]a[nn], merrily challenge us to decode the meanings of the masked ball we are witnessing.

Chiarina: Clara Wieck, aged fifteen and passionate about her future, plays an etude. From this point on, the four coded letters are reduced to three (A,C, and H), and three young people— Robert himself, Ernestine, and Clara—seem to be occupying most of the composer's interest.

Chopin: One of the most illustrious members of Schumann's imaginary Davidsbund appears at the carnaval to play the piano— and Schumann provides him with a piece that is a remarkably successful imitation of the all-but-inimitable Chopin style.

Estrella: Ernestine von Fricken, aged seventeen and secretly engaged to Robert, manifests a passion that is abruptly discontinued when someone, presumably Clara's father (who was giving piano lessons to all three young people), seems to intrude.

Reconnaisance: A masked couple at the ball decide, in this sparkling dance, to remove their masks—and they recognize each other. (Could this piece be about the growing mutual attraction between Robert and Clara?)

Pantalon et Colombine: The old rich man of the *commedia dell'arte* chases after the saucy young lady of the same troupe—and never catches her. (In later *commedia dell'arte*, Pantalon was the father of Colombine. Could this piece be about the Wiecks, father and daughter?)

Valse Allemande: A flirtatious dance, which is interrupted memorably by the appearance of . . .

. . . *Paganini*: Schumann provides the famous virtuoso, another member of his imaginary Davidsbund, with a piano imitation of one of his violin caprices. Then the carnaval couples return to their charming *Valse Allemande*.

Aveu: A couple at the ball exchange simple, somewhat sugary declarations of love. (Robert and Clara?)

Promenade: Another couple, on a quiet stroll, engage in a passionate dialogue and seem to reach a meeting of minds. (Robert and Ernestine?)

Pause: Hardly a pause, this repetition of twenty-eight bars of the *Préambule* seems rather to be a call to arms: it is time for the members of the Davidsbund to sally forth to defend their aesthetic principles.

Marche des "Davidsbündler" contre les Philistins: Schumann and his cronies march doughtily out to fight against all musical reactionaries and, to themes from the *Préambule* and *Pause* sections, vigorously put them to ignominious flight, leaving the world of music safe for innovation and imagination.

Recording
Michelangeli (Testament)

Piano Concerto in A Minor, Op. 54 (1845)

"Hats off, gentleman. A genius!" Schumann wrote to his readers when he first came across Chopin's music for the piano. And that is pretty much what the piano says about Schumann himself at the start of this, his only piano concerto. The extraverted chords and cascading A-Minor opening have always struck listeners as an enthusiastic self-portrait, even as the plaintive eight-bar melody in the woodwinds that immediately follows the cascade is a portrait of his beloved Clara. (So effective is this opening that Grieg, who adored Schumann's music, began his own piano concerto in the same fashion, in the same key, and in the same tempo.) The piano and orchestra immediately develop a fragment of the "Clara" theme in a richly Romantic style that Rachmaninoff was to remember and use. The music modulates into a major key and announces, in lieu of a second theme, a new, more tender version of Clara's theme. (She played the piano part at the work's first performance.)

The development—almost a misnomer here—eventually settles into an eighty-five-bar "love duet"—for so it is often called—between piano and clarinet (clarinet for Clara?), based almost entirely on Clara's theme. The mood changes as the initial allegro tempo returns, leading to a straightforward recapitulation and a cadenza that is, for a Romantic concerto, decidedly modest.

(In fact, both critics and public complained at first that there was no room for virtuosity in this concerto, and Liszt ruefully dubbed it "a concerto without a piano.") The movement concludes with another transformation of Clara's theme, brisk and joyous.

It might be added that this first movement was composed some four years before the rest of the concerto, as a freestanding "Phantasie in A Minor." That, perhaps, is why Clara's theme dominates it more than the second theme of an ordinary sonata-form movement is likely to do.

Schumann went through a difficult period between the writing of the first movement and the rest of the concerto. In a letter to Mendelssohn he confessed that he had experienced "nervous prostration accompanied by a host of terrible thoughts" and that he was nearly driven to despair, but that "music is again beginning to sound within me, and I hope I have quite recovered." He called his second movement an intermezzo, and gave it a childlike theme much like those he developed in the piano pieces called *Kinderszenen* (*Scenes of Childhood*). (Clara had encouraged him to work something in this vein into the concerto, saying tenderly that he often reminded her of a child.)

The lyrical middle section of this movement is developed from a little strain in the childlike first theme and given to the cello. (Robert took up the cello when he foolishly damaged his hand with a finger-stretching device, and thereafter the piano playing in the family was left to Clara. That perhaps is why the piano devotes all its attention in this movement's center to lovingly embroidering the cello's melody.)

Then Clara's theme sounds three times in the woodwinds and, without interruption, we are into the last movement, in sonata form, with a first subject that is, again, a variation on Clara's theme and a second subject in syncopated cross-rhythms. There is some fugal writing in the development section (husband and wife had done a study of Bach's works together), and the recapitulation features, at last, some virtuoso passages for the soloist, but no cadenza (Clara may have wanted to keep her part unpretentious). The whole of this last movement is simply radiant with joyful feelings. Almost ten years were to pass before the madness that temporarily intervened between the first and second parts of this concerto finally felled Clara's beloved Robert.

Recording
Perahia, Abbado, Berlin Philharmonic (Sony)

You may also want to hear...

...the other piano works that flesh out the portrait of this intriguing genius—*Papillons*, twelve early pencil sketches for *Carnaval*, inspired by a novel by Jean-Paul Richter; *Davidsbündlertänze*, eighteen more pieces in the *Carnaval* vein, some for fiery Florestan, some for reflective Eusebius; *Kreisleriana*, eight studies inspired by E. T. A. Hoffmann's demon-driven Romantic figure that are also a self-portrait of the composer in his many moods; the often played "Arabeske," which stays indelibly in the memory; and the aforementioned, poignantly naïve *Kinderszenen*. (You will recognize the familiar "Träumerei," and you may remember Meryl Streep in *Sophie's Choice* exclaiming, over the wistful "From Foreign Lands," "I luff that piece.") After that, you might move on to the more demanding *Études Symphoniques*, twelve variations in the styles of the composer's predecessors and contemporaries; the eight popular pieces in *Fantasiestücke,* Op. 12; and the *Fantasie in C Major*, the composer's grandest but hardly most characteristic work.

...the Piano Quintet, the first successful attempt to blend string quartet and piano, and very enjoyable.

...the four symphonies—the first, the vivacious "Spring" symphony, celebrating Robert's marriage to Clara; the second, written in pain and built around a motto theme; the third, the picturesque "Rhenish," which I've always thought made Wagner choose E Flat for his own Rhine music; and the Brahmsian fourth, with subtle links from movement to movement that all but make it a seamless whole. These enthusiastically Romantic works are often criticized as being the creations of an imperfect orchestrator with a pianistic imagination, but, as Schoenberg rightly remarked, if the orchestration were changed, we would lose what is most typically Schumann about them.

Johannes Brahms
1833–1897

Brahms, the lad from the slums who played the piano for pfennigs in the bordellos of Hamburg; Brahms, the devoted young friend of Robert and the platonic lover of Clara Schumann; Brahms, the sturdy upholder of classical forms when musical trends were changing inexorably with the advent of what was thought the new Liszt-Wagner formlessness; Brahms, who mastered his craft early but feared for years to undertake larger forms because he was intimidated by the legacy of Beethoven, "that giant whose footsteps I always hear behind me"; Brahms, who wrote so sweetly and powerfully for massed string sections and gave the French horn a new mellowness, but remained for all his life an intractable, solitary bachelor almost afraid to reveal in music the passions of his heart—Brahms is a fascinating study in greatness. It is difficult for anyone who has come to value his immense output to single out just a few works. These are my choices:

Piano Concerto No. 1 in D Minor, Op. 15 (1858)

Beethoven's last piano concerto, the "Emperor," was in its time the longest and most demanding concerto ever written. Brahms's first in the genre is bigger still. It is massive and massively difficult, hardly a concerto in the older sense but something of a duel, a fierce duel, between the piano and the orchestra. It was, as a result, thought presumptuous and misguided, coolly received at its first performance in Hanover, and savagely hissed a week later at the Leipzig Gewandhaus.

To some extent the audience reaction was understandable. The work was originally conceived as a symphony—the large-scale structure that Brahms was not to master for another two decades. Then, when the eighteen-year-old composer realized that he was not ready, in the shadow of Beethoven, for such an undertaking, he reworked the material as a sonata for two pianos. But the symphonic nature of the heavier piano part proved too large for such a reduction, so the piece became, finally, a piano concerto—but a concerto in which, audiences thought, the solo-ist (Brahms himself, at the age of twenty-three) was overwhelmed by the colossal statements of a thundering orchestra.

In fact, the soloist is given nothing to play for a full five min-utes, while the orchestra repeatedly hurls forth a great grotesque theme, replete with fiery trills, then sounds and repeats a couple of sorrowful strains, returns to the terrifying original theme, and then introduces a new subject in repeated quavers—to which the piano finally responds. Gradually the combat subsides as the piano restates the orchestral themes nobly and quietly, and the orchestra—Brahms's beloved French horn in particular—comes to discover how beautifully its initial statements can be made to sound. The pianist even conquers, as Orpheus conquered the beasts, that terrifying opening theme. By that time the first movement, as long as many whole concertos from earlier com-posers, has clocked in at twenty-five minutes.

A "program" interpreting this movement has persisted for almost a century. It would hold that the movement is the com-poser's depiction in music of his attempt to deal with the terrible events of the year 1854. In the very year that the young Brahms began fashioning this material as a symphony, his close friend and mentor, Robert Schumann, began showing signs of mental derangement, became violent, and tried to kill himself by leaping into the Rhine from the bridge at Düsseldorf. Two years later Schumann died in an asylum while Brahms was struggling to tame the intractable symphony-turned-sonata into a concerto.

The second movement, by Brahms's own admission, is "a tender portrait" of Schumann's widow, Clara, whom he loved himself with a discreet passion. In the score at the start of this movement, he wrote, cryptically, "Benedictus qui venit in nomine Domini." The phrase from the Latin Mass will allow a past tense for "venit," so that we may translate it here as a tribute to the dead Schumann: "Blessed is he who *came* in the name of the Lord." On the other hand, as the young Brahms often called Schumann his "dominus," his master, the phrase could be an assurance to Clara that he, Brahms, would now be her protector: "Blessed is he who *has come* in the name of his master." In any case, the movement is like a letter of condolence—comforting, understanding, and assuring continued devotion. It is built on two quiet themes, the first of which seems to be shaped by the Latin words.

The third movement, cast as a rondo, is not the bright exhibition piece customary with earlier rondos but a new sort of conclusion for a piano concerto—a vigorous D-Minor theme interrupted by lyrical episodes that are almost as weighty as those in the opening movement. There is, however, much opportunity for pianistic display—for Clara, one of the great pianists of the nineteenth century, was eventually to perform it in public. The concerto is, in short, a long personal tribute to a departed master and his beloved widow—from a terribly tormented young man.

Recording

Schiff, Solti, Vienna Philharmonic (London/Decca)

Symphony No. 4 in E Minor, Op. 98 (1885)

Brahms labored for twenty years over his first symphony, and waited till he was in his forties before he published it— understandably, for in his day the symphony, perfected by Haydn and Mozart and expanded by Beethoven to monumental proportions as a means of making monumental statements, had come to be regarded as the greatest of all forms of instrumental music. Brahms was right to be wary.

But when his first symphony was well received, three more followed with relative quickness, all of them large-scale statements of consummate workmanship but none so moving and profound as the fourth, written in the Austrian Alps in the composer's late maturity. I am not alone in believing it to be Brahms's greatest work.

"Autumnal" is an adjective often given to Brahms's late works, and it is an especially apt description of the opening movement of this symphony, which from its first measures seems to depict the ripeness and the hint of inevitable change in what Keats called the "season of mists and mellow fruitfulness." Every movement of this last of Brahms's orchestral works begins with an immediate statement of its main theme, instantly memorable, instantly evocative, invariably long-lined, and containing in itself the seeds of every melodic development in the movement it introduces. In the first movement the main theme is a superb E-Minor "autumnal" melody a full sixteen bars in length, sung by the violins, propelled at first in short two-note phrases, and soon to produce a harvest of subsequent themes. The second subject is a little fanfare in the woodwinds that will be heroically restated in the development. The prevalent mood throughout is, despite occasional forays from minor into major, melancholy. It is the music of a man in his mature years, at the height of his powers, pondering meanings. Pondering beauty and terror. Perhaps, above all, pondering what King Arkel in Debussy's *Pelléas et Mélisande* was to call "the sadness of everything one sees."

The second movement, more affecting still, is grounded in the Phrygian mode of ancient Greece. (The scale of this mode can be sounded on a piano by starting on E and moving upward, using only the white keys.) Two mellow French horns intone the archaic-sounding first melody—another long-lined opening statement containing in itself the seeds of several themes to follow. The most eloquent of these is a songful and fully developed cello melody in a major key, one of Brahms's most unashamedly Romantic statements. The classic development and recapitulation follow, and at the end the opening melody is sounded alternately in its Phrygian E-Minor and its modern E-Major modalities.

The ebullient third movement is a change of pace for Brahms: in his first three symphonies the third movement was not a scherzo or—something no longer thinkable—a minuet, but a quietly reflective, even introspective, piece. Here the third movement is extroverted and exhilarating. (I cannot agree with those who think that it is some sort of desperate attempt to force happiness to its knees.) Structurally the movement is close to the scherzos of Beethoven, and it is, like everything in this masterly symphony, beautifully crafted.

But it is the last movement that makes Brahms's fourth a symphony for the ages. It is a movement grounded on a single theme, a solemn minor-key bass tune intoned by the horns and, most notably, the trombones—those instruments long associated with the supernatural. (Witness their use at the appearance of the statue in Mozart's *Don Giovanni*.) The austere, almost forbidding theme repeats itself over and over for the full length of the movement. In technical terms, the movement is a passacaglia, more severe even than the passacaglia in which Bach made one of his greatest statements—and possibly intended to evoke comparison with that statement.

The monumental theme is eight notes in length, and each note weightily occupies a full bar. On that decidedly un-Romantic ground bass, Brahms does thirty quick, uninterrupted variations of eight bars each—not building upward, as Bach seems to do in his cathedralesque passacaglia, but progressing horizontally through a series of crises, great and small, each propelled by the massive theme that sounds, now distinctly, now almost imperceptibly, through the eight measures of each variation. For three of the variations the music moves into a major key, but then the ground bass reverts again to the minor tonality, driving the music onward with almost savage relentlessness. (It may be significant that for some time Brahms had been reading Sophocles.) Finally the eight-bar variations give way to a coda in which all the autumnal beauty of the rest of this remarkable symphony is swept away in an almost terrifying final statement. Paul Henry Lang called this fourth movement, from the entrance of the trombones in the fourteenth variation, "a Requiem Mass for the eternal rest of the soul of the symphony." Certainly it is the ultimate statement of a man who, after a lifetime of making music, remains essentially unknown to us—except that here at the end he is crying out in pain.

At first, both critics and public thought the fourth symphony unintelligible and repellent. Even Brahms's friend Elisabeth von Herzogenburg found all but the second movement difficult to understand. It took more than a decade for the symphony to find an appreciative audience—in Vienna in 1897. Brahms, who then had less than a month to live, was in attendance. The first three movements were enthusiastically applauded, and, according to Florence May in her *Life of Brahms*, "an extraordinary scene followed the conclusion of the work. The applauding, shouting house, its gaze riveted on the figure standing in the balcony, so familiar and yet in present aspect so strange, seemed unable to let him go. Tears ran down his cheeks as he stood there shrunken in form, with lined countenance, strained expression, white hair hanging lank; and through the audience there was a feeling as of a stifled sob, for each knew that they were saying farewell."

Recording
C. Kleiber, Vienna Philharmonic (DG)

Quintet in B Minor for clarinet and strings, Op. 115 (1891)

Twenty-five chamber works of Brahms survive—a goodly number, indeed, but we may be sure that there were many more that were destroyed because they did not meet their composer's exacting standards. In his youth, throughout his life, and especially when death was near, Brahms tore up manuscript after manuscript rather than allow what he thought inferior work to be posthumously published. (We must be grateful that Schubert, whose long-unpublished chamber works and sonatas are among the finest examples of his art, did not have the same scruples.) Many of Brahms's pieces lay on his desk for years, awaiting his complete revision or ruthless destruction.

Probably the most accessible of Brahms's surviving chamber pieces is the gentle, resigned four-movement work for string quartet and solo clarinet that he wrote late in life, almost seven years after he was done with large-scale symphonic writing. It may be an homage to Mozart, who pioneered the same luminous combination of instruments—but in a major key, and when he was a much younger man.

The first movement conveys, to this listener at least, the serenity and resignation of a man who feels that his titanic efforts may now cease and he can devote himself to writing for his own pleasure. The opening theme, instantly memorable and more than a little mysterious, is sounded by the strings and taken up by the clarinet. The second is intoned by clarinet and second violin. The development and recapitulation bring no surprises, nor does the coda, quietly built on the swaying, still mysterious opening theme. Not every problem need be solved, not in one's mellow years.

Similarly, the adagio, which offends some with its simplicity and sweetness, seems rather to this listener to be a straightforward confession by a man who all his life remained incorruptibly devoted to his art. I think of Mozart's own clarinet quintet, and of Brahms's characteristically modest words: "That people do not understand and do not respect the greatest works, such as Mozart's, helps our kind to live and acquire a certain fame. But if only they knew that they are getting from us in droplets what they could drink there to their heart's content."

The third movement is a subdued scherzo with a delicate prestissimo for its central section. And the final movement, cast in the theme-and-variations mold, is similarly placid and easy to follow. At its end the quintet's opening theme returns. It seems that even when life is viewed with clarity and formal perfection in four different moods, we have to confess that the mystery that prompted all our thoughts will return to stay with us, as does that opening theme.

Recording
Kell, Busch Quartet (Testament)

You may also want to hear...
...the other three symphonies, all of them masterly, all of them filled with marvelous detail, all of them ending superbly.

The ambitious first symphony (in C Minor) is Brahms's long-delayed response to the challenge of Beethoven's ninth. It is rather self-consciously long, with a portentous opening that is like a great curtain being drawn aside, and with a last movement in C Major (the key of Beethoven's finale) that is famous for its climactic French horn pronouncements and for an instrumental chorale that is deliberately reminiscent of Beethoven's "Ode to Joy."

The genial, loveable second symphony (in D Major) was written in a summery Austrian village and is full of Gemütlichkeit. (There is even an echo of Brahms's lullaby in the first movement.) Like its sister symphonies, it rises to a magnificent ending. It is often said that there is "an awful lot going on" in Brahms. Well, there is scarcely a moment in the second symphony when that is not deliciously true.

The third symphony (in F Major) seems at least in part to be another tribute to Robert Schumann: its opening "motto" phrase occurs in the second movement of Schumann's "Spring" and in the first movement of his "Rhenish" symphonies. But the haunting melody in the third movement is thoroughly Brahmsian, and the fourth movement is triumphantly so: it is always a joy to hear that jubilant French horn introduce the finale's second subject.

. . . the other great work for piano and orchestra, the Piano Concerto No. 2 in B-Flat Major. Memorably introduced by a horn call and a sweeping restatement of it on the piano, this concerto is more spacious than the first, still longer (its four expansive movements make it possibly the longest piano concerto ever written), and equally challenging to soloist and orchestra. The great difference between it and the first is that this, written almost a quarter-century later, sings with the confidence of late middle age, while the first sang with the tormented passions of youth.

. . . two more concertos, the Violin Concerto in D Major, in which the soloist can revel in passages of the utmost sweetness before demonstrating his virtuosity in the last movement's swirling Hungarian rondo; and the late Concerto for Violin and

Cello in A Minor, often called the "double concerto," as "autumnal" as any of Brahms's works, concluding with yet another Hungarian rondo.

. . . two shorter orchestral works that every music lover must hear and will likely cherish for all of his or her life. The first is the immensely enjoyable *Variations on a Theme by Haydn,* a piece grounded on an instantly memorable hymn tune, the St. Antoni Chorale, that is apparently not by Haydn at all. Brahms puts the tune through nine variations, every one of them a delight—the seventh a lilting barcarole, the ninth a passacaglia less grand than, but similar to, the great closing movement of the fourth symphony. And just as marvelous is the brief *Academic Festival Overture,* which Brahms wrote for the University of Breslau when it awarded him an honorary degree. Joyously featured are four student songs, "We Have Built a Stately House," the "Hochfeierlicher Landesvater," "The Freshman" (clownishly tootled on the bassoon), and, in a magnificent peroration, the traditional "Gaudeamus Igitur."

. . . Brahms's chamber music, a feast better saved until after you have explored his symphonic works. Once you have heard the late Clarinet Quintet (discussed above), proceed, for purposes of contrast, to the youthful, stormy, almost symphonic Piano Quintet in F Minor, which taxes the pianist to the utmost. Then move on to two violin sonatas—the very beautiful A Major, which opens with a theme that calls to mind the beginning of "Walther's Prize Song" in *Die Meistersinger,* and the D Minor, which has been thought a character study of Hans von Bülow, the conductor of Wagner's *Tristan.* (He seems an altogether more interesting figure here than in most Wagner biographies.) And don't stop browsing through the more intimate works until you have sampled some of the intermezzi for solo piano that the composer wrote at the end of his life. B. H. Haggin, no lover of Brahms, called the intermezzi "arid formulae dipped in treacle."

You'll know what he meant when you hear the Intermezzo Op. 117 No. 2 in B-Flat Minor and the Intermezzo Op. 118 No. 2 in A Major, for they are sweetness itself. I'm also sure that you'll disagree with Haggin; the pieces are formulaic, perhaps, but dipped in the most poignant sadness.

Doubtless you already know, from orchestral transcriptions, two of the Hungarian dances for piano—No. 5 in F-Sharp Minor and No. 6 in D-Flat Major. And anyone who ever took lessons at the keyboard will have coped with the charming Waltz in A-Flat Major, one of sixteen Brahmsian miniatures in three-quarter time.

As for the once ubiquitous motto "Bach, Beethoven, and Brahms"—it may still be useful as a catch phrase signifying the beginning, middle, and end of what I have called "the Germanic canon," but it simply will not do as a sloganeering statement to the effect that the three B's are the composers *par excellence*. The phrase was coined by Hans von Bülow as a retaliatory slogan when he left the Wagner camp (Wagner had, after all, stolen his wife) and joined the Brahmsians. In any case, such a listing, even one limited to the Germanic canon, must include Haydn, Mozart, Schubert—and, of course, Wagner.

And why did Brahms never write an opera? "After Wagner it was impossible," he said. But there is also the suspicion that Brahms, a classicist writing in a Romantic period, sensed that he possessed neither the passionate high-mindedness that Beethoven showed in *Fidelio*, nor Haydn's witty way with myth, nor the profound insight into human characters that animated Mozart's works for the stage. In the end he said, not without rue, "I never found a suitable subject."

More Germans

Carl Maria von Weber
1786–1826

The man without whom Wagner's early works might never have been, the composer of the breakthrough German Romantic operas Der Freischütz, Oberon, *and* Euryanthe *(all lamentably neglected today except for their overtures), also wrote several instrumental works (now equally neglected) and one small piece still performed by orchestras and corps de ballet. It would be criminal not to include its composer, related by marriage to Mozart himself, in this volume.*

Invitation to the Dance (1819)

First written for the piano, as Rondo Brillant in D-Flat Major, this charming piece has been orchestrated several times, and is most familiar in an adaptation made by Berlioz to serve as part of a ballet interpreted in the Paris premiere of *Der Freischütz*. A program was soon attached to the piece: a young gentleman (the cello) introduces himself to a young lady (the woodwind section) at a ball and, after a few polite exchanges, invites her to dance; they whirl through several discreetly passionate numbers and then graciously part with expressions of thanks.

This piece provided the two Johann Strausses with a template for their famous Viennese waltzes, each of which is a succession of several numbers in three-quarter time. It may also have provided Gounod with an idea for his waltzes in *Faust*: the French composer set a tender exchange from Goethe—the ardent young man inviting the demure young girl to walk with him—in the midst of a series of swirling waltzes.

The most notable use of Weber's piece for ballet purposes was called *Le Spectre de la Rose*—first choreographed by Fokine, presented by Diaghilev, and danced by Nijinsky and Karsavina. In this scenario, a girl brings a rose home from a ball, falls asleep, dreams that the spirit of the rose is waltzing with her, and wakes when it makes a Nijinskian leap from her window.

Recording

Karajan, Berlin Philharmonic (EMI)

You may also want to hear...

...the Konzertstück in F Minor, an enjoyable one-movement piece for piano and orchestra, for which the composer himself wrote a program: a chatelaine awaiting the return of her knight from the Crusades has a vision of him dying on the field of battle—but he returns with waving banners (to a glistening piano glissando), and she falls into his arms.

Weber also wrote several works for his clarinet-playing friend Heinrich Bärmann, of which the Concerto No. 1 in F Minor, the Grand Duo Concertant (for clarinet and piano), and the Quintet in B Flat are sometimes heard today. You may be astonished by the rusticity, the shrillness, and the sheer showiness of the runs up two and three scales in the latter piece. But these works, as well as the other concertos, the symphonies, and the piano sonatas are further indulgence. Remember Weber first as the founder of Romantic opera.

Felix Mendelssohn
1809–1847

The darling son of a wealthy and artistic Jewish family, the grandson of the philosopher Moses Mendelssohn, the young prodigy to whom composing, concertizing, and conducting were almost second nature, the Romantic who thought of himself as part of the Classic tradition reaching back past Beethoven and Mozart to Bach—Mendelssohn seems to have had an almost unrelievedly successful life. Perhaps he might have produced greater music had he had to face the setbacks that confronted his contemporaries Schumann, Berlioz, and Wagner, but it should be said that even to Mendelssohn doors were closed because of his Jewish lineage. When his father converted, with his family, to Lutheranism, he appended a Christian name to the family name, and for more than a century the composer was referred to as Mendelssohn-Bartholdy. But the name that best describes both his life and his music is his given name, Felix.

Incidental Music to *A Midsummer Night's Dream*, Opp. 21/61 (1826, 1843)

Mendelssohn wrote the overture to this orchestral suite when he was seventeen years old, and it is an absolute marvel, an encapsulation of the mood of Shakespeare's play—elfin, mischievous, delicate, imaginative, beautifully structured, full of melody, and an astonishing creation for a young man in his mid-teens. It is true that Mozart had by his seventeenth year written seven operas, ten symphonies, a piano concerto, several divertimentos, and sonatas for various instruments, and in that seventeenth year alone he produced no fewer than six string quartets. But while many of these are remarkable pieces, none of them quite surpasses, for imaginativeness and sustained inspiration, the luminous and lightsome overture young Mendelssohn wrote for Shakespeare's comedy.

With its first four woodwind chords the overture transports us to a fairy world, and it continues to cast its spell through a full-blown sonata-form movement in which the youthful composer seems to be describing scenes in the play he had just read. The gossamer opening theme (the notes all staccato, the volume pianissimo) is blasted—not quite to smithereens, but blasted quite away—by a fortissimo theme that might signify the magical power of Oberon, king of the fairies. Then a lyric, flowing second theme depicts the two pairs of young lovers, and a rambunctious third subject mimics the antics of the "rude mechanicals," including the hee-haw braying of Bottom the weaver held under a spell cast by Puck.

Most of the development section is given over to the gossamer opening theme, and then the four evocative chords return us to a recapitulation and, finally, a description in music of the closing scene, where, as the composer himself put it, "The principal players leave the stage, the elves follow them, bless the house, and disappear with the dawn. So ends the play and my overture too."

Seventeen years later (seventeen was apparently a magic number for Mendelssohn), the king of Prussia asked for more music for a performance of Shakespeare's comedy, and Mendelssohn wrote thirteen additional numbers, of which at least four are commonly heard when his *Midsummer Night's Dream* music is performed as a suite. These are the nimble, onward-rushing "Scherzo," written to illustrate Puck's second-act "Over hill, over dale, through bush, through brier"; the "Intermezzo," which, at the end of Act II, spins the most delicate of webs over "a wood in Athens"; the "Nocturne," a classic piece for French horn, to be played while the two pairs of lovers slumber in the enchanted forest; and, for Shakespeare's last act, the familiar "Wedding March" without which no bride for a century and a half felt she could leave the church properly married. (Organists who wanted to play something less secular objected that the march was originally written to celebrate the marriage of the king of Athens to the queen of the (!) Amazons. Prospective brides either didn't believe it or didn't care. Neither did it bother them much that the music they wanted for their march up the aisle before the ceremony—"Treulich gefürt" from Wagner's *Lohengrin*—was written for a marital union that was never consummated.)

Recording

Previn, London Symphony Orchestra (EMI)

You may also want to hear...

. . . the Concerto in E Minor for violin, long a concert favorite, melodious and perfect of its kind; the endearing first piano concerto; the symphonies No. 3 in A Minor (the "Scotch") and No. 4 in A Major (the "Italian"), joyous creations written when the composer first traveled to the respective countries; the Symphony No. 5 in D Major (the "Reformation"), which uses not only Luther's "Ein Feste Burg" but also the "Dresden Amen" that Wagner was to use extensively in *Parsifal*; the atmospheric "Fingal's Cave" Overture, sometimes called "The Hebrides," written after another trip to Scotland; the Octet in E Flat for Strings, the composer's best chamber work, written at the age of sixteen; and, for solo piano, the familiar Rondo Capriccioso in E Major and some of the once ubiquitous "Songs Without Words." Much of the rest, including the other piano concerto and the other chamber pieces are, I would say, on a lesser level.

Parisians

Hector Berlioz
1803–1869

Hector Berlioz used gigantic orchestral and choral forces to achieve the most precise and delicate effects. Aaron Copland rightly said that, while other composers wrote for instruments in order to exploit their individual sounds, Berlioz mixed the "colors" of instrumental sounds to produce wholly new results. He also had highly original ideas about the length and shape that melodies should take. Largely unappreciated in his day, Berlioz supported himself by writing musical criticism that was unusually perceptive and often very generous. He also left us, in his Memoirs, *a Romantic manifesto that is perhaps the best book any composer ever wrote about himself. It took the musical world a hundred years to catch up with the gifted Frenchman—and it is thought by some non-Parisians that Paris hasn't caught up with him yet.*

Symphonie Fantastique, Op. 14 (1830)

It is almost impossible to think of this extraordinary piece as written in France in the same year as Auber's *Fra Diavolo* and Hérold's *Zampa*, once popular operas long since faded into near obscurity, in the year when an audience's idea of what a symphony should be was Mendelssohn's "Reformation," with its reverential treatment of Luther's hymn, "Ein Feste Burg." The twenty-six-year-old Berlioz gave his "Grand Fantastic Symphony in Five Parts" the subtitle "An Episode in the Life of an Artist," based part of it on an irreverent treatment of the liturgical "Dies Irae," and wrote a program for it in which it seems fairly clear that each of the five movements is a dream—three of them might be thought nightmares—brought on by drugs. The artist depicted by Berlioz is, in his own words, "a young musician of morbidly sensitive character," a would-be suicide who "poisons himself with opium in a fit of amorous despair. The narcotic dose, too weak to result in death, plunges him into a heavy sleep accompanied by the strangest visions, during which his sensations, sentiments, and recollections are translated in his sick brain into musical thoughts and images."

Musically, the innovation in the *Symphonie Fantastique* is its use, in each of the five movements, of a recurrent theme. Berlioz set thereby an example for Franz Liszt, César Franck, Camille Saint-Saëns, and other Parisians looking for fresh approaches to symphonic composition. Berlioz's recurrent theme, which in view of the circumstances he quite understandably called an *idée fixe* (a then-new medical term meaning, roughly, "obsession"), is a wispy, protracted, irregularly shaped tune associated with the "Beloved" who has deserted the young man and driven him to his suicide attempt.

First movement: "Reveries. Passions." The young man, awaking from his suicide attempt, still feels the effects of the narcotic. The "Reveries" are a largo introduction and the "Passions" an allegro movement in which the *idée fixe*, the Beloved, appears as an elongated strain for unison flutes.

Second movement: "A Ball." The young man imagines he sees the Beloved in the midst of a brilliant waltzing company.

Third movement: "Scene in the Country." On a summer evening, the young man hears two shepherds (English horn and oboe) questioning and answering each other on their pipes. The trees rustle in the wind. Calmness comes to his heart. Then the Beloved appears. He wonders if she could possibly be deceiving him. One of the shepherds takes up his piping again, and the other does not respond. The sun sets. Distant thunder rolls. There is silence. (We who listen are waiting in vain for some structural guide map for these proceedings. The composer seems not to have the slightest interest in sonata form.)

Fourth movement: "The March to the Scaffold." The young man imagines he has murdered the Beloved and is being marched through the streets to his death. She appears to him for a moment just before the axe falls. The crowd roars its approval. (This movement caused a sensation at the first performance.)

Fifth movement: "Dream of a Witches' Sabbath." The young man imagines himself at the Faustian celebration of his own funeral. The Beloved appears amid the grotesque figures in the person of a hideous old crone, her *idée fixe* now turned a gnarled, snarling tune on a high-pitched clarinet. A bell clangs, and the bassoons and tuba intone the "Dies Irae." That dire chant from the Requiem Mass is opposed by the now frightening *idée fixe*, and the two tunes fight it out to an overwhelming orchestral climax.

Is this innovative work in any way autobiographical? Jacques Barzun, the tireless promoter of Berlioz at the expense of Wagner, would say, emphatically, no. Most of the rest of us are not quite so sure. Three years before the premiere of the *Symphonie Fantastique*, Berlioz had seen the Irish actress Harriet Smithson performing with an English Shakespearean company and had fallen hopelessly in love with her. He recorded that, when he saw her Ophelia, "A feeling of intense, overpowering sadness overwhelmed me and I fell into a nervous condition, like a sickness of which only a great writer on physiology could give any adequate idea." And when he saw her Juliet he said, "I was hardly able to breathe—as though an iron hand gripped me by the heart. I knew that I was lost." Thereafter he organized a concert of his works in Miss Smithson's honor; she did not attend. He tried to meet her and failed. Finally he wrote, in the throes of passion—but using ideas from earlier compositions—his *Symphonie Fantastique*. Eventually, he married his beloved. Predictably, the marriage was not a success.

Berlioz later insisted that the lady who inspired his *idée fixe* was not Harriet Smithson at all but Estelle Deboeuf, with whom he had fallen in love in the country when he was twelve and she eighteen. He had written a song for her when he and his parents moved to Paris, and he thought he would never see her again. When they did meet again, they were both in their sixties, and she could hardly believe that so famous a man was still obsessed with her. He remembered her, along with his Virgilian heroine, Dido, on the day he died. But before that he had remembered the song he once wrote for her, and he confessed that he had used it not only in his cantata *Herminie* but as the *idée fixe* of the *Symphonie Fantastique*. "I used it unchanged," he said.

Recording

Davis, Vienna Philharmonic (Philips)

You may also want to hear...

...*Harold in Italy*, a viola concerto Berlioz was not about to call a viola concerto. This is a four-movement piece, written for Paganini, ostensibly based on the adventures of Byron's Childe Harold, but closer in both spirit and subject matter to Berlioz's own recollections of his days in Italy. It has, predictably enough, an *idée fixe*, a scene with a piper, and an orgy—and yet in its melancholy way its effect is wholly different from that of the *Symphonie Fantastique*. Paganini didn't much like it and never played it. But violists and lovers of Berlioz cherish it.

Much of Berlioz's other concert music actually comes from his operas and quasi-operas—the "Dance of the Sylphs," the "Minuet of the Will-o'-the-Wisps," and the "Hungarian March" from *La Damnation de Faust;* the "Roman Carnival Overture" from *Benvenuto Cellini;* the "Royal Hunt and Storm" from *Les Troyens;* and the "Queen Mab Scherzo" and "Love Scene" from *Romeo and Juliet.* Along with the tender cantata *L'Enfance du Christ* and the massive *Requiem,* these works fall outside the province of this book. But the mere mention of them shows the ambition of the composer's search for inspiration—Goethe, Virgil, Shakespeare, and the New Testament.

Franz Liszt
1811–1886

The Hungarian-born prodigy, possibly the greatest pianist who ever lived, was long discounted as a composer, and there are still those who regard him as little more than a facile purveyor of self-aggrandizing display pieces and noisy orchestral works. They are wrong. Liszt, a sometime Parisian, occupied a central position in European culture in the nineteenth-century. His experiments with musical structure, harmonization, and orchestration have had far-reaching effects. And no man of genius was so selfless and tireless in promoting the work of others. The opera lover should know that, during his management of the opera house at Weimar, Liszt staged the premieres of Wagner's Lohengrin *and Saint-Saëns's* Samson et Dalila, *and, at a time when there were no broadcasts or recordings, he helped to publicize some thirty other operas by writing transcriptions of their overtures and "paraphrases" of their scores and performing them at his concerts. He did the same for many instrumental works of Handel, Beethoven, Schubert, and others.*

Les Préludes (1850)

This stirring piece is the most familiar of the thirteen "symphonic poems" in which Liszt rejected classical sonata form—exposition, development, recapitulation—for a less abstract, more fluid and Romantic approach to stating and developing ideas in music. In contemplating a myth (Prometheus), an author (Tasso), a literary hero (Hamlet), a legendary hero (Mazeppa), a historical event (the defeat of the Huns), or a national ideal (Hungaria), Liszt, inspired by verses of Schiller or Herder, Shakespeare or Victor Hugo—or by some famous painting or Etruscan vase—would use a single "Ur-theme" that would affect, and to some extent generate, all of the music to follow. He often gave his audiences explanatory "programs" for these works, but it is not as if, in his composing, he were providing mere pictorial effects instead of true musical substance. Actually, in his attempts to structure his music less formally and relate it to the other arts, he was introducing a whole new aesthetic, one that would lead in time to the parting of the ways of the two great claimants of Beethoven's mantle—Brahms, the staunch defender of classical forms, and Wagner, the proponent of the "unified art-work." (It is significant that Liszt's two symphonies are never referred to as No. 1 in C Major and No. 2 in A Minor but as the *Faust* Symphony and the *Dante* Symphony. The first of these actually begins as ambiguously as Wagner's *Tristan*, with a melody in a twelve-tone row à la Schoenberg!)

The "program" for *Les Préludes* is a rather overwrought poem, *Méditations poétiques*, by Alphonse de Lamartine, which Liszt paraphrased as follows: "What is our life but a series of preludes to that unknown song wherein Death strikes the first solemn note? Where is the destiny in which the first pleasures of happiness are not interrupted by a storm whose deadly breath scatters all its fair illusions? Where is the soul that, cruelly wounded, does not seek to calm its memories in the peace of the countryside? When the trumpet sounds the signal of alarms, man hastens to the post of peril, whatever the strife that calls him to its ranks, for in struggles he finds the full consciousness of himself."

The Ur-theme of *Les Préludes*, stated by the double basses at the start, is a three-note motif, a kind of musical question mark, that Wagner was to adapt for his "Fate" motif in the *Ring* cycle and César Franck was to use in the first movement of his only symphony. The theme develops into a veritable "announcement of death." Then we hear musical passages to suggest, in the order of their occurrence, "the first pleasures of happiness," the "storm" that scatters illusions, "the peace of the countryside," the "trumpet" sounding the alarm, and, finally, man's heroic discovery of "full consciousness of himself." And the Ur-theme can be traced in each of them.

But we ought not to make too much of Liszt's paraphrase. Some of the musical ideas in *Les Préludes* were used by him years earlier, for a work based on the poems of Joseph Autran. The important thing, he said, is that the listener's attention be directed to a "poetic idea." That was why he affixed "programs" to the scores of his symphonic poems.

Recording
Davis, Vienna Philharmonic (Philips)

Mephisto Waltz No. 1 (1861)

This twelve-minute tour de force—which should be heard in its unsimplified first version for piano—is, especially for the operatically literate, a better introduction to Liszt's voluminous keyboard works than are his more popular pieces. Musically unconnected with his depiction of Mephistopheles in *A Faust Symphony* (see below), and based on a poem by Nikolaus Lenau rather than on Goethe's drama, the *Mephisto Waltz* is a virtuoso piece (it has been called the most difficult thing ever written for the piano) that is also a stunningly sardonic portrait. Like much of Liszt's output, it has a program: Mephisto, in hunter's garb, arrives with Faust at a village tavern where a wedding is being celebrated. He reproaches Faust for his shyness, seizes a violin, and sets the rustic company madly whirling. Faust presses the hand of a black-eyed beauty and dances with her into a forest where the strains of Mephisto's now distant waltz mingle with the twitterings of nightingales. The critic James Huneker thought the orchestral version of this piece "one of the most voluptuous episodes outside of the *Tristan* score." Frankly, I don't hear that in the original piano version, but what is there—Mephisto tuning his fiddle, striking up menacing chords and cascading arpeggios, and launching into his satanic waltz—is quite enough.

Recording
Horowitz (RCA)

You may also want to hear...

...*Orpheus*, after *Les Préludes* the best of the symphonic poems, written to introduce the first Weimar production of Gluck's *Orphée et Eurydice*. Liszt depicts the mythical hero lifting up his lyre and taming all of nature in one extended song. Every one of the symphonic poems has impressive pages (try the exciting *Mazeppa* next). But employing a single Ur-theme instead of the multiple themes of classical form can, and in Liszt often does, result in overextension and repetitiveness. The brief and beautiful *Orpheus*, however, has no such problems.

...the Piano Sonata in B Minor, a single-movement work of monumental difficulty about which critical opinion remains sharply divided. It was dedicated to Schumann (whose beloved Clara must have been one of the few pianists who could actually play it) and described by Wagner (Liszt's son-in-law at the time) as "beyond all conception beautiful, great, lovely, deep and noble, sublime even as thyself." Alfred Brendel has suggested, in his book *Music Sounded Out*, that three of the sonata's recurrent themes can be thought characterizations of Goethe's Faust, Gretchen (the Marguerite of Berlioz and Gounod), and Mephistopheles. (Liszt's *Faust Symphony*, his most impressive attempt to build a large-scale symphonic structure without recourse to sonata form, also sketches in its three movements three portraits of Faust, Marguerite, and Mephisto. As it uses a tenor and chorus at its close, it falls beyond the scope of this book, but Wagnerites might be astonished to discover that its opening theme, depicting the aged and despairing Faust, became, note-for-note, one of Sieglinde's themes in *Die Walküre*; it occurs just before her "Kehrte der Vater nun heim!" in Act II.)

Most listeners will already know Liszt's more popular piano pieces—the Hungarian rhapsodies, the dreamy Etude No. 3 in E Flat, the dreamier Consolation No. 3 in D Flat, and, dreamiest of all, the omnipresent *Liebesträume* No. 3 in A Flat. These may not be great music, but to this listener they are preferable to the two showy piano concertos and to the variations for piano and orchestra on the "Dies Irae" (still more of the Faustian!) called *Todentanz*. Wagnerians will be interested to know that when Liszt was staying with the Wagners at the Palazzo Vendramin in Venice he was impressed by a funeral procession he saw floating down the Grand Canal, and he composed "The Lugubrious Gondola," a piano piece (existing in three versions) with strikingly new harmonies. A few weeks later, Wagner's own funeral cortège made its way by gondola from the Vendramin down the Grand Canal.

Finally there are Liszt's piano transcriptions and paraphrases of operatic music. The chief beneficiaries of these often flamboyant pieces, once flamboyantly played for an adoring public by the composer himself, were Bellini, Donizetti, Meyerbeer, Gounod, Verdi, and Wagner. But Liszt also went to bat, pianistically, for the operas of Rossini, Mozart, Halévy, Auber, Berlioz, Glinka, and Tchaikovsky. The "*Rigoletto* Paraphrase" was a popular concert piece for almost a century; today the grandiose "Reminiscences de *Norma*" is more likely to be heard, even though it dispenses with "Casta Diva." Under Liszt's fingers *Don Giovanni* becomes a whirlwind of virtuoso display. The *Tannhäuser* "Pilgrim's Chorus" and the *Tristan* "Liebestod" (which was Liszt's name, not Wagner's, for the opera's last page) are relatively straightforward, but unexpected pianistic storms come whirling through the "Sextette" from *Lucia* and the "Miserere" from *Il Trovatore*, and *Simon Boccanegra* is briefly touched by the *au courant* composer with whole-tone harmonies. Finally, Liszt turns the innocent waltz from Gounod's *Faust* into something almost as diabolical and nightingale-twittered as his own *Mephisto Waltz*.

Frédéric Chopin
1810–1849

The immensely talented and hypersensitive son of a French father and Polish mother, Chopin wrote almost exclusively for his beloved instrument, the piano, and discovered new sonorities in its sounding strings. Schumann called him one of the heroes of Romanticism. He was influenced, especially in the nocturnes, by the long-lined melodies of Bellini's Norma *and* I Puritani. *Any music lover, however remotely interested in classical music, will have already heard Chopin's ten most popular pieces, listed here in alphabetical order:*

Etude Op. 10, No. 3 in E Major
Fantasie-Impromptu Op. 66 in C-Sharp Minor
Nocturne Op. 9, No. 2 in E-Flat Major

Polonaise Op. 40, No. 1 in A Major ("Military")
Polonaise Op. 53, No. 6 in A-Flat Major ("Heroic")
Prelude Op. 28, No. 7 in A Major
Prelude Op. 28, No. 15 in D-Flat Major ("Raindrop")
Waltz Op. 18, No. 1 in E-Flat Major ("Grande valse brillante")
Waltz Op. 64, No. 1 in D-Flat Major ("Minute")
Waltz Op. 64, No. 2 in C-Sharp Minor

To my knowledge, all but three of these were turned into popular songs in the heyday of Tin Pan Alley, and every one of them has been fully orchestrated for concert use. But do not persuade yourself that you have heard any of these remarkable pieces properly until you have heard them played on the piano by the likes Rubinstein or Horowitz (on records) or (in the concert hall) by a virtuoso like Perahia or Pollini. Then you may be ready for ten of Chopin's even more extraordinary achievements. Some of these, too, may be familiar to you, not from popular songs but from film scores that used them, and to startlingly dramatic effect, as Chopin wrote them:

Andante Spianato in G Major and Grand Polonaise in E-Flat Major, Op. 22: The Grand Polonaise is the brilliant and heroic display piece that, in Roman Polanski's film *The Pianist*, the Holocaust survivor Wladyslaw Szpilman plays triumphantly in the last scene and throughout the long rolling of the credits.

Ballade No. 1, Op.23 in G Minor: Schumann thought this, the first of four dramatic pieces in this form, the composer's "most spirited, most daring work." Inspired by a narrative poem by a compatriot, Adam Mickiewicz, about the fifteenth-century uprising of Lithuanians against the Teutonic Knights, it has been seen as a protest against the nineteenth-century Russian domination of Poland. In *The Pianist* the starving and exhausted Szpilman plays the heroic opening and closing of this ballade for a Nazi officer in the hope that he will spare his life. (Actually, Szpilman in his memoir says that the Chopin piece that saved him was the posthumous Nocturne in C-Sharp Minor; in the film he is playing that nocturne on Polish radio when the Nazi bombs fall on Warsaw.)

Concerto No. 1 in E Minor, Op. 11: This is the longer and perhaps the more popular of the composer's two piano concertos. Chopin was not a gifted orchestrator, and the sonata form and rondo may not have been the structures most congenial to him, but the second movement here, a Bellinian "Romanza," is superb, and the piano parts of all three movements are impressive enough to have kept the concerto in the repertory of major pianists well into this century.

Etude Op. 10, No. 12 in C Minor ("Revolutionary"): Though each of Chopin's twenty-seven etudes is built around some pianistic exercise, there is as much variety in the collection as can be found in the scherzos, preludes, and mazurkas. This etude is a brief, tempestuous piece in which finger-stretching chords in the right hand are set against powerful, whirling arpeggios in the left. Chopin, it is popularly believed, wrote it upon hearing of the fall of Warsaw to Russian troops in 1831.

Mazurka Op. 17, No. 4 in A Minor: While the eleven polonaises give voice to grand patriotic passions, the aristocratic mazurkas, fifty-five in number, run the whole gamut of emotions, and this one, subtly and unforgettably used in Ingmar Bergman's film *Cries and Whispers*, is quietly breathtaking. The composer has never spoken more intimately to the listener than here.

Nocturne Op. 27, No. 2 in D-Flat Major: One of the best of the nineteen "night pieces," this is a prime example of the dreamy, ethereal Chopin that is indebted to the operas of Bellini.

Nocturne Op. 48, No. 1 in C Minor: This tragic statement was used in the fictionalized 1945 film biography *A Song To Remember* when Liszt hears of Chopin's death and goes to the piano to pay him tribute.

Prelude Op. 28, No. 24 in D Minor: The last of the twenty-four pieces in this form (the collection covers every one of the keyboard's major and minor keys), this hauntingly daemonic piece was effectively used in two pivotal scenes in the 1945 film *The Picture of Dorian Gray.*

Scherzo Op. 31 in B-Flat Minor: Chopin's four scherzos are hardly the amusing diversions found in the third movements of classical symphonies and sonatas. This substantial piece is a dramatic, if unsubtle, study in pianistic contrasts—heroic and almost hysterically lyrical.

Sonata No. 2 in B-Flat Minor, Op. 35: This is the most ambitious of only three Chopin works in this large-scale classical genre. Schumann thought it presumptuous, a betrayal of the sonata form; others have detected unifying elements in it that justify its fame: the funeral march of the third movement is adumbrated in, if not musically linked with, the terror of the first movement, the pathos of the second, and the daemonic intensity of the last.

Recordings

Ballades: Perahia (Sony)
Concertos: Vasary, Berlin Philharmonic (DG)
Etudes: Pollini (DG)
Mazurkas, Nocturnes, Polonaises: Rubinstein (RCA)
Preludes and Sonatas: Argerich (DG)
Scherzos: Richter (Olympia)

Masters of Opera

Giuseppe Verdi
1813–1901

The composer of the trio from I Lombardi, *the quartet from* Rigoletto, *the quintet from* Un Ballo in Maschera, *and the nonet from* Falstaff—*all of them, of course, vocal pieces—composed a string quartet when he was nearing sixty, in Naples for the local premiere of* Aida, *and thinking seriously of retirement. The production of* Aida *was delayed owing to the illness of the soprano, Teresa Stolz, and Verdi filled the interim by writing the four movements of what was to be his only chamber piece. Every opera lover should hear it. It is much more than a mere curiosity.*

Quartet in E Minor (1873)

The string quartet was a musical form appropriated and perfected by Germans and Austrians, but Italians were the first to cultivate it, and Verdi often spoke of it with respect and affection. In fact, at his home at Sant' Agatha he kept by his bedside, along with the writings of his beloved Shakespeare and Schiller, the string quartets of Haydn, Mozart, and Beethoven, and for years the tightly written Viennese masterpieces disciplined his musical thought.

Verdi had his quartet played for a few friends in his Naples hotel suite, but despite their enthusiasm he did not publish it immediately and refused permission for public performances for several years. "I have never attached any importance to the piece" was how he refused the mayor of Parma's request for a performance. That characteristically self-effacing comment has influenced popular opinion unduly. The quartet is a beautifully crafted work, with a true feeling for instrumental voices. And it provides almost our only glimpse into the private Verdi. We see him experimenting, testing, and, as always, learning. We also hear something of *Aida* and its immediate predecessor, *Don Carlo,* and, wondrously, something of what was to happen in *Otello* and, some twenty years in the future, in *Falstaff.*

First, *Aida.* In the opening movement an operagoer can feel, and occasionally thinks he or she can hear, something of the famous opera that Verdi had just composed. The restless E-Minor first subject instantly calls Amneris to mind, while a counter-melody, fugally developed, suggests Ramfis and the priests. We suspect, then, that the prayerful G-Major second subject may be Aida herself in a new musical guise—and we are sure of it when the theme climaxes in a virtual quotation from Aida's second-act "Amore, amore." The movement soon becomes a miniature drama.

A second-movement andantino follows, a free adaptation of the theme-and-variation form. Of the four movements it has always impressed listeners as the least Verdian, as the work of an Italian composer under Viennese influences. Yet the theme is not far from the instrumental music that accompanies Rodrigo's conversation with Eboli in Act II of *Don Carlo,* and the variations soon take on a characteristically Verdian intensity.

By contrast, the scherzo-like third movement fairly bursts with the spirit that will pervade much of *Otello*'s first act, even though its trio section is, in effect, a solo for a baritone less sinister than Iago: the cello sings broadly to pizzicato accompaniment, and for a few measures Verdi pays tribute to the popular songs of the city in which he is awaiting his *Aida* premiere.

Finally, in the last movement, there is *Falstaff.* The chattering ensembles of Verdi's last work for the stage are anticipated in a lighthearted fugue and all but sent up in a concluding accelerando crescendo that tests to the full the virtuosity of the four performers. Here is indisputable evidence that Verdi had complete control of the medium he was, for a moment in his life, experimenting with. As he wrote later to a friend, "I don't know whether the quartet is good or bad, but I do know that it is a quartet."

And it is a quartet that ends, as the whole Verdian operatic canon was to end, with a fugal statement that says, in effect, that "everything in the world is a jest."

Recording

Guarneri Quartet (RCA)

Richard Wagner
1813–1883

The composer who cast himself so often as a questing hero—as the Flying Dutchman, Tannhäuser, Lohengrin, and Parsifal—thought earlier in his career, in midst of scoring Rienzi, *that he might write a symphony based on the greatest of all questing dramas, Goethe's* Faust. *Every Wagnerian ought to know what happened next.*

A Faust Overture (1840)

It may come as a surprise to know that the teenaged Wagner wrote seven vocal pieces for a performance of Goethe's *Faust* in Leipzig. Nothing more came of that fledgling effort, but in his twenties Wagner planned a large-scale orchestral work on the same subject. He was clearly on to something with his *Faust* ambitions. Berlioz soon came up with a symphonic oratorio/opera on Goethe's hero; Schumann was to end his career after composing something along similar lines; Liszt was eventually to write just such a symphony as Wagner had in mind; and in a distant future Mahler was destined to write the *Faust* symphony *par excellence,* his "Symphony of a Thousand."

The young Wagner penned a first movement about the disillusioned scholar and sketched a second movement on Gretchen, the girl he dishonored. But eventually, convinced that vocal music was his true metier, Wagner abandoned his plan for a *Faust* symphony, issued the first movement as a freestanding overture, and turned to music-drama. When, some twenty years later, a sentimental Frenchman named Charles Gounod wrote the opera that was to be, for a century or more, the most popular of all musical treatments of *Faust*, Wagner, whether for personal or patriotic reasons, refused even to listen to it, though he was quick to pronounce his judgement: it was "a sweetly vulgar, affected concoction, the music of an inferior talent who would like to achieve something and in his desperation grasps at any means." The world thought differently for a long time.

Wagner's far-from-inconsequential work is composed in strict sonata form, though it is clear from the first measures that he was already thinking in terms of dramatic portraiture as much as symphonic structures. After a slow introduction in the double basses and lower brass, pointedly suggesting the darkness of Faust's despair at finding all learning useless, the first theme—a six-note motif that begins with an octave leap, sounded first by the violins—suggests the emergence of Faust's desire to find true wisdom in the exploration of his own nature. (Wagner quoted

Goethe in the published score: "The God that dwells within my breast can stir my soul through all its depths.")

The second theme, voiced first in rising woodwind chords, seems to embody what Goethe called "das Ewig-Weibliche"— the "eternal feminine," that principle within a man that leads him out of himself and onward on the quest for self-understanding.

The two themes, and others derived from them (perhaps the devil is in the details), are developed with all the earnest intensity and vehemence we expect from the young Wagner. Then there is a recapitulation and a concluding coda in which Faust is limned by the strings in unison and the "eternal feminine" hymned by the woodwind choir.

Wagner wrote in his autobiography, *Mein Leben,* that the *Faust Overture* was inspired by hearing, for the first time in years, a performance of Beethoven's Ninth Symphony. But recently it has been persuasively argued that Berlioz's *Romeo and Juliet* was a more likely stimulus. Wagner was seldom ready to acknowledge his indebtedness to anything French.

Throughout his life Wagner thought paternally of his youthful contribution to the ever-expanding number of musical treatments of Goethe's masterpiece, and he revised it several times. Concert performances of the overture use Wagner's last revision, made in 1855, where there are melodic and harmonic touches that forecast *Tristan.*

Recording
Szell, Cleveland Orchestra (Sony)

You may also want to hear...

...the Symphony in C Major, a work by a talented twenty-year-old energized by Beethoven. On the other hand, the few piano pieces that survive are only for the master's devotees.

(I presume that an opera lover in good standing will already have heard Wagner's winsome *Siegfried Idyll*, an instrumental birthday/Christmas present for his second wife, Cosima, partially woven out of motifs from the *Ring* and celebrating the recent birth of their son Siegfried.)

Slavs

Alexander Borodin
1833–1887

Borodin, a research chemist who made an important contribution to the study of catalysts, was also the senior member of the Moguchaya (The Mighty Handful), the group of five Russian composers who strove to produce an indigenous musical tradition distinct from those of the dominant Austro-German, Italian, and French schools. Amazingly, considering their remarkable success, only one of their number, Mily Balakirev, was a professional musician. The rest were largely self-taught musicians who made their livings in other fields. Cesar Cui, the most outspoken of the group, was an engineer, Nicolai Rimsky-Korsakov a naval officer, and Modest Mussorgsky a civil servant.

    As for Borodin, he wrote that composing was for him "a relaxation, a pastime that distracts me from my principal business, my professorship. I love my profession and my science." He was also a devoted teacher, a philanthropist whose doors were always open to the poor, and a pioneer for women's rights. Borodin's only opera, Prince Igor, contains his most popular orchestral showpiece, the spectacular "Polovtsian Dances." But almost as popular in recent decades is a quartet he wrote on a summer holiday and dedicated to his wife:

String Quartet No. 2 in D Major (1881)

Few chamber works are as familiar to the public as this unassuming quartet is today—and *mirabile dictu* it is written, not in the Central European tradition of Haydn, Mozart, Beethoven, and Schubert but in the quite different traditions established by the Russian "Five."

Borodin's own instrument, the cello, introduces the first subject, a suave but somehow intimate tune that the first violin quickly repeats and expands. Conversely, the second subject, subtly derived from the sixth bar of the first, is sounded by the violin and eventually taken up by the cello. Only in the development section do the inner voices, the second violin and the viola, have much more to do than accompany; density of sound is not what Borodin is aiming for. The movement, in sonata form, holds no surprises until, in the recapitulation, the second subject appears a half-tone higher than the form calls for—which is not as defiant a touch as it might seem.

The second movement, a gossamer scherzo, is given over almost completely to a waltz—a decidedly non-Viennese, quasi-oriental waltz. (Borodin was proud that some of his ancestry was Asian.) Many first-time listeners will recognize the tune immediately, never before realizing that it originated in—of all the unexpected things—a string quartet. Borodin wrote modestly that all he intended was "an impression of a lighthearted evening spent in one of the delightful suburban pleasure gardens of St. Petersburg."

The third movement, a slow and quietly charming nocturne that enjoys a special popularity apart from the quartet as a fully orchestrated piece, has a main theme as languorous as a popular song (and at twenty-four bars it is almost of standard popular-song length). A second theme also charms, descending an octave or more, trilling gracefully along the way.

The fourth movement begins with a sort of recitative between violin and cello. The critic Andrew Porter suggested that Borodin had in mind the introduction to the last movement of Beethoven's last quartet, where the composer wrote the question "Must it be?" and the answer "It must be!" over his themes. Thereafter the movement becomes a lively vivace, some of it fugally treated, some of it purposely dramatic, with yet one more of Borodin's expressively chromatic melodies.

Finally, it should be said, for fans of the Broadway musical, that the songwriting team of Robert Wright and George Forrest were much more successful at adapting the melodies of Borodin for their operetta-like *Kismet* than they were at adapting Grieg for their *Song of Norway* and Rachmaninoff for their *Anastasia*—and that the "quasi-oriental waltz" in this quartet's second movement became, in their hands, "Baubles, Bangles, and Beads," while the exotic third-movement melody became their ambitious vocal quartet, the perennially popular "And This Is My Beloved."

Recording

Haydn Quartet (Naxos)

You may also want to hear...

...the cheerfully barbaric second symphony and the orientalizing tone poem "In the Steppes of Central Asia" (notable for more reasons than for serving as material for Broadway's *Kismet*). Both opera lovers and concertgoers will already know the "Polovtsian Dances" from *Price Igor* (notable for many more reasons than for their being the source of "Stranger in Paradise" and other tunes in, inevitably, *Kismet*.)

Modest Mussorgsky
1839–1881

The composer of Boris Godunov, Khovantschina, *and four other vigorously Slavic operas that had to be completed by his friends was unquestionably a genius, but one whose life was, and whose legacy remains, a shambles. His ambition, like that of the other members of the Russian "Five," was to give musical voice to a Russia unaffected by, and in his case even opposed to, the cultures of Western Europe, and in that aim he succeeded, often magnificently. So don't look for any classical forms—sonata or otherwise—in the work of this rough-hewn Russian. For that, see Tchaikovsky.*

Pictures at an Exhibition (1874)

This is a suite of pieces for piano that describes in sound several paintings and sketches by Victor Hartmann, a friend of Mussorgsky's who, at the time of composition, had recently died at the age of thirty-nine. The composer, embittered by this "terrible blow," visited an exhibition of Hartmann's work in St. Petersburg and wrote the *Pictures* as a tribute. Only six of Hartmann's paintings have survived, and two of those—the rich Jew and the poor Jew—have been paired by Mussorgsky into a single musical portrait. All eleven of the *Pictures*, rather stark in their black-and-white piano originals, have been colorfully orchestrated by some seventeen different composers. When we refer to instruments in the following description, we are citing the brilliant orchestration by Maurice Ravel, commissioned in 1922 by Serge Koussevitzky.

"Promenade": A solo trumpet depicts a visitor confidently striding into the gallery displaying Hartmann's paintings. The art critic Vladimir Stassov, who had known Hartmann and conferred with

the composer during the composition of the suite, suggests that the "visitor" is Mussorgsky himself. And we are with him as he moves from painting to painting.

"Gnomus" (The Gnome): Hartmann depicted a wooden nutcracker shaped like a grotesque little man. Mussorgsky all but shows him pulling himself up on his feet and walking about on his deformed legs, glaring fiercely all the while. He finally sends the frightening figure scuttling away and continues his promenade, curious now about what else he might see.

"Il Vecchio Castello" (The Old Castle): A troubadour (voiced by an alto saxophone) sings a haunting strain before an Italian ruin. After gazing for some time, slowly taking in the artist's mood, the promenader strides to the next picture.

"Tuileries": The spacious Paris garden is populated, as usual, by noisy children, nursemaids, and babies bawling in their prams.

"Bydlo": A huge oxcart (depicted by a solo tuba) comes sagging and trundling into view, passes massively before us, and makes its way slowly onward. ("Bydlo" is Polish for "ox"; Hartmann painted the picture on a trip through Poland.) The promenader, now impressed by the painter's skill, passes on.

"Ballet of Unhatched Chickens": Hartmann showed a child, a diminutive member of a ballet school in St. Petersburg, emerging from a large chicken shell—a picture to challenge any composer who would choose to set it to music. Mussorgsky gives us a sprightly scherzo.

"Two Polish Jews, One Rich, the Other Poor": The wealthy Samuel Goldberg (massed unison strings in a minor tonality) seems quite pleased with himself, while the impoverished Schmuyle (a muted trumpet) stutters and whines, presumably pleading for a handout. (The names are provided by Stassov.) Of late the piece has,

I think rightly, been thought anti-Semitic: in Hartmann's two pictures, once owned by Mussorgsky himself, the figures are not caricatures.

"Limoges—the Marketplace": The women of the French town gossip at their pushcarts. Hartmann painted the picture *in situ*. Mussorgsky runs the chattering piece without pause into . . .

"Catacombs": Hartmann painted himself, together with a friend and a guide with a lamp, in a bleak Paris cemetery. Mussorgsky gives us solemn, frightening chords that lead to . . .

"Cum mortuis in lingua mortua" (With the dead in a dead language): The composer himself describes this mysterious section: "The creative spirit of the departed Hartmann leads me [through the catacombs] to the skulls, calls out to them, and the skulls begin to glow dimly from within." Mussorgsky puts himself into the picture musically by sounding the "Promenade" theme subtly, almost sardonically.

"The Hut on Fowl's Legs": Hartmann's picture showed a grotesque clock shaped like the hut of Baba Yaga, a man-eating witch from Russian folklore. Mussorgsky gives us a musical impression of Baba's wild flights through the sky, and this leads directly into . . .

"The Great Gate at Kiev": Hartmann's picture was a design for an arch and bell tower to commemorate the escape of Czar Alexander II from an assassin's knife. The "great gate" he designed was never built, but Mussorgsky's musical depiction of his sketch for it survives triumphantly. It remains, in the Ravel orchestration, one of the great orchestral showpieces.

Recording

Abbado, Berlin Philharmonic (DG)

You may also want to hear...

...A Night on Bald Mountain: A frightening description of a witches' sabbath on Mount Triglaf, near Kiev, which Mussorgsky later incorporated into his opera *Sorochintsy Fair*. You have very likely heard this piece already, in your childhood: not only is it a segment in Walt Disney's *Fantasia* but it was used when Dorothy was imprisoned in the castle of the Wicked Witch of the West in *The Wizard of Oz*.

Nicolai Rimsky-Korsakov
1844–1908

It was Rimsky-Korsakov, composer of twelve operas, who edited much of Mussorgsky's work for publication—reorchestating, smoothing away unusual harmonies, and sometimes even substituting music of his own. He has received a bad press for this, and undeservedly. His aim was generously to win a wider audience for works that were unacceptable to both critics and public in the form in which their composer left them, and he was remarkably successful in achieving that aim. Today we quite rightly want to hear Boris Godunov and the other works of Mussorgsky in their original, rough-hewn, barbaric splendor—and Rimsky would have welcomed that.

Rimsky was one of the greatest orchestrators of his or any day. And the operagoer who has enjoyed his Le Coq d'Or, Sadko, or The Invisible City of Kitezh should know his orchestral music as well—and doubtless will already have heard the most famous of them, described here.

Scheherazade, Op.35 (1888)

This "symphonic suite" is not, as is popularly believed, an attempt to tell four *Arabian Knights* tales incident-for-incident, but rather an evocation, in four contrasting movements, of the fantastic world hinted at in the titles of its four movements. At least that is what the composer insisted. And yet he did attach a note to the score to say this much: "The Sultan Schahriar, persuaded of the falseness and faithlessness of all women, had sworn to put to death each of his wives after his first night with them. But the sultana Scheherazade saved her life by arousing his interest in tales which she told him over a thousand and one nights. Driven by curiosity, the Sultan put off his wife's execution from day to day and at last gave up his bloody plan altogether."

Any listener will instantly hear, in the thunderous orchestral octaves that open the suite, the Sultan issuing his edict and, in the sinuous violin solo that follows, the beautiful Scheherazade placating him with the promise of a tale. And in a trice we are embarked on the movement titled "The Sea and Sinbad's Ship." But Rimsky was right to discourage us from constructing a story out of what we hear next, for the "Sultan's theme," if indeed that is what it is, seems now to represent Sinbad's ship, breasting orchestral waves that are suggested by, if we may call it that, "Scheherazade's theme." This fusion of storyteller, listener, and story is something new in musical narratives.

On another of the thousand and one nights, the Sultan asks for a new tale, and Scheherazade obliges. The second movement is titled "The Story of the Kalendar Prince." Rimsky is, perhaps deliberately, being unhelpful again. There are at least three separate *Arabian Knights* stories of princes who became kalendars, or whirling dervishes, and we have no idea which of them this movement is concerned with. What we do have is a new theme introduced by the bassoon and taken up by a succession of instruments, and a striking, vigorously masculine theme whose characteristic triplet, a careful listener may eventually discover, is derived from the very feminine "Scheherazade" theme. So we must put our imaginations to work without having a narrative in mind.

The third movement has a title, "The Young Prince and the Young Princess," that could apply to dozens of Arabian tales. But we are sure that both he (the violins) and she (the clarinet) are beautiful and in love when, in the words of Edward Downes, "Rimsky's orchestra displays an iridescence of tone color so rich and subtly shifting that one is reminded of the spreading of a peacock's tail." And, for reasons Rimsky kept to himself, the theme of the Kalendar Prince makes its way into this new story.

The Sultan, his theme now quivering with anticipation, hears, we presume, the last—the one-thousand-and-first—tale from Scheherazade, and this time Rimsky's title gives us some help: "Festival at Bagdad; The Sea; The Ship Goes to Pieces Against a Rock Surmounted by a Bronze Warrior." As we listen, the riotous festival at Bagdad suddenly seems, as if in a dream, to be taking place on Sinbad's ship, which is in utmost peril at sea. It is all quite breathtaking, and at the end of it, the solo violin that has been Scheherazade's voice wafts upward. She has won her Sultan's mercy by wooing his imagination.

Recording

Mackerras, London Symphony Orchestra (Telarc)

You may also want to hear...

... two glittering works for orchestra—the *Capriccio Espagnol*, a five-movement evocation of Spain replete with instrumental solos (Tchaikovsky called it "a colossal masterpiece of instrumentation"), and the *Russian Easter Overture*, which combines traditional melodies of the Orthodox Church with a celebration of pre-Christian "rites of spring."

Peter Ilyich Tchaikovsky
1840–1893

Through the first half of the twentieth century, the concert halls of America, once the almost exclusive terrain of the masterpieces of the Germanic canon, resounded to Slavic strains. The symphonies of Beethoven and Brahms were in danger of being superseded by the symphonies, concertos, ballet suites, and orchestral overtures of one Peter Ilyich Tchaikovsky. The very sound of what was at the time called "classical" music was Tchaikovskian—on radio broadcasts, in record stores, and on sound tracks. Popular music in the swing era used Tchaikovsky extensively: in an eight-month period in 1939–40 he had more "songs" on the hit parade than Jerome Kern, Cole Porter, Richard Rodgers, and Irving Berlin. (George Gershwin, who might have challenged him, had just died.)

There was, expectedly, an over-reaction from some critical quarters. Tchaikovsky was declared a shameless exploiter of sentimental melody, a hyperemotional, even hysterical, self-pitying, heart-on-sleeve exhibitionist. A just assessment of his work came only when the craze, which lasted for four decades, subsided in the sixties with the unexpected emergence of Gustav Mahler as a suddenly popular "classical" composer.

*Tchaikovsky was a cosmopolitan, a Russian willingly open to German, French, and Italian influences. As such, he was scorned by the Russian "Five," who wanted their national music to set its own trends and forge its own forms. But none of the "Five" came anywhere near achieving Tchaikovsky's fame. Oddly enough, during the decades of the composer's remarkable popularity, his operas—*Eugene Onegin, The Queen of Spades, *and eight others—were virtually unperformed outside of Russia. That situation, fortunately for us all, no longer obtains.*

Violin Concerto in D Major, Op. 35 (1878)

Immensely popular as this concerto and its sometime companion, the First Piano Concerto, eventually became, both were initially thought amateurish and unplayable. Nicolai Rubinstein, to whom the piano concerto was dedicated, thought it "utterly worthless, trivial, and vulgar" and refused to have anything to do with it. Leopold Auer, the dedicatee of the violin concerto, not only refused to play it but tried to persuade others to reject it. Years later Auer reversed his judgment on it, helpfully revising several of the "unplayable" passages and encouraging a whole generation of violinists to perform it. But the initial critical reaction had been savage. The most influential critic of the time, the same Eduard Hanslick whom Wagner caricatured as Beckmesser in *Die Meistersinger*, said of it, "We see common faces, hear coarse oaths, and smell fuel oil. For the first time we are confronted with the revolting thought that there may be music that actually stinks to the ear." Part of Hanslick's problem may have been that the violin concerto really sounds Slavic—something a Viennese steeped in Germanic traditions would not be inclined to find congenial.

The main melody of the first movement, an instantly memorable tune extending over eight measures, can be made to sound by turns insistently folk-rhythmical, or sentimental, or as sumptuous as a polonaise at the czar's imperial court. Few melodies have been so cleverly crafted for virtuoso development by a soloist. The second theme seems almost insipid by comparison. And both themes are really too long to serve the purposes of the sonata-movement structure that the Vienna musical establishment expected to hear. "The wildest Russian nihilism" was one Western critic's response.

The minor-key melody of the second movement might almost be thought a peasant's lament until, after the first eight notes,

Tchaikovsky equips it with a trill and turns it into a kind of salon piece. There is a Brahmsian major-key melody to complement it, and an expressive cadenza for the soloist—and we move without a break into the last movement, an energetic Russian rondo with plenty of opportunity for virtuoso display. Hardly "the wildest Russian nihilism," then. Today the concerto is thought a tame, Romantic, tear-inducing piece—except by the public that still clamors to hear it. In any case, it was the public, not the critics, that made the ultimate decision about it, and about the First Piano Concerto as well.

Recording

Perlman, Ormandy, Philadelphia Orchestra (EMI)

Symphony No. 6 in B Minor, Op. 74 ("Pathétique") (1893)

For many this symphony is the quintessential Tchaikovsky work. For some it is so far over the emotional top as to be an embarrassment. The composer, unembarrassed, said, "I love it as I have never loved any of my musical children."

A four-note theme emerges out of the depths of the orchestra, as if out of primeval slime, sounded by a bassoon. Eventually it quickens to life—a life of struggle and torment. Then we get, as a second theme, a fully fledged sixteen-bar melody; the composer was, as always, determined not to limit his sonata-form ideas to mere fragments. After a contrasting section, the melody returns, richly orchestrated. (Many conductors make it more lachrymose than, I suspect, the composer intended.) The solo clarinet takes the music down to the depths again—and the development begins with a terrific crash. Soon Tchaikovsky's imperial trumpet is riding an orchestral storm—and there is a brief quotation from the Russian service for the dead. In the recapitulation, the four-note first theme becomes almost desperately vehement, and the melodious second theme returns with all its charged emotion. (This time even show-off conductors have to struggle to keep the theme under control.) At last, the composer seems to realize that he has let too much emotion escape and closes the movement with a quiet, prayer-like coda.

The second movement is a waltz that is, ingeniously, not quite a waltz: it is cast not in 3/4 time but in the rarely attempted 5/4 signature, as if to indicate that the composer's attempt at light-heartedness simply cannot take hold. The contrasting section, with its insistent drumbeat and minor tonality, reinforces that impression.

A determined march emerges from a flurry of orchestral activity in the scherzo movement, as if the man whose life we are exploring has had a change of fortune and found the will to survive. In fact, there are few symphonic movements as determined and exhilarating as this one.

But we have not yet had our slow movement. Tchaikovsky has saved it for last. (Has any other composer thought to do anything so drastic?) The strings make an initial grieving statement, and in subsequent developments they have to struggle to sustain even that. Several times the bassoon takes us to the depths where the symphony began. The second theme is another full-blown song, poignantly harmonized and orchestrated, almost unbearable in its hopelessness. Its final, desperately resigned appearance comes after a discreet cymbal crash has signified what Tchaikovsky, when he first planned the symphony, said the last movement would be all about—death.

Within a week after its completion, the composer himself was dead. The critic Hans Keller wrote, "The symphonic world was never the same again." The last movement of Tchaikovsky's sixth symphony had, he said with deliberate ambiguity, "cast an illuminating shadow over the whole future history of the form."

Recording

Bernstein, New York Philharmonic (DG)

You may also want to hear...

...the Piano Concerto No. 1 in B-Flat Minor. In the mid-twentieth century, this was the very model of the Romantic concerto, and its expansive opening melody, punctuated by crashing chords from the soloist, was as much the hallmark of "classical" music as anything by Beethoven. Though nothing that follows that opening is quite so overwhelming (the famous melody is only that—an opening), the concerto remains a favorite for strong-armed pianists and swooning public alike.

...the Symphony No. 4 in F Minor, with an insistent "Fate" theme, a whirlwind finale in which Fate is trampled on and triumphed over, and much between that was either too "wild" or too "Russian" for its first audiences; and the Symphony No. 5 in E Minor, with an insistently Slavic motto theme, a dreamily Romantic slow movement, a waltz instead of a scherzo, and a triumphant finale in which the motto theme is simply unstoppable. Both symphonies are great warhorses, staples of the repertory, skillfully composed, and too often condescended to.

...the three ballets *Swan Lake*, *The Sleeping Beauty*, and *The Nutcracker*—music so beautifully crafted, evocative, and popular that comment is hardly necessary, except that we can now hear the scores complete and not, as was the case a half-century ago, reduced to "suites." As ballet music they are challenged only by three Stravinsky works—*The Firebird*, *Petrouchka*, and *The Rite of Spring*—and by Ravel's *Daphnis and Chloé*.

...the youthful *Romeo and Juliet* Fantasy-Overture, a spellbinding piece with truly impassioned love music. Tchaikovsky did not specify a program, but the work's progress is easy to follow: Friar Lawrence; the street fighting of Montagues and Capulets; the balcony scene; the second street fight, in which

Tybalt is killed; the night the newlyweds spend together; their tragic deaths; Friar Lawrence's lament. Tchaikovsky's telling of the tale is more starlit than Gounod's, more rapturous than Bellini's, more melodious than Prokofiev's, and perhaps even more compelling than Berlioz's.

. . . the other orchestral pieces, not nearly as popular as they once were. These are *Francesca da Rimini*, a tone poem that depicts Dante's lovers whirled in the inferno and then narrates their tragic story; *Capriccio Italien*, a rhapsody based on Italian folk tunes and popular songs; the Serenade for Strings, with its elegant waltz; *Marche Slave*, perhaps not as vulgar as it can seem at first (it was written for concert to benefit the families of Serbians who fell fighting the Turks); and the *1812 Overture*, again perhaps not quite as vulgar as it has seemed (it was commissioned for the consecration of a church built in thanksgiving for the Russian victory over Napoleon).

Bedřich Smetana
1824–1884

Smetana, the composer of nine operas on Czech themes and often called "the father of Czech music," was a Bohemian who spoke only German. The river celebrated in his most famous work is known not by its Czech name, the Vltava, but by its German name, the Moldau. For a hundred years the most familiar of his operas was called not Prodaná Nev sta *but* Die Verkaufte Braut *(The Bartered Bride). All of this underlines the fact that, as far back as the Middle Ages, music-loving Bohemians had wandered far beyond their borders, bringing their art to German-speaking lands. Bohemia was where Mozart's* Figaro *and* Don Giovanni *were first appreciated. And it is that Bohemia, with music at its heart, that Smetana celebrates.*

The Moldau (Vltava) (1879)

This tribute to Bohemia's river is the most familiar of the six tone poems that Smetana called *Má Vlast* (My Fatherland), a tribute in music to the history, traditions, and geographical features of his native country. (The other pieces celebrate Bohemia's meadows and forests; the river fortress Vyšekrad; the legendary warrioress Šarka; Tábor, the storied encampment of the Hussite army; and Blaník, the mountain where the soldiers still slumber, ready to defend Bohemia from attackers.) Smetana has provided his own program for *The Moldau*:

> Two springs pour forth their streams in the shade of the Bohemian forest—the one warm and gushing, the other cold and tranquil. Their waves, joyfully flowing over rocky beds, unite and sparkle in the rays of the morning sun. The forest brook, rushing on, becomes the river Vltava. Coursing through Bohemia's valleys, it grows into a mighty stream. It flows through dense woods from which come joyous hunting sounds, and the notes of the hunter's horn drawing ever nearer and nearer. It flows through emerald meadows and lowlands, where a wedding feast is being celebrated with songs and dancing. By night, in its glittering waves, wood and water nymphs hold their revels. And these waters reflect many a fortress and castle— witnesses of a bygone age of knightly splendor and the martial glory of days that are no more. At the rapids of St. John the stream spreads on, winding its way through cataracts, hewing a path for its foaming waters through the rocky gorge into the broad riverbed, in which it flows on in majestic calm toward Prague, welcomed by the time-honored Vyšekrad fortress, to disappear in the distance from the poet's gaze.

All of this is clearly indicated in the music. The theme of the river itself is a truly beautiful strain in a minor tonality, rolling onward in 6/8 time. Strangely enough, the melody may actually be Swedish in origin, and strikes some listeners as Hebraic. Not so the Czechs, however. They have claimed it as their own by turning it into a folk song.

Recording

Kubelik, Boston Symphony (DG)

You may also want to hear...

...*From Bohemia's Meadows and Forests*, from the same cycle of tone poems. An opera fan will already be familiar with the best of Smetana's other orchestral works—the overture and dances from *The Bartered Bride*.

Antonín Dvořák
1841–1904

The genial, hardworking, God-fearing composer of the opera Rusalka, the Requiem, and the Stabat Mater also wrote an abundance of instrumental music of every variety, all of it of a most agreeable spontaneity, all of it permeated with the spirit of his beloved Bohemia. He also spent several years in the United States—in Manhattan, where he received many honors and important positions, and in the Czech community in Spillville, Iowa, where he took an interest in the traditions of Negro and American Indian music. Contrary to what has been said in the past, he did not use traditional American melodies in his "New World" symphony or in his "American" chamber music. He skillfully grafted the indigenous styles he discovered in the United States onto his own Bohemian idiom—and did it so successfully that, paradoxically, Hollywood westerns have used Czech rhythms and harmonies to underscore films shot in Griffith Park and Monument Valley.

Symphony No. 9 in E Minor, Op. 95 ("From the New World") (1893)

Through an almost Wagnerian haze there eventually emerges a leaping, syncopated theme, the motto theme of the whole symphony, in a characteristic Czech rhythm and yet so evocative of folk idioms of the "New World" that it seems forever stamped with the words once associated with it—"Old Man Moses, he sells his roses." The kettledrum player, who will be having a field day throughout the symphony, gives the theme a thundering introduction and accompaniment as it takes over the orchestra. Then a quiet transitional tune, stated by flute and oboe (it will remind an American moviegoer of the soundtrack music for a dozen films set in the old South), leads to a most memorable second theme voiced first by the flute—something of an inversion of "Old Man Moses" and strongly reminiscent as well of the spiritual "Swing Low, Sweet Chariot." The development of these themes is clear-cut and powerful, and the recapitulation brings a thrilling moment when "Swing Low" changes key and flares up in the brass, for all the world like a Civil War cavalry charge in some Hollywood epic.

Seven solemn brass chords introduce the second movement, the famous "Largo," whose main theme is a melody for English horn so very like a spiritual that it has been fitted with words (by Dvoák's pupil, William Arms Fisher) and sung as one—"Goin' Home." It is complemented by a yearning second theme voiced by flute and oboe—instruments the composer seems to have thought most suited to his "New World" inspirations. A spiky woodwind call leads to an orchestral climax in which "Old Man Moses" and "Goin' Home" are stated in combination. Then the plaintive "Goin' Home" returns in its original guise—save that it halts twice, briefly, for profoundly eloquent moments of silence. Strong men may weep by the movement's end.

In the third movement Dvoák seems to turn his attention from the old South to the far West. The dance tune we expect from any scherzo might here be an American Indian tribal dance. (Dvoák thought for a while of writing an opera on Longfellow's *Hiawatha*.) There are two trios—one that can suggest Conestoga wagons crossing the prairies and, after a momentary intervention by "Old Man Moses," a jaunty second trio that seems, for once, to be purely Bohemian in idiom—though it put one *Fantasia*-influenced student of mine in mind of "buffalos prancing on hillsides." (And why should it not? This is, after all, a scherzo written by a composer celebrated for writing "humoresques.")

A fiercely determined eleven-note theme dominates the last movement like an implacable Indian chief—its last five notes anticipating Puccini's musical description of California in *La Fanciulla del West*. Then a clarinet voices a lyrical second subject. In the development section (where Dvoák seems to have playfully used "Three Blind Mice" for transitional purposes), and again in the recapitulation, themes from all of the previous moments recur. Some critics have, accordingly, called the ending "patchwork." But the audience at the first performance, in New York under the direction of the Wagner conductor Anton Seidl, did not think so. They gave the symphony a thunderous reception, as have audiences around the world for more than a hundred years since.

Recording
Masur, New York Philharmonic (Teldec)

You may also want to hear...
...the Slavonic Dances. I would not hesitate to say that, for sheer enjoyment, there is no more infectious, rhythmically inventive, easy-to-listen-to music than the eight dances that comprise the first set of Dvoák's Slavonic—or, more spe-

cifically, Bohemian—Dances. All of them are crafted from the composer's own fertile musical imagination; no actual folk music is used. (My own favorite is No. 8 in G Minor—or, then again, whichever one I last heard.) Another set of eight, written several years later, invokes the styles not only of Bohemia but of Poland, Serbia, and Ukraine as well; it is a more sophisticated collection than the first, and only slightly less infectious. The Slavonic Dances, in both the original four-hand piano versions and in the composer's beautiful orchestrations, first made Dvoák's name famous throughout Europe and America. And for exhilarating light music, the Hungarian Dances of Brahms and even the waltzes of Johann Strauss, Jr., must bow deferentially to the eight pieces in Dvoák's first set of Slavonic Dances.

. . . the Symphony No. 8 in G Major, a cherishable, almost childlike work, from its quiet opening through the deeply felt slow movement to the lilting scherzo and the heart-lifting trumpet fanfare that ushers in its exhilarating last movement. And not to be neglected are the seven earlier symphonies, especially the sixth and seventh, with their welcome traces of Brahms. (It may still need to be said that, ever since the discovery of four early symphonies in the mid-twentieth century, the old numbering has been changed, so that, for example, the G Major, once called the fourth, is now No. 8, and the "New World," once popularized as the fifth, is now No. 9.)

. . . among the other orchestral pieces, the expressive Cello Concerto in B Minor; the delectable Scherzo Capriccioso; the four symphonic poems—"The Water Goblin," "The Noon-Day Witch," "The Golden Spinning Wheel," and "The Wood Dove"—that tell frightening stories from Czech fairy tales; and the ten short, unprogrammatic "Legends" for orchestra, much admired by Brahms.

. . . among the chamber works, the popular "Dumky" Trio, a succession of six reveries that turn unexpectedly joyous; the

Piano Trio in F Minor, written in tears; the Piano Quintet in A Major, filled to overflowing with memorable themes; the Quartet in F, the first of the two chamber pieces composed in the United States, which draws partly on the indigenous styles, if not on the actual melodies, of the New World; and the Serenade in E Major for Strings, an early work in five movements, the fourth of which seems to have haunted Nino Rota when he penned his poignant "Gelsomina" theme for Fellini's film *La Strada*.

Late Romantics

César Franck
1822–1890

Franck was a Belgian of German parentage who took out French citizenship to qualify for the position of professor of organ at the Paris Conservatory, where he taught the four Ds of nineteenth-century French music—Debussy, Dukas, Duparc, and d'Indy. As a composer he was treated for most of his life with indifference or worse (Gounod called his only symphony "the affirmation of impotence pushed to dogmatic lengths.") But he wrote, in the last decade of his life, what some consider the finest of all violin sonatas and a half-dozen other pieces of stature. Much of his work is cyclic, unified from movement to movement by related and recurrent themes, composed along lines proposed by Liszt and Wagner. Neither of those predecessors wrote much in sonata form. Franck did, however, and in the best of his work he reconciled classical structures with the newer cyclic theories.

Sonata for Violin and Piano in A Major (1886)

This is a subtle work that seems to grow more impressive with each passing year. Its first-movement theme for the violin has often been identified as the "little phrase" from the (fictional) violin sonata by Vinteuil that is so important in *Swann's Way*, the first part of Marcel Proust's *In Search of Lost Time*. It is a gently curving theme, instantly appealing and rather startlingly sensuous for a composer as withdrawn and devout as Franck. (In Proust it is associated with Swann's love for the sensuous Odette.) The second theme, from the piano, is romantically Brahmsian. There is little by way of sonata-form development, and a modest recapitulation. But Franck will soon be going after bigger game.

The second movement, as stormy as the first was placid, uses the Proustian "little phrase" to link its two subjects. It is our first indication of the true nature of this sonata: themes will recur from movement to movement, and themes we think new in one movement will have been subtly anticipated earlier. This second movement actually pre-echoes a theme from the third—but the two instruments stir up such a storm that such subtleties only become apparent after repeated hearings.

The third movement, marked "Recitativo-Fantasia," begins as an extended dialogue between the two instruments (discussing, among other things, the "little phrase"), and finally develops into a fantasia out of which comes a passionate, wide-intervalled theme that instantly etches itself on the memory. After an echo of the Proustian "little phrase," this new theme returns, almost savage in its intensity. Seldom has Franck given expression to passion so ardent.

The finale is a rondo whose genial main melody is always played canonically (that is, in overlapping repetitions of itself) by the two instruments. The inner episodes of the rondo are built on the placid "little phrase" of the first movement and the passionate, wide-intervalled theme of the third. The main melody ends the sonata joyously.

Proust, perhaps wearied by those who identified his "little phrase" with the opening theme of this work, insisted in a letter to a friend that the source of his inspiration had not been the Franck violin sonata at all but a sonata by Saint-Saëns (presumably the Violin Sonata in D Minor); that the tremolos in his "little phrase" were from "a prelude of Wagner" (presumably the prelude to *Parsifal*); that its spatial qualities were derived from "the Ballade of Fauré" (presumably the one in F-Sharp Major); and that the languorous heights and depths in his "little phrase"—well, yes, those *were* from the Franck sonata. But these possibly tongue-in-cheek remarks from Proust have not stopped the Franckophiles from claiming the "little phrase" for their beloved César.

Recording
Perlman, Ashkenazy (London/Decca)

You may also want to hear...

...the Symphony in D Minor. The work that so enraged Gounod is a cyclic symphony in only three movements (and so hardly calculated to win over the traditionalists), filled with contrasting moods and changing colors. It is as if the pious Franck were seated at the organ of his beloved St. Clothilde in Paris, pulling out the "open diapason" and "lieblich gedeckt" and "great pausaune" stops and busily introducing ominous bass strains on the pedals as sunlight streams through a stained-glass window. The opening theme is (perhaps deliberately) reminiscent of the Ur-theme in Liszt's *Les Préludes* and the "Fate" motif in Wagner's *Ring*. I must confess that I find some of the other themes banal. In any case, this once very popular symphony is less often heard today. Tastes change.

...among other works, the moody Symphonic Variations for Piano and Orchestra, in effect a one-movement piano concerto, cyclic in nature. The Prelude, Chorale, and Fugue for piano is the most impressive of Franck's instrumental religious works. The *Pièce Héroïque* and the Third Chorale in A Minor are the best examples of his monumental writing for organ. The Quintet in F Minor for Piano and Strings is, even more than the sonata discussed above, a startlingly passionate composition; Liszt, Saint-Saens, and Mme Franck all found it shocking. Finally, the "chaste paganism" of the orchestral portions of *Psyché*, a symphonic poem for chorus and orchestra, may encourage you to investigate the other, lesser tone poems *Les Éolides*, *Le Chasseur Maudit*, and *Les Djinns*.

Edvard Grieg
1843–1907

Norway's leading composer captured something of his nation's spirit in the distinctive contours of his melodies, and Norwegians will be the first to tell you as much. Like his favorite composer, Chopin, Grieg was essentially a miniaturist. His one attempt at opera came, almost predictably, to naught, but he excelled at writing songs, lyric pieces for piano, and incidental music to plays. His only real success with large-scale writing came when he was only twenty-five, newly married, under the influence of Schumann, and able to benefit from the pianistic advice of the always helpful Franz Liszt. That great success was:

Piano Concerto in A Minor, Op. 16 (1868)

Though this familiar work conjures up for most people vast vistas of the wintry fjords of Norway and is popularly thought to be fashioned out of folk materials, it was actually written in Denmark in the summer and contains of Norwegian folk tunes nary a one. It begins, as every concertgoer will know, with a kettledrum roll, an orchestral crash, and a downward pianistic flourish in the "cold" key of A Minor. Thereafter a first subject, introduced by woodwinds and almost immediately taken up by the piano, is tense and rhythmic; and a second theme, introduced by the cello and, again, almost immediately taken up by the piano, is dreamy and fashioned much like the lyrical short pieces for which Grieg is most admired. There is minimal development, and the recapitulation is predictable. The real effects are saved for the cadenza, which is extended and, with a good pianist at the keys, brilliantly effective.

The second movement is an adagio built from a very tender theme on the strings that is embroidered, and then given an almost heroic cast, by the piano. As this idyllic reverie ebbs away, the last movement all but bursts in without pause; it is a rondo whose main theme is based on the rhythm of a Norwegian dance called the halling. The contrasting section is a rather insipid tune first introduced by a solo flute. Some commentators have insisted that the tune is actually a Bavarian folk song, which seems most unlikely; certainly it is an inadequate theme on which to structure the concerto's noisy finale.

In none of the three movements is there much evidence of the compositional skill demanded by conservatories and critics, but this has made little difference to pianists grateful for the concerto's opportunities for display, or to the concertgoing public that has, for a century, responded to its picturesqueness and abundance of melody.

Recording

Zimerman, Karajan, Berlin Philharmonic (DG)

You may also want to hear . . .

. . . the incidental pieces, somewhat faded now from too frequent performance, written for Ibsen's picaresque drama *Peer Gynt*; the Holberg Suite for string orchestra, a charming blend of Nordic idiom and eighteenth-century form; and, among the many piano pieces, the familiar "Nocturne," "To Spring," and "Wedding Day at Trollhaugen," the four Norwegian Dances, and the once popular fourteen-variation Ballade in G Minor. Not for nothing did Wagner's conductor Hans von Bülow call Grieg "the Chopin of the North."

Max Bruch
1838–1920

Bruch, the composer of three symphonies, three operas, and much choral music that was famous in its day, is now remembered almost exclusively for his writing for the violin, which offers a skilled soloist ample scope for expressiveness and virtuoso display.

Violin Concerto No. 1 in G Minor, Op. 26 (1866)

I have a special affection for this concerto because it begins with a brief theme in the orchestra very much like a recurrent strain in Joseph Kosma's score for what I consider the finest of all films, Jean Renoir's *Grand Illusion*. The film is a valedictory for the long and honorable European tradition of chivalry, and Bruch's popular work is one of the last in a line of Romantic violin concertos—from Beethoven to Mendelssohn to Brahms and Tchaikovsky—that find their roots in much the same tradition. (With the Sibelius violin concerto we have already moved beyond that tradition.)

The "valedictory" theme in the orchestra promptly introduces the soloist, who enters with a flourish that calls the previous Romantic violin concertos to mind. The soloist and orchestra then enter into a kind of dialogue, a minute-long prelude leading directly to . . .

. . . the first movement, which starts off as if in sonata form, with an upwardly leaping first theme and a sweetly descending second subject. But what follows is more a rhapsody than a development section, and, instead of a recapitulation, the orchestra leads the soloist back to the music of the introductory "valedict-dory" theme and dialogue, and then we proceed without pause into . . .

. . . the second movement—a rich, warm, lyrical adagio. One of the themes seems prescient of Mahler to come—especially the adagietto of his fifth symphony. The lyricism lifts briefly to a dramatic climax before the Mahleresque theme returns to end the movement. And this leads without a pause to . . .

. . . a fiery Hungarian "gypsy" rondo that is not quite a rondo, with a vigorous main theme that will be instantly familiar to anyone who has ever listened to much orchestral music. Here one is put in mind of the last movement of Brahms's violin concerto, which was to follow twelve years later. Both the Brahms and the Bruch are dedicated to the virtuoso Josef Joachim, who advised the two composers on matters of technique.

Recording

Heifetz, Sargent, New Symphony Orchestra of London (RCA)

You may also want to hear . . .

. . . the Scottish Fantasy for violin and orchestra, which borrows liberally from Scottish melodies, and the touching Variations on Kol Nidrei for cello and orchestra, which is indebted to Jewish musical traditions—and responsible for the mistaken notion that Bruch himself was Jewish.

Anton Bruckner
1824–1896

Bruckner, a naïve but determined Austrian who composed only religious choral music until he mastered the symphonic form—and then wrote nothing but symphonies—has only come into his own in the last few decades. His works, it was said, were too long, too formless, too brassy. But he got his ideas of length and form from Beethoven and his ideas of orchestration from Wagner. No disciple ever worshipped his masters more, and no master ever had so difficult a time simply getting his own works performed. The initial opposition came from Eduard Hanslick, the Viennese critic Wagner caricatured in Die Meistersinger *as Beckmesser. Today there are still doubters—some of them real Beckmessers—but the symphonies, now that they have become better known, have found a large, vocal following.*

Symphony No. 4 in E-Flat Major ("Romantic") (1874)

Bruckner constantly revised his symphonies, sometimes in attempts to measure up to his own unattainable standards of perfection, sometimes at the insistence of friends who thought that, if simplified, the huge works would meet with more success in the concert hall—or, in the case of some of the symphonies, actually get a hearing there at all. The composer gave this fourth symphony two major revisions and several minor ones. The first two movements were reworked, the finale rewritten, and the original third movement replaced by a wholly new "Hunting Scherzo." Today the symphony exists in two performing editions. The following summary follows that of 1880, the version that Hans Richter conducted at the first public performance of the work, in Vienna.

The opening horn call is quintessential Bruckner—lushly Romantic in sound and instantly evoking a world of forests, valleys, and mountains. As is almost inevitably the case with the composer's main themes, the horn call is soon taken up by other instruments and then emphatically stated by the entire orchestra. A heavy, six-note descending theme leads, in this sonata-form movement, to an ingratiatingly feminine second subject. After a development in which the themes conjure up Alpine visions (this, along with the Saint-Saëns "Organ" symphony, is ideal music for train-travel headset listening), the recapitulation is worked out predictably, and the movement ends with several orchestral restatements of the horn call. It is small wonder that Bruckner's friends urged him to name this symphony the "Romantic."

Two details should be noted before we leave this movement: the descending fifth of the opening horn call also appears in the main theme of the second movement, in the hunting call of the third, and throughout much of the fourth. And the six-note descending theme is cast in a rhythm—two quarter notes, a triplet, and a final half note—that will permeate the third-movement "Hunting Scherzo." So, while the symphony may be structured in a very large-scale sonata form, much of its working out is cyclic.

The second movement is a slow march with muted fanfares. Perhaps it depicts a religious procession: its second section, a devout solo for the violas accompanied by plucked violins and cellos, reaches a climax in a sonorous chorale for the brasses. The last thing we hear are hushed footfalls sounded by the kettle-drums.

The third movement, a "Hunting Scherzo" with an Austrian Ländler for its middle section, is as enjoyable as anything Bruckner ever penned. Bruckner, too ready to listen to the suggestions of friends, provided some programmatic titles for it that have proved an embarrassment. No titles are necessary. Simply enjoy the music while your train speeds onward past Austria's forests and rivers into the mountains.

The last movement, in sonata form, begins with an inversion of the first-movement horn call and builds, in long but never overextended segments, to several impressive climaxes, quoting—or doing variations on—themes from the previous movements *en route*. The movement's principal theme is a descending passage to match that in the first movement, thundered out by the brasses in unison. As with every Bruckner symphony from the third onward, the "Romantic" ends with a restatement of the main theme of the first movement: everyone who knows this symphony identifies it from that opening horn call. And many regard it as the most melodious and least pompous of all the composer's orchestral works.

Recording

Jochum, Berlin Philharmonic (DG)

You may also want to hear...

...some of the other symphonies, including, out of curiosity if for no other reason, the discarded one, which Bruckner called—whether with naïveté or cunning it is difficult to say— his Symphony No 0. But not the first or the second, which are tentative, and not the turgid third, which Bruckner, hoping hard for support, called the "Wagner": in its early, longer versions it quoted several times from "the Master," but only a single motif from the *Ring* (the theme Deryck Cooke called "The Magic Sleep") survived revisions. Longer still is the fifth, the longest symphony Mahler didn't write, and probably one that should be saved till one is thoroughly into—that is to say, convinced by—Bruckner's idiom. That leaves the Symphony No. 6 in A Major, a work that requires a virtuoso conductor and has, for the Wagnerian, a suggestion of the Rhinemaidens' music in its rippling scherzo; the beautiful and relatively understated Symphony No. 7 in E Major, with a slow movement written in memory of the recently deceased Wagner; the massive Symphony No. 8 in C Minor, the most successful of the series in the composer's lifetime, with an adagio that virtually quotes the *Ring*'s "Siegfried" motif; and the unfinished three-movement Symphony No. 9 in D Minor—the same key in which Beethoven began his ninth.

The dying Bruckner suggested that his earlier, choral "Te Deum" might be performed as a fourth movement to this ninth symphony to match the "Ode To Joy" that concluded Beethoven's ninth. This is seldom done today. Bruckner's ninth is now allowed to end with its surpassingly beautiful third movement—and the humble composer has, in the last half-century, taken his place with Beethoven, Schubert, Dvoák, and Mahler as a nine-symphony composer of the first rank.

Gustav Mahler
1860–1911

Who was the greatest composer of the twentieth century? Surely, whoever he was, his last name began with the letter S. At different points in the troubled twentieth, critics (and possibly even the public) might have agreed that the most important figure was Sibelius, or Schoenberg, or Stravinsky, or Shostakovich, or Strauss. But by the century's end, to the surprise of many, the answer to the question seemed almost overwhelmingly to be the once neglected Gustav Mahler, whose creative genius climaxed at the century's beginning. "My time will come," he once said ruefully. It did.

Unlike the other five, he wrote no operas. But like any conductor in the Central European tradition, he received his early training in the opera house. In Hamburg he once conducted nineteen different operas in a single month. He labored for four years at the Metropolitan Opera in New York, where he conducted Don Giovanni, Fidelio, Die Walküre, Tristan, The Queen of Spades, *and* The Bartered Bride. *He also edited and completed Weber's unfinished opera* Die Drei Pintos. *And all the while he worked unheralded on his mighty symphonies. It is because of those nine masterpieces that we now see him dominating the twentieth century as Beethoven did the nineteenth—like a colossus.*

Four of Mahler's symphonies contain prominent vocal parts, so singling out one of them for discussion here is not as difficult as it might have been. Only five of the symphonies—the first, the fifth, the sixth, the seventh, and the ninth—are strictly instrumental works. (The so-called tenth is instrumental but fragmentary.) Those ready to plunge into the exclusively instrumental Mahler might start, then, with . . .

Symphony No. 5 in C-Sharp Minor (1902)

"A symphony," Mahler once said to Sibelius, "must be like the world. It must embrace everything." This symphony without song moves from terror and grief to joy and sorrow to a finale that really does seem to reach out and embrace the world.

A ringing, unaccompanied trumpet begins the first movement, issuing a call to the orchestra, which takes up the rhythm of the trumpet call and turns it to a funeral march (the movement is, in fact, called "Trauermarsch") that seems written for the death of a soldier. The measured processional is interrupted—even assaulted—at unexpected moments by fierce orchestral storms. A second section features muted strings in anguished battle against solo brass instruments.

At the start of the second movement, the storms of the first break upon us again, and some of the motifs of the first recur. Then we hear another march. There are no military overtones this time; the funereal melody is treated with alternating poignancy and savagery, and a hopeful chorale sounded in the brass seems at the end to go down in defeat. (These first two movements, so similar in mood, are thought by most commentators to form a single whole; perhaps they give pessimistic view, in 1902, of the havoc dealt to Europe, to both military and civilian populations, in the wars of the century just past.)

Mahler then sends his massive orchestra through a series of dances in a brilliantly orchestrated scherzo that is almost as long as the two desperate marches together. The listener will be reminded, here of *Der Freischütz*, there of *Der Rosenkavalier*, here of a Brahms scherzo, there of Ravel's *La Valse*—some of it throbbing with Mahlerian joy, some of it succumbing to Mahlerian Weltschmerz.

The fourth movement, liked with the fifth in the overall structure of the symphony, is Mahler's most famous single piece—the poignant adagietto for strings and harp so memorably conducted by Leonard Bernstein at the funeral service of John F. Kennedy and so persistently throbbing on the soundtrack of Luchino Visconti's film *Death in Venice*, where Thomas Mann's tormented Aschenbach was all but made into a figure not only of Mann, as was expected, but of Mahler as well. The adagietto is so straightforward and heartfelt a statement that it all but compels listeners to rethink their reactions to other, more oblique and opaque moments earlier in this symphony.

With no break, a single prolonged note on the horn introduces the final movement, a rondo with jubilant themes for almost every section of the orchestra. It is an unexpectedly joyful, eminently fugal conclusion to a symphony in which the contrasts are extreme and each of the five movements is—unthinkable in a classical symphony—set in a different key. Yet the jubilant orchestral chorale that is the crown of this movement had already been adumbrated in the despair of the second. And at some point in this mighty work one can find the "everything" that Mahler told Sibelius a symphony should embrace. For Mahler that meant compassion for human suffering, pessimism about the human condition, a pantheistic love of nature, and an almost mystical sense of the wonder of the world.

Recording

Bernstein, Vienna Philharmonic (DG)

You may also want to hear...

...among the strictly instrumental works, the first symphony, which is accessible and relatively short despite its title, the "Titan"; the sixth, aptly named the "Tragic" and a favorite of those serious twelve-tone serialists Schoenberg and Webern; the seventh, titled "Song of the Night," which mixes Weltschmerz and Gemütlichkeit in about equal proportions; and the ninth, a grim valedictory from an embittered composer who had still not found his following.

It was not until the LP era, when listeners were able to hear all of Mahler's symphonies in succession—in complete cycles by Leonard Bernstein, Georg Solti, Rafael Kubelik, Claudio Abbado, Klaus Tennstedt, Bernard Haitink, and others—that the composer emerged from relative obscurity into wide international acceptance. In the troubled 1960s, especially amid the confusion and despair following on the assassination of President Kennedy, Mahler touched a nerve. His time had finally come, a full half-century after he had succumbed to the death he had anticipated for so long in his music.

More Parisians

Camille Saint-Saëns
1835–1921

Composer, conductor, critic, caricaturist, poet, playwright, pianist, organist, essayist, amateur scientist—Saint-Saëns busied himself with music and many other things through a very long life. Innovative in many ways, and formidably talented (so much so that his works have often been called facile), he lived to see everything change in the twentieth century. He was outspoken in his antipathy to Debussy, had little good to say about Richard Strauss, and was reported to have walked out at the premiere of Stravinsky's Rite of Spring *(though Stravinsky himself claimed that Saint-Saëns had remained bravely in his seat to the very end). Most music lovers will be familiar with his opera* Samson et Dalila, *but there is much in his instrumental output to enjoy as well.*

Symphony No. 3 in C Minor, Op. 78 ("Organ") (1886)

This hugely (some will say shamelessly) enjoyable work for orchestra, organ, and two pianos was commissioned by the London Philharmonic Society and conducted at its premiere by the composer himself, along with his fourth piano concerto, over which he presided from the keyboard. He and his new symphony were enthusiastically received, not least by the Prince of Wales. Only a few Germanophiles withheld their praise. Saint-Saëns had made it practically a lifelong mission to counteract the pervasive influence of German music on French composition; he saw no real need for a Frenchman of his day to adhere either to the sonata form still dutifully practiced by Brahms or to the densely woven web of symphonic leitmotifs that Wagner had proclaimed "the music of the future." In this signature work he opts for the cyclic construction favored by César Franck, with the deployment of a motto theme that pervades the entire work, changing its form with each succeeding movement—a device as old as Berlioz and most fully developed in the tone poems of that sometime Parisian Liszt. In fact, Saint-Saëns dedicated this "Organ" symphony to the memory of Liszt—who had recently died and was, like himself, a composer, conductor, pianist, and organist.

Out of a slow, mysterious eleven-bar introduction emerges the motto theme, which will recur in different guises in all four movements. Here it is an agitated, propulsive figure on the strings, relentlessly forward-moving. (I have found this symphony, like the Bruckner fourth, ideal for headset listening on rapidly moving European trains.) Two other themes soon appear, themes that would not seem out of place in the orchestral work of César Franck—and beneath them both we can hear the propulsive motto theme, racing on its way. Just when we sense that this unusual movement may be shaping itself into a sonata form, the music slows to a moment of near stillness (though not to a complete stop), and the organ signals . . .

. . . the beginning of the second movement, quietly but sonorously supporting a broad, prayerful melody in the strings, in the mellow key of D-Flat Major. Then the organ takes up the theme, and for some listeners its ambiance gives an uncanny feeling of moving in some conveyance under water, as if through some Neptunian kingdom. Other listeners feel themselves, more conventionally, in a Gothic cathedral. As for me, my train is now making a less propulsive and incredibly awesome journey past snowy Alpine peaks. (It's that kind of symphony.) For several measures the strings turn themselves into a kind of organ, reprising the prayerful melody with Bachian figures. There is no question that the sound and feel of the movement is extraordinary. The composer himself called it "mystical." He also saw to it that his motto theme, reduced to gentle pizzicato outlines, eventually emerges to accompany the "mystical" prayer.

There is a break after this second movement but none thereafter, so that, in effect, this is a symphony in two, not four, movements. In the rapid scherzo that ensues, the motto theme, in its third guise, takes control again, in a minor (the composer's word was "diabolic") tonality, sending off piano arpeggios "swift as lightning." It is opposed briefly by an expressive trio, and then it sends my train hurtling on again till I came to a solemn transitional theme on the brasses—and the violins, taking up that new theme, reverently invite me, without a break in the music, to diesel ahead into . . .

. . . the last movement, introduced by a great, crashing chord on the organ. The motto theme returns in its last and most majestic guise, intoned by orchestra and organ, accompanied by sweeping arpeggios on the two pianos and adorned with fanfares. Soon the omnipresent theme is turned into to a Bach-like fugato; then it starts churning like the wheels of my Trans-Europe-Express; then it is radioed ahead like a signal; and finally—summoned by a repeated, arching phrase—it climbs higher and higher past cascading mountain waterfalls until it reaches its Alpine summit in a trumpet-blasting, kettle-drum-thumping climax. Liszt, if during the premiere he heard all of this from some heavenly vantage point, must have approved. He was not just the nineteenth century's organist and pianist *par excellence*, not just an apostle of cyclic construction, but also a flamboyant celebrity, not always subtle in his musical ways. And this, again, is that kind of symphony.

Recording

Barenboim, Chicago Symphony (DG)

You may also want to hear...

...the Piano Concertos No. 2 in G Minor and No. 4 in C Minor. Cynics may call these Saint-Saëns's rearrangements of all the music he liked best by other composers, but both concertos are, again, hugely enjoyable—and if I were Saint-Saëns I would have stolen the thumping themes in the second movement of the second and in the last movement of the fourth myself, if I hadn't already written them.

...among the works for string instruments, the familiar Introduction and Rondo Capriccioso for violin and orchestra, the Violin Concerto No. 3 in B Minor, and the Cello Concerto No. 1 in A Minor, all of them favored by virtuoso soloists.

...*The Carnival of the Animals*, a lightweight but literate satire for orchestra and two pianos. Saint-Saëns, ostensibly depicting in music a series of animate creatures, amiably spoofs Offenbach (turtles lumber lethargically through the can-can from his *Orpheus in the Underworld*), Berlioz (an elephant galumphs through the delicate "Dance of the Sylphs" from *The Damnation of Faust*), virtuoso pianists (characterized as wild asses on the loose), and piano students (fumbling up and down their beastly scales). And in a section wryly called "Fossils" we hear bits from Mozart, Rossini, and Saint-Saëns's own "Danse Macabre." There are straightforward pieces, too: "The Swan," which became a palm-court favorite, and "Aquarium," which was memorably used to underscore Terrence Malick's classic film *Days of Heaven*.

Claude Achille Debussy
1862–1918

The composer of Pelléas et Mélisande *had a few complimentary things to say about his fellow countrymen Gounod and Massenet, but he was not at all kind to his former teacher César Franck, and of Berlioz he said, "He has always been the favorite musician of those who do not know much about music." Predictably, he had even less love for the Germans. Beethoven "wrote very badly for the piano," Schubert's most famous symphony "couldn't decide once for all whether to remain unfinished," and, as the sonata form was "obsolete," Brahms couldn't help being "a bore." Above all, Debussy strove mightily to dismiss Wagner, but succumbed finally to* Parsifal—*to its stained-glass-window translucence, but not to the frenzied cries of its tormented characters.*

Debussy could not love the great ones of the past because he was, at the turn of the century, music's foremost harbinger of the new. With impeccable taste, he blended Western medieval modes with Eastern pentatonic and whole-tone scales, discovering hitherto unknown sonorities in the piano and devising a new palette of sounds for the orchestra, and thereby he matched in music the achievements of his day in the other arts—by Monet and Manet, Mallarmé and Verlaine. The operagoer who does not respond to Pelléas—*and his number is, sadly, legion—may profit by an exposure to the instrumental Debussy. We'll need to concentrate on two works of his, for he was equally innovative with the orchestra and the piano.*

La Mer (1905)

A masterpiece, beyond a doubt. Debussy's symphonic seascapes are worthy to stand alongside those in Homer, Virgil, Conrad, and Turner. Debussy called the three movements of *La Mer* "symphonic sketches," implying that any attempt to find formal or structural niceties in his impressions of the sea would be futile—and it is. *La Mer* is an ever-changing series of brilliantly evocative impressions. That leaves a commentator like the present one helplessly adrift. Shall he record his own, perhaps illusory, impressions?

> "From Dawn Till Noon on the Sea": Rays of light play on the surface. The sun clears away the mist. We realize that we are near to port, that this is the China Sea, that strange cargoes are coming in from Arabia. We venture farther out where the waves are stronger, and we come mysteriously to a sudden calm. The water changes colors. Finally we sight a great ship, sailing straight at us. It bears a Chinese dragon on its prow . . .

Or shall he single out instrumental features in the score and offer the kind of program note provided for concertgoers a century ago?

> "Play of the Waves": We hear exhilarating whole-tone- scale splashes from the harp and woodwind trills illustrating the sea's trembling surfaces. The flute whistles up a gale that exulting strings take up in full chorus. Finally we peer down, to a delicate cymbal crash, into the lucid watery stillness . . .

Or shall he combine the two approaches and say, in what words he can find, that the third movement, entitled "Dialogue of the Wind and the Sea," is not a dialogue at all but a kaleidoscope of changing effects?

> Amid rumbling bass viols and kettledrums, shrill cries from the trumpet, and warning calls from the French horn sounding across the swirling water, an insistent melody emerges to see us through a storm. Then, in the midst of a calm, a solo flute takes up the same melody, and the orchestra rides it, with impressive brass chords, to a triumphant, windswept conclusion.

Debussy, let it be said, would be furious were he ever to read those descriptions. But a critic of his day complained that in

La Mer he could neither hear nor see nor feel the sea, and while no twenty-first-century listener is likely to be so obtuse, prose descriptions can sometimes be helpful—though any listener's own impressions will likely be of more use to him or her in appreciating these three masterly seascapes than any further comment from this hapless landlubber.

Recording
Karajan, Berlin Philharmonic (DG)

Préludes, Book 1 (1910)

Debussy wrote for the piano with a deftness unequaled even by Beethoven, Liszt, and Chopin. The twelve pieces of Book 1 of his *Préludes* find him very much in character—the master of carefully nuanced moods, now witty, now profound, always luminous, always subtle. No music is more familiar to me, as I misspent my teens playing the *Préludes* over and over with one friend and listening to them over and over with another. It should be said that anyone who plays or listens to them is invited to wonder what the subject of each prélude might be. Only at the end of each piece does Debussy tell us what he has given us his impressions of.

1. *"Danseuses de Delphes"*: A stately piece inspired by three female Delphic dancers on a frieze in the Louvre.
2. *"Voiles"*: A shimmering depiction, in whole-tone patterns, of sails (not veils) moving in the wind. This is like a watercolor sketch for the seascapes in *Pelléas*.
3. *"Le vent dans la plaine"*: A windswept study in pianistic arpeggios inspired by Paul Verlaine's poem "The Wind on the Plain."
4. *"Les sons et les parfums tournent dans l'air de soir"*: A study in synaesthesia that takes for its title the third line of Baudelaire's famous sonnet "Harmonie du Soir": "Lo, the time is here

when every flower, swaying on its stem, / Sends out its perfume like a censer. / The sounds and scents swirl on the evening air."

5. *"Les collines d'Anacapri"*: An Italian tarantella transformed into a French impressionist picture of "the hills of Anacapri."

6. *"Des pas sur la neige"*: A remarkably evocative depiction of the slow progress of a lone figure making "footprints in the snow" on the way, perhaps, to his death.

7. *"Ce qu'a vu le vent d'ouest"*: A tumultuous piece that tests the pianistic skill of its performer to the utmost. Debussy, in a rare and almost surely tongue-in-cheek concession to a puzzled questioner, said that "what the West Wind saw" was the history of the world. This listener thinks rather of Shelley's "breath of Autumn's being / . . . from whose unseen presence the leaves dead / Are driven, like ghosts from an enchanter fleeing."

8. *"La fille aux cheveux de lin"*: A recreation in luminous sound of the poet Leconte de Lisle's Scottish "girl with the flaxen hair" singing at her work.

9. *"La sérénade interrompue"*: An engaging little drama in which a would-be serenader, an Andalusian with a guitar, clumsily strikes up several strains, only to have his "serenade interrupted" when his lady pines for a more Romantic lover.

10. *"La cathédrale engloutie"*: A depiction in sound of the city of Ys rising momentarily from the sea after its engulfment, with its cathedral organ still sounding, its bells, great and small, still ringing, its choir still singing amid the surging waves. (Edouard Lalo also treated the Breton legend of "the engulfed cathedral" in his opera *Le Roi d'Ys*.) This is the crown piece of the collection.

11. *"La danse de Puck"*: A trifle, perhaps inspired by the quip of Shakespeare's quicksilver imp, "What fools these mortals be!"

12. *"Minstrels":* A shambling cakewalk of the sort popularized by minstrel shows. Debussy liked to amuse himself with various jazz rhythms, and in another piano piece, the "Golliwog's Cakewalk" from his *Children's Corner* suite, he quoted the opening phrase from Wagner's *Tristan und Isolde* amidst the merriment. We wait for it here, but we seem to get a strain from Massenet's *Manon* instead.

Recording
Gieseking (EMI)

You may also want to hear...

... among the other piano works, the immediately accessible *Arabesques* and the familiar "Reverie"; the *Suite Bergamasque,* which contains the best known of all Debussy's piano pieces, "Claire de lune"; the enjoyable *Children's Corner* suite, with its "Golliwog's Cakewalk"; and the *Petite Suite,* written for two pianos but often played as an orchestral favorite, with the idyllic "En Bateau" and the uncharacteristically jolly "Ballet." Other piano pieces require more sensitive listening: *Estampes* (etchings), with its early impressions of Spain; the two series of *Images* (containing "Reflets dans l'eau" and "Poissons d'or"); and the second book of *Préludes,* especially "La Puerta del Vino," "Ondine," and "Feux d'artifice."

...among the orchestral works, the famous *Prélude à l'Après-Midi d'un Faune,* inspired by Stéphane Mallarmé's poem and shockingly in advance of its time in 1892; the impressionistic *Nocturnes* ("Nuages," "Fêtes," and Sirènes"); and "Iberia," the second of the composer's *Images for Orchestra.* For further indulgence there is the young Debussy's only string quartet—a brief, cyclic, atmospheric work that is much more Parisian than Viennese.

Maurice Ravel
1875–1937

The composer of the one-act operas L'Enfant et les Sortilèges *and* L'Heure Espagnole *is often mentioned in connection with Debussy, but has an aesthetic all his own. His output is small but impeccably crafted, curiously detached, witty sometimes to the point of cynicism, and masterly in its orchestration. Ravel, ever aware of where his strengths lay, reworked much of his piano music for orchestral performance, and is almost as well-known as the orchestrator of Mussorgsky's* Pictures at an Exhibition *as he is for his own symphonic scores.*

Daphnis and Chloé Suite No. 2 (1911)

Daphnis and Chloé, one of the great scores of the twentieth century, was composed, as were Stravinsky's *Firebird, Petrouchka,* and *The Rite of Spring,* for Serge Diaghilev's Ballets Russes. It was subsequently adapted by the composer into two suites of what he modestly called "orchestral fragments." But neither suite is really fragmentary, and the second is a triumph of musical imagination. In performance totals it has now far surpassed the ballet for which it was written. (The choral parts that the composer thought indispensable for theater performance are generally omitted in concert performance.)

The ballet's scenario was adapted by Ravel and Mikhail Fokine from a pastoral romance—the closest thing to a novel in ancient Greece—by a virtually unknown fourth-century writer called, simply, Longus.

The first section, "Daybreak," begins with rippling figures in the woodwinds, and beneath them the suggestion of a theme that eventually, to the sounds of twittering birds and plaintive shepherds' pipes, becomes a soaring panoramic description of a classic Greek landscape—clearly the inspiration for (but charged with more eroticism than) the wide-vistaed themes favored in Hollywood westerns.

The beautiful Chloé has been carried off by pirates, but her lover, Daphnis, has prayed to the rustic god Pan, and now, in the second section, "Pantomime," she is restored to him, and together they mime, in gratitude, the myth of Pan and Syrinx: how the god—half-man, half-goat—wooed the woodland nymph; how she, a devotee of the chaste Artemis, rejected him and fled; how he pursued her; and how, at the moment he caught and kissed her, she was changed beneath his lips into the sylvan reeds that became his musical instrument, the Pan pipe. One of the most charming stories told by Ovid in his *Metamorphoses* here receives its classic treatment in music.

The third and final section is a "General Dance" in which the hitherto idyllic youths and maidens become veritable bacchants, dancing to a whirling vortex of sound that comes close to sending them, and the awed listener, into the very panic to which Pan gave the name.

It is impossible to describe in words what Ravel achieves in these three uninterrupted sections of his ballet—in the massed singing of the strings and the cascading of the woodwinds as the light spreads in "Daybreak"; in the luxuriant caress of the violins, the priapic piping and fluttering of the flute, the fountains of explosive sound sent aloft by harp glissandos in the "Pantomime"; in the skirling, circling figures, trailing fiery colors in their wake, in the "Dance"; in the headlong yelping of evoës there, and the exultantly pagan abandon of it all! And yet the fastidious composer keeps everything in complete control—which may be the hallmark not just of his own art but of classic Greek art itself.

Recording

Monteux, London Symphony Orchestra (London/Decca)

You may also want to hear...

. . . three other works conceived for the orchestra: the familiar *Bolero* (which Ravel regarded as of minimal importance); the exotic *Rhapsodie Espagnole*, a four-movement evocation of Spain; and *La Valse*, a glittering and utterly cynical depiction of a desperately waltzing Europe that, with World War I, had lost its moorings.

. . . two piano concertos—the so-called "jazz" Concerto in G Major, written in homage to George Gershwin, and the Concerto in D Major for the Left Hand, commissioned by the pianist Paul Wittgenstein, who had lost his right arm in World War I.

. . . five keyboard works subsequently orchestrated—the *Valses Nobles et Sentimentales*, some of which anticipate *La Valse*; *Le Tombeau de Couperin*, a sophisticated collection of dances in the style of eighteenth-century French music; the Sonatine, which deftly blends eighteenth- and twentieth-century styles; the heartfelt *Pavane pour une Infante Défunte*; and the charming *Mother Goose Suite* (Ma Mère L'Oie), a personal favorite of this author in its four-hand version, but also utterly magical in its orchestral garb.

. . . three works for solo piano—*Jeux d'eau*, a display piece of almost Lisztian difficulty; *Miroirs*, six impressionistic miniatures; and above all *Gaspard de la Nuit*, three macabre pieces inspired by the poems of Aloysius Bertrand.

. . . two chamber works—the early string quartet and the *Introduction and Allegro* for harp, flute, clarinet, and string quartet. In other words, virtually everything the man wrote is worth seeking out.

The Twentieth Century

Leoš Janáček
1854–1928

The composer of Jen fa, Katya Kabanová, The Cunning Little
Vixen, The Makropoulos Case, From the House of the Dead,
*and five other operas achieved the recognition he deserved only in
the last years of his life. His highly original style—it seems to owe
nothing either to his Slavic predecessors Smetana and Dvo ák or to
his international contemporaries Debussy and Strauss—is characterized by repeated, curiously elusive musical phrases derived from
Czech speech rhythms. His work has had to survive any number of
adaptations by both friend and foe (he had many of those), but by
the century's end he was firmly established as one of its half-dozen
greatest composers—a solitary, compassionate voice.*

String Quartet No. 1 ("The Kreutzer Sonata") (1923)

This astonishing quartet, composed in white heat in eight days, is
almost unique in the canon of chamber music: it is programmatic,
based on Tolstoy's controversial novella "The Kreutzer Sonata."
Janá ek had made two previous attempts at depicting the Tolstoy
story in music—an earlier string quartet and an unfinished piano

trio. Neither work has survived, but possibly some of their material made its way into the finished quartet.

It is perhaps best to think of this work not so much as detailing the action of Tolstoy's story as expressing the feelings of
revulsion and compassion of the composer as he remembers it
in music. (The operas, too, seem to express not the tormented
inner feelings of the characters onstage, but the pity lavished on
them from without by the dramatist/composer.) All the same,
it will help the listener deal with the pain and the pathos in the
music, and the abruptness of many of its passages, if he has an
outline of the story:

> The author is traveling by rail with an elderly tradesman, a
> clerk, a mannish woman, her lawyer friend, and a gray-haired
> man with flashing eyes—all of whom have pronounced opinions
> on the subject of marriage. Eventually the gray-haired traveler
> calmly confesses that he is the very man they have been alluding
> to—the notorious Pozdnyshev, who has recently murdered his
> wife. Only the author remains in the compartment to hear him
> tell, neurotically, with astonishing frankness, and with repeated
> denunciations of marriage as an institution, how he and his wife
> quarreled; how they used their children to hurt each other;
> how he became insanely jealous, especially when, at his own
> invitation, she accompanied a young violinist in Beethoven's
> "Kreutzer" sonata; how he drove her to a suicide attempt; and
> how, returning from a business trip, he found her and the vio-
> linist dining together in his home, and stabbed her to death. He
> was tried for the offense, denied custody of his children, but
> acquitted (we may presume, as he is too overwrought to finish
> his story) on a plea of justifiable homicide.

The story was thought shocking and immoral in the 1890s, not
least because Tolstoy refrains from comment while the husband
expounds his unacceptable views about the sexes. Janá ek, for

his part, tells the story in music filled with terror and with pity
for the wife.

Each of the four movements of the quartet is somewhat less
than five minutes in length. The first begins with a poignant six-
note rising-and-falling phrase that will be movement's—indeed
the quartet's—major theme. It is instantly followed by chattering
comments of the solo instruments—perhaps the conversation of
the characters in the railway carriage. Most of the brief movement is characterized by the compassion for human suffering
that an operagoer will already know from *Jen fa* and *Katya*, and
that—"compassion"—is what I shall call the main theme. The
movement, largely introductory, ends with just the first three
notes of the theme, suspended like a musical question mark.

The second movement, a scherzo that proceeds by fits and
starts, is more clearly programmatic: it may be thought to depict
the quarrels that disrupt the married life of Pozdnyshev and his
wife. We first hear his jauntily defiant seven-note theme. There
is an eerie passage where the strings, played *sul ponticello* (near
the bridge of the instrument), seem to depict his suspicions—and
thereafter Pozdnyshev's jaunty theme becomes increasingly
sinister. Equally important in the movement is the wife's pleading five-note theme, which memorably expresses, to use the
composer's words, "the suffering of a passive, enslaved woman,
beaten and tortured to death." Both themes are reiterated by
solo instruments underscored by tremolos and pulsing figures in
the other strings, till the composer mercifully ends this stressful
musical chapter with a quiet chord.

The third movement begins with an eight-note musical idea
that is almost, but never quite, the second theme in the first
movement of Beethoven's "Kreutzer" sonata—and so may be
thought to mark the appearance, in the musical narrative, of the
young violinist. The "Kreutzer" theme is opposed by a vehement,

almost irrational, outburst—first stated *sul ponticello*—that soon dominates the movement. Intermittently a new melody, lyrical and pleading, intrudes, but the movement ends as it began, with the now-thickened plot unresolved.

The final movement opens with a poignant adagio based on the quartet's opening "compassion" theme; the first violin has an extended solo marked "as in tears" in the score. An agitated development section is built up largely from the "compassion" theme, and the tension increases for several minutes. At one point the lower instruments seem to imitate the ostinato onward motion of the train speeding the narrator to the end of his story. Finally, we reach a climax, marked "ferociously," in which the "compassion" theme is subjected to terrifying violence. The moment of the murder is not, however, clearly suggested. Instead there is an abrupt ending derived from the "compassion" theme. We are left, not with the ambivalent feeling of Tolstoy's story, but with the humane and pitying emotions of the composer retelling the story in music.

Recording
Guaneri Quartet (Philips)

You may also want to hear . . .
. . . the String Quartet No. 2 ("Intimate Pages"). In this intense work, on the same level of achievement as the first quartet, Janá ek gives expression to the passionate but probably platonic love that he, a married man, felt late in life for Kamila Stosslová—a married woman thirty-eight years younger than himself and the inspiration for the heroines of *Katya Kabanová*, *The Cunning Little Vixen*, and *The Makropoulos Case*.

If the quartets are too daunting at first, you might start your exploration of Janá ek's instrumental works with some more accessible pieces: the six early Lachian Dances; *Taras Bulba*, a nationalistic tone poem in three movements; and the brassy, exuberant Sinfonietta, a "little symphony" in five movements. Any of these will help you approach not just the quartets but the operas as well with fresh ears.

Richard Strauss
1864–1949

The famous orchestral works of Richard Strauss, one of the foremost composers of the twentieth century, were actually written in the nineteenth century—along with his fledgling, failed, forgotten opera Guntram *and long before those twentieth-century operatic master-pieces* Salome, Elektra, *and* Der Rosenkavalier. *After the immense success of these works, Strauss turned almost exclusively to operatic composition for more than thirty years, even though both critics and public were slow to take to his subsequent operas, including those—* Ariadne auf Naxos, Die Frau ohne Schatten, *and* Arabella—*that have now found a large following. During World War II and its aftermath, Strauss, living with the taint, almost wholly undeserved, of having been pro-Nazi, seemed to have gone into an irreversible decline. (Stravinsky called him "a talent that was once a genius.") Then, in his penultimate year, he startled the world with the autumnal* Four Last Songs, *which initiated a wholesale reevaluation of his earlier work, including the operas. It was, all told, an extraordinary career, and its first successes were instrumental works.*

Don Juan, Op. 20 (1888)

This has been called the first *modern* tone poem. That is to say, it is a musical description, incident by incident, of a piece of

literature—the narrative poem *Don Juan* by Nikolaus Lenau—
rather than, as with earlier tone poems, a work inspired by
literature in which the structure is still determined by musical
demands. Lenau's Don Juan is not the amoral sexual predator we
know from Mozart and Molière; he is a heroic quester driven by
an ever-unsatisfied desire to find the ideal woman. He meets his
death not when he is confronted by a stone guest from hell, but
when, admitting defeat in his questing, he purposely lowers his
guard in a duel, even though he is on the point of overcoming his
opponent. And it is that heroic, soul-searching, ultimately disillusioned man we hear limned in Strauss's explosive music.

After a few orchestral flourishes, the young Don Juan is memorably characterized by a ten-note theme that leaps impetuously
upward and recurs whenever the hero sets out on a new amorous
conquest. The first of his ladies is voiced by a solo violin, the
second by solo oboe. In each amour a Romantic melody eventually emerges though an orchestral web of ever-changing colors.

Then, to a tremolo in the upper strings, four unison horns
sound the great theme of the piece—a musical depiction of the
mature man who has come to see his questing as more than just
youthful dalliance, as positively Faustian in its ambition. More
conquests ensue in rapid succession, but the musical comment
implies, with touches of irony, that they are increasingly less
satisfying. Finally, the big Faustian theme sends the hero on his
greatest exploit. It is not to be, this time, a sexual conquest.
It is to be a face-off with Fate. The orchestra builds to a great
climax—and suddenly we hear the thrust of the deliberately
summoned sword point, a moment of silence, the sword's extrac-
tion, and the blood dripping from its blade.

The audience at the first performance at Weimar went wild.
It was as if, in a quarter-hour of music, a twenty-five-year-old
composer had expanded the frontiers of orchestral music beyond

anything even Wagner had thought of. Four more remarkable tone poems followed. Straussians will extend that number to seven. See below.

Recording
Muti, Berlin Philharmonic (Philips)

You may also want to hear...

...*Tod und Verklärung* (Death and Transfiguration), a twenty-five-minute tone poem that reverses the pattern Strauss had begun the year before with *Don Juan*: it was not inspired by a work of literature, but rather it inspired one—*Death and Transfiguration*, a poem by Alexander Ritter that Strauss suggested and had printed in the score. The poem details the musings of a dying man searching through his life for some meaning and finding transcendence as he loses his battle with death. This was no doubt a presumptuous theme for a composer in his mid-twenties, but Strauss, inspired by a performance of Wagner's *Tristan*, brought it off with his virtuoso orchestral writing and substantial musical themes—including the famous rising melody he was to use again, instrumentally, in the last of his *Four Last Songs*.

...*Till Eulenspiegel's Merry Pranks*, the shortest of the tone poems, detailing the adventures of a legendary player of practical jokes. Till's main theme (oddly reminiscent of the opening phrase of the popular song standard "How High the Moon") recurs a hundred times in a hundred guises, and his execution as a public nuisance quotes, with delicious irony, the main theme of Wagner's "Siegfried Idyll." Some Straussians see the whole merry sketch as a self-portrait—for that, to a degree, is what the Strauss tone poem was fast becoming.

...*Also Sprach Zarathustra* (Thus Spake Zarathustra). This is not, of course, a detailed account of Nietzsche's famous book, even though Strauss affixed some of the philosopher's chapter titles to sections in the score. As he explained, "I meant to convey by means of music an idea of the development of the human race from its origin, through the various phases of evolution, religious as well as scientific, up to Nietzsche's idea of the Superman." Stanley Kubrick was not wrong, then, in using the work's first measures for the opening scene of his evolutionary *2001: A Space Odyssey*. Potheads who loved the film in the 1960s found, however, that the rest of Strauss's score was something of a letdown, and they were not alone.

. . . *Don Quixote*. Perhaps Strauss's most admired orchestral work, this set of variations for cello and orchestra is also an elaborately descriptive tone poem detailing twelve incidents in the life of the Knight of the Doleful Countenance. The cello speaks for the quixotic hero, the viola for the faithful but uncomprehending Sancho Panza.

The three other tone poems—*Ein Heldenleben* (a massive work whose hero is, to all appearances, Strauss himself), the *Symphonia Domestica* (an orchestral depiction of life in the Strauss household), and *An Alpine Symphony* (a work of glacial brilliance written when the composer was settled at Garmisch-Partenkirchen)—I find less interesting. They are Strauss overly concerned with descriptive and imitative sounds and operating on a scale that is, in the end, too vast for the rather second-rate musical ideas at work. But on a smaller scale the two horn concertos—one early, one late, and both surprisingly retro for Strauss at either time in his career—are enjoyable pieces. And *Metamorphosen*, an intense one-movement lament for strings written in 1945 after the bombings of Munich and Dresden, poignantly marks the twentieth century's pivotal year and may be thought the turning point in Strauss's late career, forecasting the resurgence and renewal of his once considerable powers.

Jean Sibelius
1865–1957

By the time Sibelius and Mahler, perhaps the two greatest symphon-ists of the twentieth century, met in Finland in 1907, the former had opted decisively for compactness of expression in his third symphony, and the latter had completed his decidedly un-compact eighth, the "Symphony of a Thousand." Together they discussed "the great ques-tions of music." Sibelius said that he thought the most important aspect of a symphony was "its severity of style and the profound logic that creates an inner connection between the motifs." To which Mahler replied, famously, "A symphony must be like the world. It must embrace everything."

When this incident is recalled by the Mahlerists, they usually neglect to say what Sibelius responded. It tells us as much about his formal artistic purposes as Mahler's exclamation does about his life-affirming ones: "If we understood the world, we would realize that there is a logic of harmony underlying its manifold apparent dissonances."

Sibelius, a patriot and national hero in a period when his coun-try was struggling to win its independence from imperial Russia, was nothing if not original. The "profound logic" he sensed in an apparently chaotic, fragmented world drove him to write symphonies that were pervaded by, propelled by, an inevitability that was like a force of nature. Each symphony strove in a different way to find some unifying factor that would make sense of the diversity it discov-ered. Continental Europe, where a different kind of music—atonal music—was stirring, was almost indifferent to Sibelius, while in England and America his brooding Nordic melodies and majestic orchestral conclusions were regarded as the real continuation of the Central European symphonic tradition. By the end of the century, things had leveled off, and Sibelius had been reconsidered and recorded by both Colin Davis in Britain and Herbert von Karajan on the Continent.

Symphony No. 2 in D Major, Op. 43 (1901)

Over quiet, insistently pulsating string chords, the oboes and clarinets, followed by the French horns, sing the folklike song that will serve as the first movement's main subject. There follows an anguished recitative for strings, and eventually, from an orchestral swirl, a second subject with an unusual turn appears in the woodwinds. These and other musical elements, in the unique Sibelius sound, seem to conjure up images of the lakes and forests of the composer's native land. And as we proceed through a sonata-form movement, the themes are reduced to fragments that take on an energetic life of their own. Some critics have likened this fragmentation—which is a mark of Sibelius's style—to the process in nature in which living organisms are dissolved into the seeds that were their original components.

A low drumroll and a long succession of pizzicato notes in the lower strings introduce the main theme of the second movement, a sad and somewhat Slavic melody for the bassoons. A dark and powerful drama ensues, punctuated by swelling brass chords and cries of pain from the violins, with a hymn-like theme sounded by divided strings as the second subject. One thematic phrase sounds startlingly like the glorification of Siegfried's horn call in the funeral march of *Götterdämmerung*. The last measures are gloomily heroic. Is it too much to say that all of this represents a Finland yearning to throw off the yoke of imperial Russia?

The whirring of wings (which we seem to hear often in Sibelius's symphonies) sweeps us quickly and quietly through the scherzo movement, which pauses twice for an extended, plaintive oboe melody, and finally swells without a break into . . .

. . . a triumphant finale, with a broad melody in the strings adorned with trumpet fanfares, and with a fervent second theme evolving in the woodwinds and set to a swirling string ostinato. These two themes are developed in a series of long, sweeping crescendos that lead to a finale of stupendous orchestral grandeur. More than one critic has felt that the whizzing wings of the third movement represent the awakening of Finnish nationalism and the exultant close of the last movement expresses the hope that Finland would soon achieve its goal of independence. That goal was reached in 1917.

Recording

Davis, London Symphony Orchestra (RCA)

You may also want to hear . . .

. . . the other symphonies, each quite different from the others, each more compact and precise than the one that precedes it. The first symphony, melodious and somewhat Tchaikovskian, reaches typical Sibelian structure and sound only in the last movement. The third has less thematic development and is reduced almost to the texture of chamber music. The fourth is introspective and ascetic, the strangest and perhaps the most critically admired of the works. The fifth, written during the First World War, is restless and pessimistic, but rises—again after much whirring of wings—to a stirring finale driven home by six affirmative chords. The sixth is curiously tranquil and unexpectedly mellow, almost a landscape painting. The seventh, a valedictory, compresses a dramatic first movement, a scherzo, and a triumphant finale into one terse, uninterrupted whole. In all seven symphonies one has the sense of formal design serving a powerful emotional purpose and leading inevitably to the only conclusion possible after the previous movements.

...the tone poem *Finlandia*, perhaps the most incendiary expression of nationalism in music; another tone poem, *The Swan of Tuonela*, which seems to give off Technicolor images; the violin concerto, impressive in its first two movements but almost risible in the third, which Sir Donald Tovey called "a polonaise for polar bears"; and, mainly for purposes of comparison with Debussy's gossamer opera, the heavier incidental music Sibelius wrote for Maeterlinck's play *Pelléas et Mélisande*. (Schoenberg and Fauré also wrote works on the subject.) The other orchestral pieces, not nearly as popular as they were in the composer's mid-twentieth-century heyday, I find less interesting.

Sergei Rachmaninoff
1873–1943

Conductor, composer, concert pianist—Rachmaninoff was all three, and to a degree that any musician who chose only one of the three careers might envy. He had great international success, yet he was profoundly melancholy, the last of the Romantics—and it is the Slavic pessimism, the unashamed emotional opulence in his compositions, that have, in the twentieth century, secured him lasting fame. Though his operas are rarely performed, Rachmaninoff succeeded notably in almost every other form of musical composition.

Piano Concerto No. 2 in C Minor, Op. 18 (1900)

This concerto, perhaps the most popular piece of classical music written in the twentieth century, may be said to owe its existence to a certain Dr. Nicolai Dahl, who through hypnotism relieved the young Rachmaninoff of the "composer's block"—not to say the three-year depression—that beset him after the failure of his first symphony. "Day after day," Rachmaninoff said, "I heard the same hypnotic formula repeated while I lay half-asleep in an arm-chair in Dahl's study: 'You will begin to write your concerto.... You will work with great facility.... The concerto will be of an excellent quality.'" Soon thereafter the composer produced this torrent of passionate melody. He dedicated it to Dr. Dahl.

The piano alone begins the first movement with nine solemn chords, like the tolling of a bell. Then, in an unforgettable moment, the orchestra enters with the broad, ever-expanding C-Minor melody that came to signify "concert music" to a half-century of listeners. This is not, like the famous opening of the first Tchaikovsky concerto, a mere introduction; it is the commanding main theme of the movement, sung by the strings while the piano provides a sweeping accompaniment. The second theme—a long lifting-and-gently-falling melody, if anything more familiar than the first theme—is introduced by the piano, though one of the best-known moments in Rachmaninoff comes when, after an impassioned development of both themes, the second theme is sung by a solo French horn. The movement ends with a whirling coda.

The spirit of Frédéric Chopin seems to hover over the second movement, a nocturne developed out of a single strangely elusive theme that emerges from a dreamy arpeggioed figure on the piano. At first, the woodwinds develop the subtle, shifting theme while the piano provides accompaniment. Then the roles are quietly reversed. The poetic mood turns from major to minor, increases in passion, is quickened for a few minutes by some pianistic flourishes—including a brief cadenza. But soon the nocturnal melody returns, sounded now on the strings to the same haunting piano arpeggios.

The marking "allegro scherzando" attached to the third movement doesn't promise much more by way of Romantic melody. But in fact once the first, driving, scherzoesque theme has had its say, the most expansive melody Rachmaninoff ever wrote appears, and it is this familiar melody—quietly lyrical at first but building to arcs of passion—that dominates the movement and has made the whole concerto famous around the world. It returns at the end, after an extended cadenza for the soloist, thundering from the orchestra while the piano sounds crashing, Tchaikovskian chords. Yes, we are reminded of Tchaikovsky. But Rachmaninoff puts his signature to the concerto, as he does in several other works, by thumping out four rhythmic syllables at the end—RACH-man-i-NOFF!

The concerto owes some of its immense popularity to the fact that three of its melodies have been turned into popular songs, and that it has provided a background score for more than a few movies. It is sturdy enough to have survived these mistreatments, and, in fact, one of the films, David Lean's classic *Brief Encounter*, uses passages from all three movements with great sensitivity.

Recording

Ashkenazy, Previn, London Symphony Orchestra (Universal Classics)

You may also want to hear…

. . . Piano Concerto No. 3 in D Minor. This is the enormously difficult piece that became unexpectedly popular when it was featured in *Shine*, the film biography of child prodigy David Helfgott. Those who love the second piano concerto may find this quasi-cyclical, muscular showpiece somewhat lacking in lyricism, but afficionados of pianistic technique have much to wallow in—right up to the signature RACH-man-i-NOFF.

. . . Symphony No. 2 in E Minor. Written during a sojourn in Dresden—where the composer was "delighted" with Strauss's new *Salome* and "laughed like a fool" at Lehár's "absolutely wonderful" *The Merry Widow*—this is, nonetheless, a very Slavic piece, with a solemn motto theme that comes to full flower in the sumptuously romantic third movement, and with a final movement that ends with another RACH-man-i-NOFF!

...Rhapsody on a Theme of Paganini. A great piano virtuoso of the twentieth century pays tribute to a great violin virtuoso of the nineteenth by pacing one of the latter's vigorous themes through twenty-four variations in what is, in effect, a one-movement piano concerto. All of it is enjoyable, but the eighteenth variation is the one that fans of the lyrical Rachmaninoff will take to their hearts; perhaps inevitably, it became a popular song and found its way into more than a few movies, most notably as rearranged by Miklos Rozsa for *The Story of Three Loves*.

...*The Isle of the Dead*, a churning, Stygian tone poem inspired by Arnold Böcklin's painting of the same name, and using the medieval hymn that had a special fascination for the often morosely pessimistic composer—the "Dies Irae" of the Requiem Mass. (The "Dies Irae" also appears in three of Rachmaninoff's Paganini variations, in the *Symphonic Dances*, and in other compositions.)

...the preludes for piano, especially the famous "C-Sharp Minor," with its tolling bells, which the composer wrote when he was nineteen and which became—eventually to his dismay—his most frequently requested concert encore.

Igor Stravinsky
1882–1971

Stravinsky still holds a place as one of the twentieth century's most important composers, though it is not any longer thought improper to suggest that he peaked early, that the three great ballet scores he wrote as a Russian nationalist in Paris are his best work, and that his later internationalist excursions into neo-Classic and serial composition are of lesser importance and lesser stature. The fact remains that, in whatever genre or style he worked, his was always an individual voice. His only full-scale opera, The Rake's Progress, *shocked and surprised a half-century ago and still surprises, though seldom shocks, today. His great shocker, perhaps the most controversial work of the entire twentieth century, was his score for Sergei Diaghilev's ballet . . .*

Le Sacre du Printemps (The Rite of Spring) (1912)

This evocation of pre-Christian rituals in Stravinsky's native land (*Pictures of Pagan Russia* is its subtitle) marked the beginning of "modernism" in music. The Romantic and post-Romantic eras may be said to have ended when, in the opening measures of *The Rite of Spring*, a bassoon straining at the top of its register gave voice to what seemed like some unspeakably primitive passion, and Saint-Saëns reportedly stormed out of the Théâtre des Champs-Elysées, grumbling, "What instrument is *that?*" Paris, the site of the greatest musical scandal of the nineteenth century—the tumultuous first performance of Wagner's *Tannhäuser* at the Opéra—was about to witness the greatest musical scandal of the twentieth. As catcalls and hisses filled the auditorium, as critics shouted "fraud" and ambassadors guffawed and society ladies spat, as a princess fled her box saying, "This is the first time anyone dared to make a fool of me," Debussy pleaded for silence, Ravel shouted, "Genius!" and Stravinsky himself held back his choreographer, Nijinsky, to keep him from leaping into the audience and starting a fistfight. The American critic Carl van Vechten recorded that a young man in his box, carried away by the primitive rhythms, actually began beating him on the head with his fists. Diaghilev was delighted. A scandal was just what he wanted.

So what happens in the course of this extraordinary music? The composition falls into two large uninterrupted sections, "The

Adoration of the Earth" and "The Sacrifice." The opening bassoon that so enraged Saint-Saëns calls plaintively for the return of spring to the earth, and before long it is joined by other woodwinds, pushing up like shoots and luxuriating in the growing light. (The bassoon's phrase, by the way, is actually a Lithuanian folk tune—the only such material used in the work.)

A prolonged trill from the woodwinds introduces "The Adoration of the Earth" with a movement titled "Harbingers of Spring—Dance of the Adolescents," a foot-stomping dance with jarring rhythms, brutally dissonant chords, shrill woodwind shrieks, and with a muted second theme first sounded by the French horn. Soon we find ourselves in the midst of a presto section, "Game of the Abduction," that depicts, with violent kettledrum beats, the ritual seizure of a young woman. A woodwind tremolo leads to "Spring Rounds," which begins quietly with a melody fashioned from only four tones that is eventually fitted with harmonies hitherto unknown to the Paris conservatories and then turned on the wheel of a dragging ostinato. (One can easily imagine the Paris crowd rising in fury at the sheer oppressiveness of it.)

It is a relief when "Spring Rounds" returns to the initial woodwind tremolo and quiet melody. Then the tempo picks up for "The Games of the Rival Tribes"—a depiction, in thumping kettledrum rhythms and explosions of sound from the rest of the orchestra, of primitive contests between two neolithic communities. Soon four unison horns sound "The Procession of the Celebrant," a *really* wild section in which a tribal wise man consecrates the earth for the coming sacrifice. (Stravinsky introduces here an ancient percussion instrument carved out of bamboo, which scrapes away frighteningly.) There is a terrible moment of silence as the dancers prostrate themselves in adoration. And finally the full orchestra bursts into an abandoned

"Dance to the Earth" that rises in a vortex of sound to fever pitch and a sudden stop.

The ballet's second part, "The Sacrifice," begins with a hushed, gently swaying section Stravinsky called "The Pagan Night" (a title not in the score itself) and proceeds to the aptly named "Mysterious Circles of Adolescent Girls," a near-silent passage in which the strings are divided into thirteen parts to truly eerie effect. Eventually a melancholy Slavic melody is passed from instrument to instrument as the young girls circle about and choose the one among them who will be the sacrificial victim offered to the earth. Savage kettledrums then introduce "The Glorification of the Chosen One," a ritual dance of barbaric splendor, and they pound away through the slower "Evocation of the Ancestors" and the sinister "Ritual of the Ancestors." The final section is a long "Ritual Dance of the Chosen One," more horrifying and at the same time more rhythmically and harmonically sophisticated than the "Dance of the Seven Veils" in Strauss's *Salome*. (This section, with its ever-changing meters and key signatures, must have been a challenge for the young conductor, Pierre Monteux, who was just at the start of his long career.) Finally, in a moment of sheer terror, the chosen victim falls dead.

Moviegoers will already be familiar with much of *The Rite of Spring* from its use in Walt Disney's *Fantasia*—where, with some rearrangement, it illustrated H. G. Wells's theory of "the survival of the fittest," underscoring the struggles of primeval creatures (ranging from protozoa to brontosauruses) with their environment and with one another. Stravinsky was, at least at first, enthusiastic about reaching out to the movie masses, but *Fantasia* audiences were more enthusiastic about other, jollier, Disney animals cavorting to the strains of "The Dance of the Hours" from Ponchielli's *La Gioconda*. Concert audiences, however, have continued to flock enthusiastically to Stravinsky's abandoned primeval rituals.

Recording

Muti, Philadelphia Orchestra (EMI)

You may also want to hear...

... *The Firebird*. Stravinsky's first worldwide success, this ballet, composed for Diaghelev's Ballets Russes and choreographed by Mikhail Fokine, tells in astonishing orchestral colors the fairy-tale story of a young czarevitch who captures a mythic firebird and, armed with one of its magic feathers, rescues thirteen maidens from the castle of the evil King Kastchei. Of the three suites that the composer arranged from the score, the second, which highlights the story from fiery start to jubilant finish, has been the most often performed. But today we can often expect to hear the entire ballet in concert.

... *Petrouchka*. This second of Stravinsky's three great ballet scores poses, in the context of a Petersburg carnival, the question "What is real and what is illusory?" One of the carnival puppets, the everyman Petrouchka (Poor Peter), is rejected onstage by his ballerina sweetheart and killed by her Moorish lover. A policeman assures the shocked crowd of coachmen and nursemaids that the victim was, after all, only a puppet. But when all have left, the puppet master sees the smashed puppet threatening him from the roof of the theater. The music, which sounded strange in 1911, is to twenty-first-century ears immediately accessible. The only word for the orchestration is "brilliant."

The later ballet scores—*Pulcinella* (based on melodies of Pergolesi), *Le Baiser de la Fée* (based on melodies of Tchaikovsky), *Apollo*, and *Orpheus*—all of them couched in neo-classic styles—are estimable but do not reach the level of the earlier ballets, the operas *Oedipus Rex* and *The Rake's Progress,* and the choral work *Symphony of Psalms.* Two idiosyncratic works from that pivotal year for Europe and America, 1945—the *Symphony in Three Movements*, a personal reaction to what the composer called "our arduous time of sharp and shifting events," and the *Ebony Concerto*, commissioned by jazz clarinetist Woody Herman for small combo—show, if nothing else, the composer's protean adaptability. The later ballet *Agon* contains Stravinsky's first attempt at serial technique. All of these are the monochromatic works of what we might call Stravinsky's "New Testament"; I do not foresee any of them ever superseding his colorful "Old Testament"—the three great ballet scores that, together, set the musical course of the twentieth century.

Sergei Prokofiev
1891–1953

*The tough-minded composer who survived the ideological storms of Soviet policy by moving first to America—which he didn't much like—and then to Paris, chose an inauspicious moment (1932) for his return to Russia, escaping the purges but having to answer to the Central Committee's disapproval of his modernizing tendencies. Actually, Prokofiev saw no need to comply either with "socialist realism" or with the atonal dissonances of his German and Austrian contemporaries. He chose to work on his own terms, in mostly tra-ditional forms, and produced a sizeable body of energetic, often sardonic, occasionally profound, almost always enjoyable work. His operas—*The Gambler, The Love for Three Oranges, The Fiery Angel, War and Peace, *and four others—*have had more than moderate success, but he is likely to be longest remembered for his instrumental works, most notably . . .*

Romeo and Juliet (1935)

Perhaps not as exalted in its love music as Berlioz's *Romeo and Juliet*, or as rapturous as Tchaikovsky's, or as melodious as Bellini's, or as sweetly sentimental as Gounod's, Prokoviev's ballet treatment of Shakespeare's play is nonetheless consistently imaginative and often very impressive indeed. Until recently it was more familiar in the form of two suites arranged by the composer. But now we can and should demand the whole score, the sweep of which can hardly be grasped in excerpts. The following description follows the plan of the complete recording by Valery Gergiev and his Kirov forces. (The numbers in the parentheses below indicate the places the more popular movements occupy in the two suites Prokofiev fashioned from the full ballet.)

Act I

Introduction: The orchestra gives musical expression to Shakespeare's line: "In fair Verona where we lay our scene."

Romeo: The ballet's young Montague seems here to be nothing more than an insouciant young blade footing it home after a night with the fair Rosalind.

The street wakens (suite 1, number 2): This charming bit of descriptive music is based on a piquant theme that will recur in several of the upcoming movements.

Morning dance: The "street wakens" theme quickens into a bustling scherzo.

The quarrel: There is mayhem in the wakened street as the servants of the Montagues and Capulets brawl. Peace is restored by the imperious Duke of Verona.

Interlude: At first, this before-the-curtain movement is alternately frightening and eerie, the anticipation of tragedy to come. Then it evolves into a prolonged brass fanfare depicting the pride of the Capulets.

At the Capulets: The "street wakens" theme goes indoors as preparations get under way at the Capulets for the ball at which Juliet will be introduced to Veronese society.

The young Juliet (2,2): The charming young girl, asked by her nurse to think of marriage to Count Paris, shows herself—in four successive themes—to be skittish, courtly, lissome, and wise beyond her years. An absobloomin'lutely loverly movement.

Arrival of the guests (1,4): The hosts are depicted in the pompous main subject while the guests, a varied crew, arrive in a series of contrasting episodes.

Masks (1,5): Romeo, Mercutio, and Benvolio crash the Capulet ball in capes and dominos. They are a somewhat Slavic threesome as depicted here. Romeo, rejected by his Rosalind, is melancholic.

Dance of the knights (2,1): A famous movement. The overweening, heavy-footed theme of the proud Capulets, wielding their arms, shimmers in the strings to the accompaniment of snarling brasses. Juliet is depicted in a gently contrasting middle section for solo flute (which is very much her instrument in the score). Her theme here is a variation on the almost inhuman "Capulet" theme—rendered human and vulnerable.

Juliet's variation: Juliet dances with Paris as the orchestra develops the flute melody from the preceding section.

Mercutio: Romeo's quicksilver friend tries to cheer him up with a bit of braggadocio and a description of Queen Mab, "the fairies' midwife."

Madrigal (1,3): Romeo follows Juliet with his eyes, and the lovers converse in the midst of the ball—Romeo in the violins, Juliet in the flute (which repeats phrases from her "variation" above). The encounter ends all too quickly, as . . .

. . . *Tybalt recognizes Romeo*: Tybalt is enraged when he finds a Montague in the crowd, and it takes all of Capulet's powers of persuasion to calm him down.

Gavotte: The Capulets and their guests dance to the third movement of Prokofiev's Classical Symphony (see below). While it comes as a nice surprise to hear the symphony's familiar gavotte in this context, it must be admitted that a twentieth-century imitation of a courtly eighteenth-century dance seems as out of place here as Romeo does to Tybalt at the ball.

Balcony scene (1,6): The most famous scene in the play begins here with an evocation of night on the strings and harp and continues, in the movement called "Romeo's variation and love dance," with themes from the "madrigal" movement—Romeo's on the strings and Juliet's on the flute. A separate love theme is appropriately impassioned, but most of the section is sotto voce: the lovers are whispering, as in Shakespeare.

Act II

Folk dance (1,1): The Veronese dance a tarantella in which the tune is tossed from instrument to instrument—among them a cornet and a saxophone.

Romeo and Mercutio: The two young gentlemen's themes from previous movements] express both the differences between them and the friendship that binds them together.

Dance of the five couples: A lively street in Verona grows livelier as a parade passes by.

Dance with mandolins: A street group dances a veritable "carousel waltz."

The nurse: Woodwinds delineate the slow-footed beldame; then her "at the Capulets" theme recurs.

The nurse and Romeo: The beldame takes a message from Juliet (as her "skittish" theme indicates) to Romeo. A secret marriage is imminent.

Romeo with Friar Laurence (2,3): As Romeo awaits the arrival of his Juliet, the friar who is to marry them is characterized by a simple melody of cloistered neatness.

Juliet with Friar Laurence: A pure flute responds to the quiet imprecations of a pious choir of cellos.

Public merrymaking: More dancing from the "five couples" we met above.

Further public festivities: More of the act's initial "folk dance," with Mercutio and Benvolio participating.

The meeting of Tybalt and Mercutio / The duel / The death of Mercutio / Romeo decides to avenge Mercutio / Finale (1,7): Furious swordplay, two tragic deaths, and, for Tybalt, a great, spiky Capulet funeral procession with lugubriously wailing brasses. (The concert version omits the third and fourth movements of this sequence.)

Act III

Introduction and Romeo and Juliet / Romeo bids Juliet farewell (2,5): After an ominous introduction, a gentle flute depicts Juliet, and a mellow horn-and-clarinet duo depicts Romeo, on their one night together. Then her flute and his viola sing another long, coiling, amorphous, rhapsodic melody. Dawn breaks. He leaves her and, banished, heads for Mantua. (This section is generally known at concert performances as "Romeo and Juliet before parting.")

The nurse: The nurse tiptoes in (to her Act I theme) and advises Juliet (to the "minuet" theme) to forget Romeo and marry Paris.

Juliet refuses to marry Paris: Juliet, her "skittish" theme now more determined, faces her father's Capulet wrath.

Juliet alone and Interlude: A full orchestral development of one of the themes from "Romeo bids Juliet farewell."

At Friar Laurence's cell and Interlude: After a quiet development of another theme from the "farewell," the friar suggests that Juliet take a potion feigning death till he can reunite her with Romeo. This is done to an ostinato figure with a frightening "potion" theme in the lower orchestra. Juliet's determination is expressed in a rapturous melody that confronts, once again, her father's Capulet wrath.

Juliet's room: A flute sings Juliet's Act I "variation" as, concealing her true purpose, she tells her parents she is ready to marry Paris. But the orchestra reminds her of the potential horror she will have to face when she awakes in the family crypt.

Juliet alone: Haunted by the ostinato and the "potion" themes, but strengthened by memories of Romeo's "farewell," Juliet drinks the potion and succumbs to its influence.

Aubade: As Paris comes in the morning with wedding gifts, the orchestra strums, and then trumpets forth, a lightsome "dawn song." An utterly magical moment.

Dance of the girls with lilies (2,6): Maidens in the Capulet palace prepare for Juliet's wedding.

At Juliet's bedside: The maidens come to wake the slumbering Juliet and find her, to all appearances, lifeless.

Epilogue

Juliet's funeral (2,7): We are in the Capulet crypt. The music of Juliet's funeral procession begins high in the strings, softly, as if at a distance. Woodwinds and brass join in as the cortege draws nearer, its arching theme shuddering with grief. Romeo appears, to one of his "balcony scene" themes, and hides in the crypt till the mourners depart. Muted strings rise to ethereal heights as Romeo contemplates the seemingly lifeless Juliet and suddenly, to a quiet throbbing in the orchestra, drinks poison.

Juliet's death: Juliet awakes, finds her Romeo lifeless, and joins him, ecstatically, in death. The warring families are reconciled over the dead bodies.

Recording

Gergiev, Kirov Theater Orchestra (Philips)

You may also want to hear . . .

. . . Symphony No. 1 in D Major (The "Classical" symphony). This is Prokofiev's most often performed work, slyly written in his own style but with the formal precision of Haydn and Mozart. The composer did not scruple to include its third-movement gavotte in his *Romeo and Juliet* score (see above). Of the later symphonies, all six of them of interest, your first choice might be the kaleidoscopic fifth, in B flat, with a brilliantly satirical second movement and a third movement that some have thought a meditation on the tragic losses on both sides during the Second World War: written in the summer of 1944, it seems to quote sympathetically from German composers Beethoven (the familiar triplets of the "Moonlight" sonata are omnipresent) and Wagner (there is a recurrent hint of Hans Sachs's "Wahn, Wahn" from *Die Meistersinger*).

. . . Piano Concerto No. 3 in C Major, one of the half-dozen most popular piano concertos of the twentieth century, with a second-movement theme and variations that is among Prokofiev's best inspirations and a third-movement allegro that boasts an instantly memorable, soaring theme. This being Prokofiev, we are not surprised to find that the soloist's part is percussive and extraordinarily difficult. So are those in the four other piano concertos, all of which are worth hearing. (The fourth, for the left hand alone, was written, like the similar concerto by Ravel, for the one-armed pianist Paul Wittgenstein, who ruefully returned it unplayed.) The two violin concertos, rather unendearing pieces, have nonetheless stayed in the repertory—the first the inventive but almost cynical work of a young man on the make, the second, written twenty years later, unashamedly melancholy and even sentimental until its skittish, off-kilter finale.

. . . *Visions fugitives*, twenty remarkable piano pieces in varying moods, each only two minutes or less in duration, often harmonically complex, and reflecting the lines of the poet Konstantin Balmont: "In every fugitive vision I see worlds / Full of the changing play of rainbow hues."

Other works, immediately accessible, are *Peter and the Wolf*, a very successful attempt to introduce children to the instruments of the orchestra; the *Scythian Suite*, the young Prokofiev's prickly, primitive response to Stravinsky's *Rite of Spring*; the ballet *Cinderella*; and three film scores—for Eisenstein's classics

Alexander Nevsky and *Ivan the Terrible*, and for *Lieutenant Kijé*, a cinematic satire that no one alive seems to have seen, though many will remember the music's use later in Alec Guinness's film *The Horse's Mouth*.

Dmitri Shostakovich
1906–1975

The composer who incurred Stalin's wrath with his opera Lady Macbeth of Mtsensk *also wrote, among much other music, fifteen symphonies and fifteen string quartets. Most of his life he spent quietly asserting the right of the artist to function independently of the state, though in some circles he is still thought, quite wrongly in this writer's opinion, to have been a Soviet toady. (*Testimony, *the "memoirs" that, in 1970, detailed his rueful resistance, may possibly have been, in part, a hoax perpetrated by Solomon Volkov, but that does not mean that Shostakovich caved in to Kremlin pressures.)*

The symphonies veer from the formally classic to the blatantly patriotic to the defiantly ironic, and in them Shostakovich became, more than any other composer, the historian of the worst war in human history. The quartets, profoundly introspective, constitute one of the most moving personal documents of the twentieth century. A music lover should treat himself to one of each if he is to begin to understand the complex personality of this beleaguered and important composer. Here are my choices:

Symphony No. 5 in D Minor, Op. 47 (1937)

Still the most popular and accessible of the fifteen symphonies, this *may* be a dutiful attempt, after the fierce criticism of *Lady Macbeth* and other "unsuitable" works, to conform to Soviet-approved conventions—or it may instead be a cynical serving-up of what Soviet conventions demanded. In either case, it became the composer's first big international success, and it sent him directly and almost exclusively into the composition of instrumental music.

The first movement, of epic length, begins with a bleak, steely theme (now one of the most familiar musical statements of modern times), slowly gains momentum, bustles with music that calls up movie images of the workers' uprising in Eisenstein's *Strike*, climaxes in a thoroughly blatant march, and ends with an ethereal canonic duet for solo flute and horn. The evolution, struggle, triumph, and apotheosis of Communism, perhaps?

The second movement scherzo is the Shostakovich of popular works like the ballet score *The Age of Gold*, whooping it up with what seems like cynical glee. Many commentators have taken the trio, with its "Viennese" solo violin, as a send-up of the peasant dances in Mahler's big symphonic works.

There is much sensitive writing for strings in the third-movement largo, a long, searching, and obviously sincere meditation—perhaps on the sufferings Leningrad endured under Soviet repression in 1937. The occasional division of violins and violas into separate "choirs" is reminiscent of Samuel Barber's *Adagio for Strings*, composed at almost the same time.

The final movement, with its Tchaikovskian trumpets and thundering kettledrums, is, once again, a bid for popularity, and, as it turned out, the Soviets were pleased. And not only the party officials. One of the Tolstoy family, Alexei, called Shostakovich's fifth the "Symphony of Socialism" and offered a program for the four movements: the first was "gigantic factory machinery victorious over nature"; the second, "the athletic life of the happy people of the Union"; the third, "the synthesis of Soviet culture, science, and art"; and the last, "the gratitude and enthusiasm of the masses." I like to think that Shostakovich regarded at least the last suggestion as going too far.

Recording

Rostropovich, National Symphony (Teldec)

String Quartet No. 12 in D-Flat Major, Op. 133 (1968)

As a necessary antidote to the rambunctious excesses of the fifth symphony, and to assure yourself that Shostakovich was indeed a serious and even great composer, turn to this impressive chamber work. Its first section, in sonata form, begins with a grave, persistently weaving theme on the cello (I think of the old monk Pimen writing the chronicle of Mother Russia in Mussorgsky's opera *Boris Godunov*). Then, for its second subject, the music shifts to an atonal context, a serial row—but not one to throw the average listener off base, for the tonal first theme is what dominates this brief first section. (For more pervasive atonality, see the entry on Alban Berg, below.)

The second section, three times as long as the first, is cast in four movements that make a continuous whole. The opening allegretto bursts on the ear with wild, birdlike cries of anguish, and eventually sets them against an obsessive five-note theme, passed from instrument to instrument. This is followed, at the heart of the quartet, by an adagio, a sorrowing meditation for the cello—interrupted by, and eventually haunted by, ghostly chords from the other three instruments, as if the solitary composer were being visited by the three Fates.

In the ensuing moderato, a serial row is announced with insistent pizzicatos and developed with frightening violence. The ghostly chords threaten again—an altogether extraordinary effect—and the cello, as if in answer, humbly takes up the "Pimen" theme of the quartet's opening. Finally the anguished cries and the obsessive five-note theme return, only to be pulled aggressively into a major tonality. Somehow, the struggle—with Fate or Death or the Unknown—has been won.

Recording

Fitzwilliam String Quartet (London/Decca)

You may also want to hear...

...among the symphonies, the first, an often astonishing work for a nineteen-year-old; the still controversial seventh ("Leningrad"), in C Major, with a half-hour first movement that depicts in brutally programmatic terms the Nazi march on the composer's native city—though the author of *Testimony* (Volkov or Shostakovich?) insists that it is a depiction of Soviet, not Nazi, oppression; the eighth, in C Minor, with a long, awe-inspiring first movement and a moving passacaglia that commemorates the fallen in the war; the ninth, in E-Flat Major, which the Soviets regarded as insultingly lightweight for an end-of-war statement; the tenth, in E Minor, generally accounted the composer's orchestral masterpiece, which soprano Galina Vishnevskaya called "a testament of misery, forever damning a tyrant" (i.e., Stalin). Opinion is still divided about the fifteenth and last, in A Major, but opera lovers should at least know about it. It may be thought of as a kind of "four ages of man"—with an opening movement set in a toy shop (the little soldier struts to Rossini's *William Tell* overture) and with a final movement that begins with Wagner's *Walküre* "Fate" theme, the timpani thuds of Siegfried's Funeral March, and a wisp of *Tristan*, and ends back in the toy shop with a question mark. (Some of Shostakovich's other symphonies are estimable, but, with their vocal parts, are here *hors concours*.)

...among the string quartets, the tormented No. 11 in F Minor; the introspective No. 13 in B-Flat Minor; the haunted No. 14 in F-Sharp Major; and the death-obsessed No. 15 in E-Flat Minor (which casts elegy, serenade, intermezzo, nocturne, and funeral march in the same adagio tempo). The earlier quartets are interesting as marking the composer's spiritual progress from relatively untroubled extraversion through his years of personal

crisis toward the inwardness of the final five. The best known
of these is No. 8 in C Minor, occasioned by Shostakovich's visit
in 1960 to the still-devastated city of Dresden. Dedicated to the
victims of war, it contains a number of musical quotations from
the composer's earlier compositions, including a bit from his *Lady
Macbeth*, and is reported to contain as well a number of encoded
messages highly critical of the Communist Party he had just been
compelled to join. The book on Shostakovich is hardly closed.

Béla Bartók
1881–1945

*Bartók the Budapest barbarian, Bartók the Transylvanian languish-
ing in American exile, Bartók the Nietzschean atheist, Bartók the
mad genius unable to get his works performed—these are the stuff
of musical legend. And mostly legend they are. The composer was
a thorough professional, respected by the musical greats of his day,
and he built his strange-sounding compositions out of Hungarian
folk materials that he and his compatriot Zoltán Kodály collected.
Listening to his string quartets is about as demanding as listening
gets, but they and much of the rest of his musical legacy, it seems
clear in this new century, will survive.*

String Quartet No. 2, Op. 17 (1917)

There was a time when listeners were encouraged to approach
Bartók via the Joseph Szigeti arrangements for violin and piano
of his simple Hungarian folk songs. But Bartók's six string quartets constitute, with the fifteen quartets of Shostakovich, one of
the enduring personal testaments of the twentieth century. So
my choice, if I am limited to one work by Bartók, falls on this

quartet, begun after World War I and written almost coterminously with the opera *Bluebeard's Castle*. To some listeners it is more mysterious than that cryptic castle. (I once used this quartet as background music for a showing of the weird silent-movie classic *The Cabinet of Dr. Caligari*.) Certainly it is more *demanding* than Bartók's now popular opera: here there are no sudden revelations, no blinding climaxes as locked doors are opened. With this work, the first of the quartets to be recorded and to win a measure of popularity, the composer has passed beyond the German Romanticism that had marked his first quartet, written nine years earlier, and has forged his Hungarian folk music traditions into a wholly new, personal, not-yet-atonal style.

Though the opening moderato is in sonata form, it is developed almost entirely from the theme on the viola that occupies its first six bars. Those bars are nominally in A Minor, but, like the opening of *Tristan*, they seem, with their welter of sharps and double sharps, not really to be in any fixed tonality, while their rhythm changes with virtually every measure. But the melody, adorned with the triplets Bartók found in many of the folk tunes he assembled, is nonetheless memorable: its first four notes become, in fact, something of a motto for the whole quartet. Close attention to the four strands of string-quartet sound is needed for a listener to appreciate what Bartók is attempting here. Much is angular, abrupt, and full of pain. But the movement also has passages of expansiveness and lyrical beauty; the recapitulation brings a sense of unity and completeness; and the coda, says Mosco Carner in his essay on Bartók's chamber music, is "sheer poetry."

There can hardly be said to be poetry of any conventional kind in the second movement, marked "allegro molto capriccioso." This is something more than a capricious allegro, and more than a conventional scherzo. It is a bitter statement, marked by clashing dissonances, slashing rhythms, grieving statements from all four of the instruments and, eventually, by spasms of pain. Yet it too is composed from Magyar dance rhythms—several dances, it seems, in succession. Bartók had clearly learned to use his unusual source materials to make impassioned personal statements.

The final lento takes us to a desolate landscape where, once the scene is set, the first violin introduces a three-note motif that is soon taken up by all four instruments. Thereafter the movement develops into a slow, halting march toward what can only be called the most mysterious of silences. It is one of the most extraordinary endings ever given a string quartet.

Arthur Honneger and Darius Milhaud, two members of "Les Six," the avant-garde of early twentieth-century French music, joined two other musicians to play through this quartet privately, and Honneger wrote, "We of the younger musical generation were captivated by Bartók." It is, of course, easier for the members of a quartet than for a mere listener to see into a chamber work's essence. But I hope that, with repeated listenings, this wonderful piece will eventually speak to you.

Recording
Takács Quartet (London)

You may also want to hear . . .
. . . the hallucinatory ballet score *The Miraculous Mandarin*; the energetic *Dance Suite* for orchestra, based on Hungarian folk tunes; the brooding *Music for Strings, Percussion, and Celesta*; the Piano Concerto No. 3, the last work from the composer's pen; and above all the increasingly popular *Concerto for Orchestra*, which points up, with a wickedly funny interruption in its otherwise very moving fourth movement, the similarity between the "Nazi army" theme in Shostakovich's seventh symphony (see above) and the rollicking "I'll go back to Maxim's" in Lehár's *The Merry Widow*.

Then by all means return in time to the string quartets—the almost Romantic first, which seems indebted to Wagner; the difficult third, thrusting into new, experimental territory; the eerie fourth, in which two percussive scherzos surround an extraordinary slow movement for cello; the eerier fifth, in which two extraordinary slow movements surround a percussive scherzo; and the sixth, combining traits of all the previous five in a relatively simple, personal statement. Traversing these works is quite an odyssey.

Arnold Schoenberg
1874–1951

Still the most daunting twentieth-century name for the average concertgoer (the only real competition for the title would come from his pupils Alban Berg and Anton Webern), Schoenberg began composing while still an avid Wagnerian under the spell of Tristan. But eventually he began to see Western traditions in music as having spent themselves, and attempted the most ambitious restructuring of music since Guido introduced the scale in the eleventh century. Schoenberg's twelve-tone system (actually the invention of one Joseph Matthias Hauer) allowed him to derive wholly new means of musical expression in harmony, counterpoint, and rhythm—and these he put to work with innovative spirit and scientific precision. Simply put, the system treated all twelve tones of the Western scale as of equal importance. For any given piece of music, Schoenberg would arrange the twelve tones in a sequence that suited him and, before any one of the twelve tones was sounded again individually, he would repeat that first "row"—sometimes inverting it, sometimes using it backward, sometimes combining the original sequence with one or another of its inversions. It was ingenious, but the results seemed terribly abstract and cold to most listeners. Webern pushed the twelve-tone system further with serialism, a method in which there is no harmonic center at all. The results were even more abstracted and distant. Some would say ear-splitting.

By the end of the twentieth century the system, which for decades had been a kind of new orthodoxy in conservatory schools of composition, was largely abandoned. But it left us a few masterworks, among them Schoenberg's opera Moses und Aron *and Berg's* Lulu.

Verklärte Nacht (Transfigured Night), Op. 4 (1899)

Schoenberg is less daunting in this famous half-hour work, which is both early (note that it is the composer's Opus No. 4) and accessible to anyone who knows Wagner's *Tristan*, from which it derives something of its chromaticism, and *Parsifal*, which is suggested here and there in melodic phrases. It is completely tonal, perhaps the last major work of German Romanticism. Schoenberg wrote it 1899 as a string sextet, rescored it in 1917 for full string orchestra, and simplified it, toning down some of its Romantic excesses, in 1943. It has been, for the better part of a century, the composer's most popular work. Wilhelm Furtwängler, who disliked Schoenberg's later works, declared it the composer's "most outstanding and most important composition."

Though *Verklärte Nacht* is written in five movements, it proceeds without interruption and is perhaps best approached by a first-time listener in its orchestral version, as a tone poem, based as it is on a narrative in verse by Richard Dehmel, a lyricist who bestrode the movements of impressionism and expressionism in poetry. Schoenberg wrote his five movements to correspond to the five sections of Dehmel's poem, the first in a cycle called "Woman and the World." What follows is a paraphrase of the poem, with musical descriptions in parentheses:

First movement: Two people are walking through a bare, cold

wood of lofty oak trees, with the moon sailing above them and illuminating their faces. Jagged peaks reach up to the clear sky. (A falling phrase recurs over a slowly plodding bass line; this will recur at the end of the movement, just as the last line of the poem will recall the first. High violins suggest the shimmer of the moonlight.)

Second movement: The woman confesses to the man that she is carrying a child that is not his. She had been so desperate to find meaning in life that she gave herself to a stranger. "Now," she says, "life has taken its revenge, for I have found you." (The music is agitated as the woman confesses her fall from grace; then a cello theme expresses her longing for motherhood, and the first violins tell of her newly found love.)

Third movement: The woman stares upward into the moonlight. (The first movement's "walking" theme gives way to a solo violin, introducing the man.)

Fourth movement: The man consoles her. "The child you have conceived must not be a burden to your soul. See how all the world shimmers in the moonlight. Here we are adrift together on a cold sea, but a warmth reaches from you to me, and from me to you, and that warmth will transfigure the child. You will bear the child to me, from me. You have brought glory to my soul. You have made me a child again." (In this longest of the sections, the man restates themes introduced by the woman in the second movement, but with a new tenderness—the solo violin soars over a quivering orchestra. There is an impassioned climax.)

Fifth movement: They embrace and continue their walk through the transfigured night. (The music, like the poem, ends with a reminiscence of its beginning.)

Recording

Karajan, Berlin Philharmonic (DG)

You may also want to hear . . .

. . . *Pelleas und Melisande* (note the "und"). This long, heavily orchestrated, leitmotific, and very Germanic tone poem follows Maeterlinck's play scene by scene, and could hardly be more different from Debussy's impressionistic French opera on the same subject. It has not attracted as many listeners as *Verklärte Nacht,* but it is still wholly tonal, the composer's Opus No. 5.

For the rest, the first string quartet (Op. 7) is an accessible, post-Brahmsian piece. (Atonality first appears in the last movement of the second string quartet [Op. 10] when a soprano marks the new divide in twentieth-century vocal and instrumental music by singing, over the four string lines, Stephan Georg's words "I breathe the air of another planet" and "I lose myself in sounds.") Thereafter, Schoenberg's completely atonal works are mainly for listeners who have already come to grips with the composer through the operas *Erwartung* and *Moses und Aron.* The dramatic action in the stage works gives direction to uninitiates who might find themselves hopelessly adrift in Schoenberg's instrumental atonal mazes. An exploration of the atonal works should start with the piano concerto (Op. 42), a one-movement work that has, with repeated hearings, spoken to many who have felt their way through earlier concertos by German composers.

It should be said, finally, that Schoenberg did not make the extreme claims for his new system that his disciples did. "There is plenty of good music," he said, "still to be written in C Major." But he could be eloquent in defense of atonality: "To future generations music [built on the traditional scale] will seem incomplete, since it has not yet fully exploited everything latent in sound, just as a sort of music that did not yet differentiate within the octave would seem incomplete to us." When asked later in life why he didn't write more music like *Verklärte Nacht,* he replied, "I am doing precisely that, and I cannot understand why people do not see it." Maybe, with patience and persistence, *you* will understand.

Alban Berg
1885–1935

Berg, the meticulous disciple of Schoenberg, wrote only a handful of large-scale works, all of them charged with his intense feeling for the marginalized figures of society—witness his operas Wozzeck *and* Lulu. *Far more than Schoenberg and Webern, he used the twelve-tone method to express human emotions. Sibelius once referred to him as "Schoenberg's best work." His is atonal music that can still seem to the first-time listener discordant, hypersensitive, even neurotic, but one can always sense a human mind and heart at work in it, and for that reason I have chosen a twelve-tone work by him rather than by Schoenberg for discussion here. The greatest of his instrumental pieces is unquestionably his...*

Violin Concerto (1935)

Berg was working on *Lulu* when he received a commission for a concerto from the American violinist Louis Krasner. He was still planning its composition when he heard that an eighteen-year-old girl named Manon, the daughter of Mahler's widow and the architect Walter Gropius, had died from infantile paralysis after a year of intense suffering. He gave his concerto the name "To the Memory of an Angel" and wrote what was, in effect, a requiem. Within a month he was dead himself. The work is thus a valedictory as well as an elegy.

While the opening movement seems mainly concerned with setting up a twelve-tone row and using it to establish a Viennese atmosphere, the other three are quite clearly programmatic—

depicting, in turn, the charming character of the beautiful and promising young girl, her suffering and death, and the ultimate journey of her soul.

The first movement, a four-and-a-half-minute andante, begins with a delicate statement, by alternating clarinet and solo violin, of the perfect fifths that sound naturally on the four strings of a violin. There follows a passage of restless but surprisingly tonal music, and ultimately the solo violin rises over soft instrumental chords to state pianissimo (it might have been better for a first-time listener if it were stated more obtrusively) the row of twelve ascending notes that will provide the main structure of the piece. Each of the first nine of these notes is a third higher than its predecessor. (A trained ear will know that, if played as overlapping triads, they form the chords of G Minor, the key of Bruch's traditional violin concerto; D Major, the key of Beethoven's; A Minor, the key of Dvoák's; and E Major, the key of one of Bach's.) The last of these nine notes forms, with notes ten, eleven, and twelve, a seemingly skeletal twelve-tone-row theme that will, at the end of the concerto, result in something absolutely unique in the history of atonal music.

In the rest of this short movement Berg inverts the row, sets the solo violin to playing it in triplets, lengthens and shortens its note values, and develops it further, perhaps, than a first-time listener can follow. But far from blistering the ear, as twelve-tone music is notoriously said to do, the movement invites the listener to a kind of reverie, remarkably Romantic in sound and feeling. There is a return, finally, to the original material, and then the first movement flows without any pause into . . .

. . . the second movement, a six-minute scherzo in which Berg proceeds—admittedly through a maze of twelve-tone busyness—in the style of a Viennese waltz ("wienerish" is his marking in the score) and then in the style of Austrian folk music (with the marking "rustico"). The row of twelve notes figures prominently as we move to the trio, the main feature of which is a folk song of Carinthia, the Austrian province where Berg was composing.

Then the third movement begins with a scream of pain and a cadenza for the soloist that seems to be an expression of the composer's own grief over the suffering and death of Manon Gropius. In the seven-minute movement, a convulsive figure takes over the musical texture; in rhythm it is similar to a "death" theme used in both *Wozzeck* and *Lulu*. There is a period of calm, in which reminiscences of the second movement recur. Then a terrifying outburst from the full orchestra, clearly built on the row of twelve notes, seems to sound the moment of the young girl's death. Finally, something completely unexpected happens: the musical texture thins out, the last four notes of the twelve-tone row begin to shape themselves into a melody . . .

. . . and we move without any pause to the eight-minute final movement. The melody from the top of the twelve-tone row is now stated clearly, harmonized on the clarinets. It is the chorale "Es is genug" from Bach's Cantata "O Ewigkeit, du Donnewort." (That is to say, the four last notes of the row have all along been, as we now see, the first four notes—"It is enough"—from Bach's cantata about death and the final journey of the soul, "O Eternity, Thou Thund'rous Word.") Nothing like this had ever happened before in twelve-tone music, nor has it since. It comes like a benediction.

The soloist then leads the orchestra through two variations of the chorale—an elegy for the loss of Manon and a devastating adagio that contains echoes (Berg's marking is "as seen from afar") of the Carinthian tune. And finally there is a sublime coda, in which the chorale is intoned with full harmonies on the woodwinds and the brass. The solo violin then restates the basic tone row, rising to an ethereal high G. The twelve-tone row has done its work—and the concerto finishes, amazingly, in an unambiguous B-Flat Major.

There are those who say that with this ending Berg has felt compelled, in order to give adequate expression to his sorrow, to reach back beyond his troubled twentieth-century atonal style to an age of faith and rock-solid musicality. That is true enough, but it was an atonal row that first sent him on his way to finding that affirmation.

Recording
Mutter, Levine, Chicago Symphony Orchestra (DG)

You may also want to hear...
...the *Lyric Suite,* one of only two works Berg wrote for string quartet, and one of his masterpieces. It is as impossible to decode its cryptic musical references to his beloved Hanna Fuchs-Robettin as it is to follow, without a score, the partially serial structures at work, but there is no mistaking the intensity of the feeling expressed. (Berg quotes the opening measures of Wagner's *Tristan* in the last movement.) Andrew Porter, offering an analysis in mid-century, when the public was not yet receptive to this work, said confidently of the *Lyric Suite* that "the music, like that of *Wozzeck* or the Violin Concerto, speaks to everyone." All the same, one is advised to be familiar with both *Wozzeck* and the Violin Concerto before wading in here. Berg later orchestrated three of the movements, but the piece is best heard when sung by only four haunted string voices.

Ernest Bloch
1880–1959

Bloch, Swiss-born, professionally trained in Germany and France, found his true métier when, emigrating to America, he resolved to write "Jewish" music in classical forms, much as Vaughan Williams strove to capture Englishness and the "Mighty Five" the spirit of Mother Russia in their musical output. But unlike the others Bloch did not avail himself of traditional religious and folkloric material; he claimed rather to be listening to "an inner voice . . . which seemed to come from far beyond myself, far beyond my parents." His ambition—to convey "the despair of Ecclesiastes, the sorrow and immensity of the Book of Job, the sensuality of the Song of Songs"—was realized in a cycle of works written more than two decades before the Shoah. But some listeners think that, for a musical understanding of Jewishness, of what Bloch called "the venerable emotion of the race that slumbers in our soul," Bloch's works still surpass anything written since. Many of these are choral, but the single best-known work is instrumental:

Schelomo, Hebrew Rhapsody for Cello and Orchestra (1916)

Bloch had long thought of writing a work on the Book of Ecclesiastes for voice and orchestra, but was uncertain about what language to use. On a visit to the Geneva home of cellist Alexander Barjansky and his wife, he was inspired by a statue of King Solomon by Madame Barjansky and convinced by the cellist himself that the cello could provide a truer and more expressive voice than any words. Bloch dedicated the completed work to Barjansky and his wife.

Much of the idiom Bloch uses in the rhapsody is characterized by orientalizing half-step phrases and dotted rhythms that anticipate, rather unfortunately, the music by lesser composers that was soon to underscore three decades of cinematic biblical epics. But the musical powers at work here are more potent and purposeful than those heard on most sound tracks. First a solo cello, as if in wordless recitative, speaks as Schelomo, the Preacher of Jerusalem, long believed to be King Solomon. The instrument seems to be saying in sound the famous words "Vanity of vanities, all is vanity. What profit hath a man of all his labor which he taketh under the sun? In much wisdom is much grief, and he that increaseth knowledge increaseth sorrow."

Then the viola section states the main musical theme, which undergoes a series of exotically colored developments—the successive quests of man for pleasure, for conquest, and for wisdom. And throughout these we hear the voice of the cello, questioning, sorrowing, and finally descending in contemplation to its lowest range. Solomon himself seems to be speaking through the most expressive of all instruments.

Recording

Isserlis, Hickox, London Symphony Orchestra (Virgin)

You may also want to hear...

...the unethnic and eminently listenable Concerto Grosso No. 1, which is almost to Bach and Handel what Prokofiev's "Classical" symphony is to Haydn and Mozart, and a violin concerto that may sound Hebraic but actually uses an authentic American Indian melody for its motto theme.

Edward Elgar
1857–1934

Sir Edward has been thought pompous by non-Englishmen, and even by some of his fellow islanders. Ingrates, all of them! It took a composer with extraordinary talent and an unshaken (and touchingly vulnerable) faith in himself and his country to lift English music out of its long doldrums and establish a new and vital tradition. Witness, above all:

The "Enigma" Variations, Op. 36 (1899)

This is the work that advanced Elgar to the front rank of British composers and in fact made him the first British composer in more than a century to secure a place among composers of the world. The "Enigma" Variations began simply as an improvisation at the piano: Elgar worked out a theme, did a little variation on it for his wife, and asked, "Who is that like?" After a moment's thought she remarked that it was "exactly the way Mr. Baxter goes out of the room." Within a short time Elgar had used the theme to typify several more of his friends, identifying them by affixing their initials (or appropriate pseudonymns) to their variations. What resulted is a veritable gallery of Victorian personages, as well as a most enjoyable and often moving half-hour of music.

The theme is a tender, long-spanned, instantly memorable melody that hovers between major and minor—not at all the sort of thing you would think susceptible to variations. But Elgar works wonders with it, as follows:

Variation 1. *C.A.E.*: Elgar's wife, Alice. The melody is hardly changed, but is more richly, not to say lovingly, orchestrated, and it rises to a Romantic climax before it subsides.

Variation 2. *H.D.S-P.*: H. D. Stewart-Powell. The tempo picks up, as did Mr. Stewart-Powell's warming-up exercises at the piano when he, Elgar, and Basil Nevinson (see variation 12) got together for a session of chamber music.

Variation 3. *R.B.T.*: Richard Baxter Townsend. The woodwinds—especially the bassoon, the clown of the orchestra—do a sly, slithering, slouchy imitation of a man who was known for his clever imitations of others.

Variation 4. *W.M.B.*: William Meath Baxter. The variation is exactly how the headstrong, unstoppable Mr. Baxter would order his guests around and then storm out of the room. Ask Mrs. Elgar.

Variation 5. *R.P.A.*: Richard P. Arnold, the son of Matthew Arnold, is depicted as a young man who could sink moodily into a daydream and then rouse himself with excited laughter.

Variation 6. *Ysobel*: Isabel Fitton, an amateur violist who had difficulty crossing from one string to another (hence the opening phrase). It seems, however, that she could sustain a lovely melody on her instrument.

Variation 7. *Troyte*: Arthur Troyte Griffith. Tempestuous tympani typify temperamental Troyte, who wanted to be a pianist but whose technique never succeeded beyond the glissando.

Variation 8. *W.N.*: Miss Winifred Norbury. A portrait of a lady of refined manners who, it seems clear, loved lively conversation.

Variation 9. *Nimrod*: August Jaeger. Elgar's best friend is affectionately presented with the longest and most famous variation, perhaps the most moving expression of friendship in all of music. The theme is played broadly in the major, with rich harmonies and special emphasis on its wide intervals. Elgar said it was a personal memoir of "a long summer evening walk when Jaeger grew nobly eloquent—as only he could—about Beethoven, especially the slow movements." (In German, Jaeger means "hunter." Hence, the variation is named for the biblical man with the bow.)

Variation 10. *Dorabella*: From what the strings and woodwinds say, Miss Dora Penny must have been pretty and prim, and something of a chatterbox, with a slight hesitancy in her speech.

Variation 11. *G.R.S.*: Some say that this is George Robertson Sinclair, the organist of Hereford Cathedral, enthusiastically blasting and pedaling away at his instrument. On the other hand, one Sir Ivor Atkins says that this variation is really a musical depiction of Sinclair's retriever, Dan, leaping down into a river to fetch a stick for his master.

Variation 12. *B.G.N.*: Basil G. Nevinson, a cellist (see variation 2), is given a slow movement for cello—Brahmsian, serious, and full of expression. A wisp of Mr. Nevinson's cello sound leads into . . .

. . . Variation 13. *X.X.X.*: Lady Mary Ogdon. The introduction to this variation suggests that X.X.X. is a quite sensible lady, but the composer has his fears for her: she is about to take an ocean voyage. The solo clarinet, the undulating strings, the ominous soft drumroll, and the mysterious brass all seem to indicate, despite a quotation from Mendelssohn's "Calm Sea and Prosperous Voyage," that the sailing might be misty and perilous. (Perhaps the lady knew her Greek and Latin poetry, where there is a long tradition of *propemptica*—poems written in apprehension for a friend about to sail the sea.)

Variation 14. *E.D.U.*: Since "Edoo" was Mrs. Elgar's affectionate name for her husband, this variation must be a portrait of Sir Edward himself—a high-spirited man who obviously loved his friends and delighted in celebrating them in music. The quotations from the C.A.E. and Nimrod variations indicate his special indebtedness to the two people closest to him. And lest anyone accuse Elgar of overlong self-congratulatory flourishes, let it be said that this variation was expanded at the insistence of the champion and first conductor of the "Enigmas," Wagner's protégé Hans Richter, who recognized the value of the work and knew what needed to be added if it was to attract the attention of the world.

It is interesting to note that two variations were eventually dropped and have not been heard since. These were musical portraits of Sir Charles Perry and Sir Arthur Sullivan. They were identifiable partly from imitations of the oratorio style of the former and the operetta style of the latter, and thus did not fit with Elgar's eventual scheme—to delineate some endearing personality trait of each of his subjects. All the same, I wish we had the two additional portraits.

But when we have identified all of the personages depicted, we still have not solved the "enigma" of the variations. "Through and over the whole set," Elgar insisted, "another and larger theme 'goes,' but is not played." What could this unidentified theme be? Apparently, like the Countess in Tchaikovsky's *Queen of Spades*, Elgar told the secret to three initiates—and all of them have since taken it to their graves. Was the composer only teasing us, as Jaeger suggested? Or is there really a hovering theme—a "dark saying," to use Elgar's own words—that can be identified? Suggestions from musically ingenious opera fans have ranged from *Parsifal* to *Pagliacci*! But no one has yet solved the enigma.

Recording

Boult, London Philharmonic (EMI)

You may also want to hear...

... the first of the two symphonies, with a typically Elgarian motto theme and an intensely personal slow movement that Hans Richter thought worthy of Beethoven; the Violin Concerto in B Minor, which—breaking all precedents—makes its most searching statement in an extended last-movement cadenza; the Cello

Concerto in E Minor, with a short adagio movement that elegizes on the twilight that settled on the Edwardian world after the Great War; the "Cockaigne" Overture, a jaunty, expansive tribute to Cockneydom; and *Falstaff*, a half-hour "symphonic study" that treats the events of Shakespeare's two Henry IV plays in realistic detail and—in two "interludes"—with Elgarian introspection.

You will already know at least two of the five "Pomp and Circumstance" marches. No one ought to condescend to the broad ceremonial strain in the first. "A tune like that," Elgar said, rightly, "comes once in a lifetime."

Ralph Vaughan Williams
1872–1958

It was Elgar who revived the long-slumbering tradition of English music, but he was at heart a Brahmsian post-Romantic; Vaughan Williams, the heir to his throne, was an Englishman with an intense interest in local musical folklore and an orchestrator who captured uncannily in music the look and the feel of his beloved homeland. Ask any Englishman. Vaughan Williams was particularly fond of the Elizabethan tune "Greensleeves" (rumored to have been written by Elizabeth I's father, Henry VIII). It fits nicely into his Falstaff opera Sir John in Love*, gets a royal treatment in a fantasia all its own, and crops up elsewhere in the composer's work. One almost expects to hear it in his operas* Hugh the Drover *and* Riders to the Sea*. But his best-known work is . . .*

Fantasia on a Theme by Thomas Tallis (1909)

In this haunting, awe-inspiring piece, Vaughan Williams takes a tune from a sixteenth-century English composer of church music (the third of the eight tunes Tallis wrote to illustrate the eight modes of the Middle Ages) and sets two string choirs of different sizes to singing it slowly and antiphonally—with the occasional use of a solo viola, a solo violin, and a string quartet—sometimes with sonorous gravity, sometimes with ethereal echoing softness. Not since Wagner divided his violins into choirs for the prelude to *Lohengrin* had there been such effective writing for massed strings. Vaughan Williams wrote the piece with the acoustics of Gloucester Cathedral in mind, and he conducted its first performance there. The audience, assembled to hear Elgar conduct his oratorio *The Dream of Gerontius,* knew from this introductory piece that Sir Edward had found a worthy successor.

Recording
Boult, London Philharmonic (EMI)

You may also want to hear...

...Vaughan Williams's other short pieces—*The Lark Ascending, The English Folksongs Suite,* and the aforementioned *Fantasia on "Greensleeves."* Among the nine symphonies, three of which have vocal parts, the second (the "London" symphony), deeply felt and more atmospheric than pictorial, should be your first choice.

Gustav Holst
1874–1934

The composer who—in an England that still regarded operatic composition as suited only to non-English composers—dared to write Savitri, The Perfect Fool, *and several other works for the stage fell for a spell under the influence of Wagner, and it is no surprise that his handling of orchestral textures is masterly. He also shared*

Vaughan Williams's interest in English folk music. The two strains came together to produce one undisputed masterpiece.

The Planets, Op. 32 (1917)

This brilliant suite of seven movements—descriptive, despite the composer's insistence to the contrary, not only of the planets but of the Roman gods for whom they have been named—became by the century's end one of the most popular of all orchestral showpieces, all but eclipsing Rimsky's *Scheherezade*, Ravel's *La Valse*, and Strauss's *Alpine Symphony* on concert schedules. For the foreseeable future, continental orchestras will no longer be able to overlook, as they have in the past, the instrumental music of Albion's sceptered isle. (It will be noted that there is no movement describing Pluto; in 1917 that planet had not yet been discovered.)

"Mars, the Bringer of War": Possibly the most relentlessly brutal, implacable, inhuman piece of music ever written by an Englishman. (That the composer's ancestry was partly Swedish and Russian may have made the difference.) Holst wrote this unforgettable movement in the last year of World War I, of which it is most definitely not a celebration.

"Venus, the Bringer of Peace": A piece as serene, subtle, and complex as "Mars, the Bringer of War" is chilling, unsubtle, and single-minded.

"Mercury, the Winged Messenger": The most versatile and light-footed of the gods is depicted in contrasting keys and rhythms, with quicksilver orchestration.

"Jupiter, the Bringer of Jollity": The most popular and kingly of the movements, with six different themes, all of them exhilarating, all of them very English in spirit. The last, broadly Elgarian

strain has been fitted with the patriotic words, "I vow to thee my country, all earthly things above, / Entire and whole and perfect, the service of my love," and has been known to stir even the most un-English of hearts.

"Saturn, the Bringer of Old Age": For most of its length, this movement depicts the chilling inexorability of time—tolling, chiming, ominously ringing. But by the end, the oppressiveness has ceased, and the mood changes to an unearthly suggestion of cosmic peace.

"Uranus, the Magician": A four-note "hocus-pocus" theme characterizes the oldest of the gods as a mountebank who conjures up terrors and tricks.

"Neptune, the Mystic": Here we have reached the rarefied atmosphere, the timeless seas of space. A wordless women's chorus adds to the awesomeness until all is silence.

Recording

Dutoit, Montreal Symphony Orchestra (London)

Benjamin Britten
1913–1976

The composer of the operas Peter Grimes *and* Billy Budd *also wrote much choral music and many songs, but his instrumental output is small. All the same, anyone who has trouble remembering whether the plaintive solo instrument that begins the second movement of Tchaikovsky's fourth symphony is an oboe or a clarinet could profit, and also derive much pleasure, from the following item, regardless of how old or young he or she might be.*

The Young Person's Guide to the Orchestra, Op. 34 (1945)

Commissioned by the English Ministry of Education for a film that would introduce children to the wonders of the orchestra, and in particular to the special sounds of the different instruments, this enjoyable piece is cast in the form of theme and variations with spoken commentary. It is often performed under the title *Variations and Fugue on a Theme of Purcell*.

Theme: The full orchestra states a spirited and slightly sinister minor-key tune from Henry Purcell's incidental music to a seventeenth-century tragedy, *Abdelazar, or The Moor's Revenge*, written by a proto-feminist spy improbably named Aphra Behn. It is as if we listeners are embarking together with the orchestra on an exciting tale from the *Arabian Nights*. Next, the four sections of the orchestra—woodwinds, brass, strings, and percussion—introduce themselves successively by giving five quick major-key variants of the intriguing tune. And then they join forces once more to reiterate, indeed, to celebrate, that tune from *Abdelazar*.

Thirteen variations on the theme follow: Two flutes and piccolo, leapfrogging. Two oboes feeling sentimental. Two clarinets strutting like peacocks. Two bassoons, one melancholy, one jaunty. Violins dancing a polonaise. Violas singing a long legato melody punctuated by staccato chords from the rest of the orchestra. Unison cellos singing an expressive, yearning song. Deep-voiced double basses keeping their calm in the midst of distractions from the woodwinds. A harp glistening with chords and glissandos, with a tremulous accompaniment. French horns calling us to the hunt. Trumpets sounding the climax of our adventure. Trombones and tubas leading our victory march. Percussion instruments, underscored by strings only, completing the celebration.

Fugue: Finally the instruments, entering in the same order in which they were introduced, whirl through the main tune in a headlong movement that, to these ears at least, owes something to Prokofiev's *Classical Symphony*. Finally the theme from *Abdelazar* emerges in full splendor from the orchestral swirl.

The Young Person's Guide is usually performed without commentary at concerts and has been successfully mounted as a ballet.

Recording

Bernstein, New York Philharmonic (Sony)

You may also want to hear...

... the early *Variations on a Theme of Frank Bridge* for string orchestra (Op. 10)—Britten's own "Enigma" Variations, in which he pays homage to his first composition teacher; the piano concerto (Op. 13) and violin concerto (Op. 15), post-Romantic showpieces for their soloists, each of them concluding in a passacaglia that forecasts the climax of *Peter Grimes*; and the ballet *The Prince of the Pagodas*, in which Britten imitates the sound of the Balinese gamelan, as he was to do again in the dance sequences of his opera *Death in Venice*.

George Gershwin
1898–1937

The Russian immigrants' son fascinated by Manhattan is the only composer of American popular song who succeeded in scaling the heights of concert music. Jerome Kern and Richard Rodgers, who wrote songs equally distinguished, were less successful with large-scale pieces, and Irving Berlin, Cole Porter, and Harold Arlen never made the attempt. In this respect, Gershwin stands alone. Porgy and Bess *may be his masterpiece, but operagoers will find their admiration for it greatly enhanced if they listen with fresh ears to its composer's concert pieces.*

Concerto in F (1925)

Commissioned by New York's musical doyen Walter Damrosch and composed and scored in white heat, Gershwin's only concerto begins noisily, almost crudely (some will say unconvincingly), but the piano soon introduces a lyrical first theme that seems instantly to evoke the lonely, glittering Manhattan that the composer knew in the 1920s. After a nervously rhythmic passage, the orchestra introduces a second theme, a rather self-conscious attempt at symphonic writing. There is some development, but no real recapitulation—only the "New York" theme driven forcibly home.

The slow movement, the most successful of the three, features in succession an unforgettably melancholy song for muted trumpet, a strutting, frankly bawdy tune first sounded on the piano, and a sweepingly Romantic effusion for massed strings. The movement closes with a return to the melancholy opening.

The third movement, a freewheeling rondo, is propelled by an energetic, insistently percussive main theme. Between its periodic recurrences, the best themes of the first two movements are passionately restated.

The Concerto in F shows how much Gershwin had grown as a composer in the year since he wrote his sensational *Rhapsody in Blue*. The rhapsody owed a good deal to Paul Whiteman's improvisational musicians and to his orchestrator, Ferde Grofé. Here Gershwin goes it alone. And his instrument of instruments, the piano, discovers exciting sonorities unexplored in the rhapsody or, for that matter, in the innovative piano works of Chopin and Debussy.

Recording

Previn, London Symphony Orchestra (EMI)

You may also want to hear...

... the *Rhapsody in Blue*, of course. Its sassily defiant opening clarinet slide is still the most famous moment in American music, classical or otherwise, and its big emotional tune is a stunning, if overly familiar, melodic achievement—the American popular song *in excelsis*. Most impressive of all, the rhapsody conjures up what was then a new sound, instantly recognizable as Gershwin's and Gershwin's alone.

Try listening as well to *An American in Paris* without images from the MGM movie intervening, and see if, at the close, you can resist surrendering to the American tourist's nostalgic memories of bluesy Charleston. And after that, listen with fresh ears to the songs—perhaps especially "Love Walked In," an artfully structured product of Gershwin's last year, with a melody and harmonies he liked to call "Brahmsian." It is a small-scale intimation of what we might have had in his vocal and instrumental music had the composer lived past his thirties.

Samuel Barber
1910–1981

The composer of the beautiful elegy for soprano and orchestra called Knoxville: Summer of 1915 *and of the operas* Vanessa *and* Antony and Cleopatra *(the work that opened the new Metropolitan Opera House in 1966) refused to take sides in the controversies that raged in twentieth-century music and wrote in a personal style—lyrical and listenable but hardly a throwback—that has weathered change better than the styles advanced by his trendier contemporaries.*

Adagio for Strings, Op. 11 (1938)

The single piece of American music most often played in the concert halls of the world, this adagio for the massed string choirs of the orchestra began life as the second movement of a string quartet, and consists of a single long-lined melody beginning quietly, slowly shaping itself in one vast arc, widening to a great poignant climax, and then subsiding. Barber, a literary man, was inspired by a passage in the third book of Virgil's *Georgics*:

> As when a wave starts to whiten in the midst of the sea,
> And from the depths shapes itself into a widening curve,
> Then rolls massively shoreward, sounding rough on the reef,
> And falls, mountainous . . .

But Virgil's lines, even in their original Latin hexameters, do not have the emotional depth, the inevitability, and the moment of transcendence one finds in Barber's adagio. It is a demonstration, much needed today, that a great piece of music can be composed from a single idea.

The piece was played at the funeral service of President Roosevelt, flooded the airwaves after the funeral of President Kennedy, and added a whole dimension to Oliver Stone's film on the Vietnam War, *Platoon*. But it is not—it should be remembered—an elegy, let alone a dirge.

Recording

Bernstein, New York Philharmonic (Sony)

You may also want to hear...

. . . the early Violin Concerto, Op. 14, a post-Romantic work, and the late Piano Concerto, Op. 38, which is not entirely convincing in its attempt at 1960s modernism.

Olivier Messiaen
1908–1992

Partly Flemish in origin but born and bred in France, Messiaen, best known as the composer of the four-hour opera Saint François d'Assise, *was schooled from childhood in both sounds and letters: he was composing by the age of seven and had reportedly read all of Shakespeare aloud, in his father's French translations, by the time he was eight. Debussy's* Pelléas *sent him early into an exploration of the modes and rhythms of Eastern music and Gregorian chant. A later enthusiasm was the notation and analysis of birdsongs, which he proceeded to work into his compositions. But perhaps the most important influence on his art was the fervent Catholicism that prompted works of ecstatic—and very noisy—celebration. He sought "a music that touches everything and at the same time touches God." Of no composer may it more truly be said that he conjures up a world all his own. It is, however, a world that many have found difficult of access.*

Turangalîla-Symphonie (1948)

This weirdly exultant celebration of God's teeming creation is written for "grand orchestra" (and that includes a whole forest of percussion instruments), piano (so prominent that the work might be thought a piano concerto), and *ondes martenot* (an electronic keyboard—also used by Maurice Jarre in his score for *Lawrence of Arabia*—that lends a quivering, metallic aura, sometimes mysterious, sometimes lacerating, to most of the ten movements). Messiaen has written that the "lîla" in the title is Sanskrit for "play—but play in the sense of the divine action upon the cosmos, the play of creation, of destruction, of reconstruction." The word also means "love." "Turanga," the composer wrote, is "time that runs, like a galloping horse" or "time that flows, like sand in an hourglass."

This *symphonie*, then, is a hymn to "joy that is superhuman, overflowing, blinding, unlimited," and to "love that is fatal, irresistible, transcending everything, suppressing everything outside itself." In the latter connection, Messiaen mentions the legendary Tristan and Yseult and Marc Chagall's floating lovers as images of what he is attempting to express in music. It may be pertinent that Yvonne Loriod, whom Messiaen married after the death of his first wife, has faithfully played the (extremely demanding) piano part in virtually every performance of this immense "song of love."

I. Introduction: Two of the four major themes are introduced in the first few minutes. The first is a massive, lumbering, frightening motif played fortissimo by the trombones: the composer, remembering a story by Prosper Mérimée (and not, apparently, Mozart's *Don Giovanni*), called it the "statue" theme. After several cascades of sound from the orchestra and the *ondes martenot*, the second motif, a four-note figure, is sounded pianissimo by the clarinets; the composer called it the "flower" theme, suggestive of "a delicate orchid, a florid fuchsia." The piano then plays an extended cadenza, and the orchestra, with its myriad percussion instruments, begins a wild celebration—which the "statue" theme brings to an abrupt halt.

II. Chant d'amour 1: No "song of love" in Messiaen is likely to be amorous in any romantic sense. This is a rhythmic, jangling, whistling, trumpeted jamboree relieved occasionally by what might be called echoing caverns of mysterious quietness—wherein the *ondes* is put to good use. While a second listening will reveal a rondo-like structure, it is best at first simply to revel in the movement's primitive splendors.

III. Turangalîla 1: Many people—those of us who have not been blessed with Messiaen's cosmic sensibility—would say that this movement could more fittingly be called "song of love" than the former. There are three sections: the haunted clarinet that introduces the movement gives way to a chorale-like chant on the trombone, and that yields to quiet oboe-and-flute duet.

IV. Chant d'amour 2: Again, this is not a "song of love" in any conventional sense. But the jaunty, wood-block- accompanied tune in the woodwinds—more an American in Paris than an Adam in Eden—does give way to an extended, quietly introspective section that *mutatis mutandis* could stand in for the slow movement of a symphony by, say, Sibelius. There is a multi-layered climax, with the "statue" theme lurking within the orchestral mix. Then the piano has an extended cadenza, the "flower" theme resonates as it did in the first movement, and—despite a fortissimo reappearance of the "statue" theme—this "song of love" ends quietly.

V. Joie du sang des étoiles: Quite the wackiest, most exuberant, and entertaining of the movements, this is an orchestral outburst alive with joy—and it is derived from, and ends with, the once menacing "statue" theme! "The joy of the blood of the stars," you say? All I can say is "Mon Dieu! These stars really sparkle!"

VI. Jardin du sommeil d'amour: Perhaps a first-time listener should start here, in "the garden of love's sleep." This is wordless music worthy of comparison with the most magical moments in Berlioz's love duet for Dido and Aeneas. Muted strings and the *ondes* conjure up the night via the third major theme in this work—the "love" theme, and the piano gives stylized impressions of the songs of nightingale, blackbird, and garden warbler—all wreathed about with whispering woodwind sounds. We might want to think of this as the innocent slumber of a prelapsarian

Adam and Eve, but the composer actually had in mind legendary lovers of a later age—Tristan and Yseult: "Time flows forgotten," he said. "The lovers are outside time. Let us not wake them."

VII. Turangalîla 2: The *ondes martenot* confronts the menacing "statue" theme. Here the composer introduces his fourth major theme, the "chords" theme—not a melody so much as a quick progression of chords. He compared the slash of the menacing statue's blade to the pendulum's swing in Poe's story "The Pit and the Pendulum."

VIII. Développment de l'amour: This is the symphony's proper "development" section. All four themes are clearly sounded—the "chords" theme now sounding not unlike the "silver rose" in Richard Strauss's *Der Rosenkavalier* and the "love" theme resounding as loud and languishing as anything in Strauss's *Salome*. The composer has told us, without referring to Strauss or Wagner, that his Tristan and Yseult are here united as in one person (Tristan-Yseult) in the ultimate "development" of their love. But why, we wonder, does the movement end as the "statue" theme, in the composer's words, "bends over the abyss"?

IX. Turangalîla 3: Even the composer called this a "strange movement." Five "percussion timbres"—woodblock, cymbal, maracas, Provençal tabor, and tam-tam—join with piano and *ondes* in what might be thought of as a transitional passage to . . .

. . . *X. Final*, in which brass fanfares introduce the clangorous final movement and the "love" theme serves as a luxuriant second subject. The *symphonie* ends with bursts of joy and, as a last creative touch, what has been called "the greatest chord ever sounded."

Recording

Loriod, Chung, Orchestre de l'Opéra Bastille (DG)

You may also want to hear...

... *Quatuor pour la fin du temps* (Quartet for the End of Time), a forty-five-minute work in praise of Jesus as the Word of God and center of creation, written for violin, cello, clarinet, and piano when Messiaen was interned in a German prison camp during the Second World War, and first performed by and for the prisoners and the guards there. The *Quartet* takes its title from chapter ten of the Book of Revelations, where the seventh angel of the apocalypse declares to heaven, earth, and sea that henceforth "time shall be no longer." It could almost be said that in this now-celebrated work Messiaen, whose new sense of rhythm was partly derived from Eastern cultures, made an end to the time structures so long observed in Western classical music. Certainly he made a demanding but rewarding musical statement—one that contains what critic Alex Ross has called "the most ethereally beautiful music of the twentieth century."

... *Oiseaux Exotiques* (Exotic Birds), a fifteen-minute suite for piano, winds, and percussion that is the most accessible and enjoyable of Messiaen's collections of birdsongs. Some forty species are here in succession—twittering, caroling, squawking—and all of their exotic calls, however impressionistic they may seem in performance, have been carefully researched and lovingly scored.

Impressive but less accessible works of Messiaen are *Vingt regards sur l'enfant Jésus,* a two-hour set of decidedly unsentimental nativity scenes for piano; *Et expecto resurrectionem mortuorum,* a monumental, five-movement, Scripture-based work for winds, brass, and percussion commissioned by André Malraux to commemorate those fallen in the two World Wars; *Des canyons aux étoiles,* a hundred-minute celebration, for horn, piano, and a very percussive orchestra, of the colors, sounds, and natural splendors of the American West; and *Le Livre du Saint-Sacrement,* a hundred-minute set of contemplative pieces that is perhaps the most important work written for organ since Bach.

Arvo Pärt
1935–

The first Estonian to reach international status in music began composing along accepted Soviet lines, moved to an almost defiant attempt at Soviet-disapproved serial methods, and then progressed to experimentation with collage techniques. Finally, after a long period of silence in which he studied Gregorian chant, Renaissance music, and the liturgy of the Russian Orthodox Church, Pärt reappeared with the highly individual style that has since won him a host of devout listeners. Tabula rasa *was the name he gave one of his pivotal works: it was as if he had wiped the slate clean and started again with new musical techniques, a new sensitivity to instruments, and, most importantly, a new and luminous spirituality. Much of his music is written for voice, but the best introduction to his art is, I think, through the instrumental works, most of them only ten minutes or less in duration.*

Cantus in memory of Benjamin Britten (1976)

This very moving piece was written when Pärt heard of the death of the English composer, whom he had only recently come to admire—for "the unusual purity of his music"—and whom, he now realized, he would never be able to meet. Written for string orchestra and a tolling bell, it lasts only six minutes and consists entirely of repetitions of a descending A Minor scale. But, as in another marvelous short piece, *Festina Lente*, the "theme" is played simultaneously at three different speeds. This most respectful of requiems crescendos gently until the bell seems to speak with its own voice. (Pärt called his instrumental works of the 1970s and 1980s "tintinnabuli," and explained, "I work with very few elements—with one voice, with two voices. I build with primitive materials—with the triad, with one specific tonality. The three notes of a triad are like bells. And that is why I call [my method] tintinnabulation.")

As with some of the greatest art, the overwhelming effect of the *Cantus* is out of all proportion to the simple means used. Pärt's music might at first be thought similar in nature to the minimalism of Philip Glass (whom operagoers will know from *Einstein on the Beach*, *Satyagraha*, and *Akhnaten*) or John Adams (the composer of *Nixon in China*). But, in fact, Pärt's music is *sui generis*. There is no striving for effect; in fact, there is virtually no striving at all. A prayerful, peaceful, monumental stasis is what Pärt aims for and, in this luminous piece, quietly reaches.

Recording

Studt, Bournmouth Sinfonietta (EMI)

You may also want to hear…

…the cloister-like, eleven-minute theme-and-variations movement called *Fratres*, best heard in its 1980 version for violin and piano, where the penultimate variation becomes a veritable "dark night of the soul"; the six-minute *Summa*, originally a vocal setting of the Christian Creed, best heard in its 1978 reworking for string orchestra; the extraordinary six-minute *Festina Lente* for string orchestra and harp; and the famous but difficult twenty-five-minute *Tabula Rasa*, a double concerto for two violins and string orchestra that also features a piano specially adapted to give the impression of bells. Note the Latin names given all of these quasi-liturgical pieces.

It is also worth noting that, at the end of the twentieth century and the beginning of the new millennium, as popular music worldwide sank further and further into commercial ruts, classical composers turned in increasing numbers to spiritual and often specifically religious subjects for inspiration. Witness, in addition to Arvo Pärt, the work of Krzsztof Penderecki, Einojuhani Rautavaara, Alfred Schnittke, Peter Maxwell Davies, John Tavener, Jonathan Harvey, James MacMillan, Steve Reich, and Wolfgang Rihm. Witness also the unexpected popularity on records of Gregorian chant, of the liturgical and paraliturgical pieces of the abbess Hildegard of Bingen, of the "Symphony of Sorrowful Songs" by Henryk Gorecki, and especially of the all-but-Franciscan raptures of Olivier Messiaen.

Glossary

These are basic terms not always explained at every recurrence in the text of this book.

accelerando (It.) a tempo designation meaning "with increasing quickness"; a movement in that tempo.

adagietto (It.) an adagio (slow) movement that is shorter than the typical adagio.

adagio (It.) a tempo designation meaning "slow"; a movement in that tempo.

allegretto (It.) a tempo designation meaning "rather fast"; a movement in that tempo.

allegro (It.) a tempo designation meaning "fast"; a movement in that tempo.

andante (It.) a tempo designation meaning "at a walking pace"; a movement in that tempo.

atonal music post-Romantic music with no fixed key center; see "twelve-tone music."

ballade a single-movement orchestral or keyboard composition that is often inspired by a literary source and may attempt to tell its story.

Baroque music	music composed in Europe in the seventeenth to mid-eighteenth centuries.
cadenza	(It.) a passage near the end of a concerto movement that provides an opportunity for the soloist to demonstrate, unaccompanied, his or her virtuosity; it may be improvised by the soloist or written out in full by the composer or the soloist.
canon	a composition in which a tune is introduced and then followed by one or more overlapping statements of itself, as in "Row, Row, Row Your Boat."
capriccio	(It.) a single-movement orchestral or keyboard composition in quick tempo, usually playful.
chaconne	(Fr.) a series of variations over a repeated bass melody, usually in the major; originally a Spanish dance in slow tempo (compare "passacaglia").
chamber music	music written for small combinations of instruments in semi-private performances, but often as extensive and important as that written for full symphony orchestra.
chorale	in instrumental music, a hymn-like passage.
Classical era	the period that followed the Baroque era, extending roughly from the mid-eighteenth century to the nineteenth-century "Eroica" symphony of Beethoven.
clavier	(Fr.) the generic term for a stringed keyboard instrument of Bach's day. Music originally

	written for clavier is most often played today on the piano, occasionally on the harpsichord.
coda	(It.) a musical "tail," the concluding section, usually brief, of a movement that is already virtually completed.
concertante	(It.) a composition for orchestra using two or more solo instruments.
concerto	(It.) a musical composition, usually in three movements, in which a soloist plays with a large orchestra.
concerto grosso	(It.) the concerto as it existed in the seventeenth century, consisting of several movements in which solo instruments played with a small orchestra.
counterpoint	music in which two or more melodies are heard simultaneously, often without underlying chords.
crescendo	(It.) gradual intensification of volume.
cyclic form	a musical structure in which one or more themes recur from movement to movement throughout the entire work; sometimes in cyclic form a single theme is the germ for all the main themes.
decrescendo	(It.) gradual diminishing of volume.
development section	the middle section of a movement in sonata form, in which themes already stated in the "exposition" are reshaped, opposed, sent through various tonalities, and poised to return in the "recapitulation."

double concerto	a concerto for two soloists and orchestra.
etude	an exercise or "study" by which a musical technique can gradually be acquired; Chopin and others wrote etudes that were also impressive concert pieces.
exposition	the first main section of a movement in sonata form, in which two or more themes are stated. Subsequently the themes are treated in a "development section" and then restated in a "recapitulation."
fantasia	(It.) a musical composition in free form.
finale	(It.) the last movement of a work with several movements.
forte	(It.) loud; *fortissimo*, very loud.
fugato	(It.) in the style of a fugue.
fugue	a composition in which a theme "flees" before two or more other themes, some of them derived from it, until there are three or four continuous lines of "flight" sounding at once.
glissando	(It.) a "sliding," usually up or down the keys of a piano or the strings of a harp.
impressionism	a late nineteenth-century musical style, using hitherto disapproved harmonies, inspired by French impressionist painting and symbolist poetry.
impromptu	(Fr.) a short piece, usually for piano, that gives the impression of being improvised.

intermezzo	(It.) an orchestral interlude played between the scenes of a stage work; a short piece for piano.
key	one of twenty-four options on the Western scale that serves as the center or home base for a piece of music. See "major" and "minor."
ländler	(Ger.) an Austrian country dance in slow three-quarter time.
largo	(It.) tempo designation for "very slow"; a movement written in that tempo.
legato	(It.) a style of playing in which the notes of a melody are "connected" rather than played staccato ("disconnected").
leitmotif	(Ger.) a short recurrent musical theme or fragment, often representing a person or idea; the term is most properly applied to Wagner's work, but is often applicable to the music of subsequent composers.
lento	(It.) tempo designation for "rather slow."
major	the basic tonality, derived from a scale (C to C′ on a piano keyboard) that usually expresses a "happy" mood. See "minor."
mazurka	a national dance of Poland, usually with a strong accent on the second beat.
minor	the alternative tonality to "major," derived from a scale that flattens the third and sixth notes of the major scale and often seems to express a "cold" or "sad" mood.

minuet	a courtly dance in three-quarter time that became the usual third movement in sonata-form compositions until it was replaced, in the Romantic era, by a scherzo.
moderato	(It.) a tempo designation for "moderately paced."
motto theme	a theme that, in music of the Romantic era, pervades a composition, often from movement to movement, in various guises. Berlioz called his motto theme an *idée fixe* (obsession).
movement	a complete, self-contained part of a larger musical work.
nocturne	a "night piece," a slow, often melancholy composition favored by Romantic composers.
opus	(Lat.) a musical work; the number given it to indicate what position it holds, chronologically, in a composer's output.
ostinato	(It.) a rhythmic pattern that repeats itself obstinately, often as a bass part for upper parts that change.
overture	an orchestral piece that introduces a work for the musical stage or a suite of musical numbers; sometimes a freestanding composition that is dramatic in nature.
partita	(It.) a series of dance movements, usually for keyboard instrument.
passacaglia	(It.) a series of variations over a repeated bass melody, usually in a minor key; originally

	a Spanish dance in slow tempo (compare "chaconne").
pavane	(Fr.) a stately dance in four-quarter time.
pentatonic music	music based on a scale composed of only five notes (for example, the five black keys on the piano).
piano	(It.) softly; *pianissimo*, very softly. (The instrument we call the piano is more properly the pianoforte, so named because its hammer mechanism enabled the performer to play both softly and loudly.)
pizzicato	(It.) the musical effect that results from the strings being "plucked" with the fingers, rather than bowed.
polonaise	(Fr.) a Polish march-past, strongly accented and, with Chopin, nationalistic in spirit.
polyphony	music in which in two or more independent lines of melody play simultaneously.
prelude	an introduction to a work for the musical stage, more concentrated than an overture; less often, a short piece for keyboard instrument.
presto	(It.) tempo designation for "very fast."
program music	music that has a descriptive or narrative purpose over and above its thematic development.
rallentando	(It.) a tempo designation meaning "with increasing slowness."

recapitulation	the final section of a movement in sonata form, in which the themes stated and developed earlier are restated in the movement's original tonality, with the stresses and discords resolved.
rhapsody	an exuberant one-movement work for orchestra or piano, often nationalistic in character.
ritornello	(It.) in the earliest concertos, the opening section of an orchestral movement that "returns" periodically between sections performed with the soloist.
Romantic era	the period in nineteenth and early twentieth-century music that extends roughly from Beethoven's "Eroica" Symphony to the Ninth Symphony of Mahler.
rondo	(It.) a lively movement, often the last movement in a work in sonata form, that follows the form ABACABA.
scherzo	(It.) the brisk "joking" movement that replaced the minuet as the third movement in sonata-form compositions in the Romantic era; *scherzando*, jokingly.
serial music	see "twelve-tone music."
siciliana	a Sicilian country dance in slow six-eight time.
sonata	(It.) a composition in three or four movements for one or two instruments.
sonata form	the structure most often used in the first and sometimes in other movements of

symphonies, sonatas, concertos, and chamber music from the eighteenth century to the present. See "exposition," "development section," and "recapitulation."

staccato   (It.) a style of playing in which the notes of a melody are "disconnected" with each other rather than played legato ("connected").

subject   a theme or group of themes in a sonata-form movement.

suite   in the Baroque period, a succession of musical pieces, usually dances; later, instrumental excerpts from an opera or ballet score played in succession.

symphony   a large-scale composition for orchestra, usually in four contrasting movements that make a unified musical statement; in the Romantic era it was widely considered the most exalted of all musical forms.

tempo   (It.) the rate of speed at which music is played, ranging from "presto" to "largo."

theme   a melody or melodic fragment that becomes the subject of extensive treatment in a musical structure.

theme and variations   a musical form in which a fully developed theme is subjected to four or more successive variations in melodic outline, harmony, or rhythm while still maintaining its basic structure; one of the most often used musical structures from the Baroque era to twentieth-century jazz.

toccata   (It.) a keyboard piece characterized by rapid finger work (from the Italian for "touched").

tonality   the dominant key (or key relationship) of a section of music.

tremolo   (It.) the rapid reiteration ("trembling") of a chord for dramatic effect.

trio   a composition for three instruments; the middle section of a minuet or scherzo movement.

triplet   a group of three notes to be played quickly, in the time two ordinary notes would take.

twelve-tone music the twentieth-century system of musical composition (also known as serial music) in which all twelve tones of the scale are treated as of equal importance and used in a predetermined sequence or "row"; now largely fallen into disuse.

vivace   (It.) a tempo designation for "lively."

whole-tone scale a scale, favored by Debussy, that consists exclusively of whole tones; for example, C, D, E, F♯, G♯, A♯, C′.

CD Track Listing

CD 1

1–4. BEETHOVEN, Symphony No. 5 (35:45)
Béla Drahos, conductor, Nicolaus Esterházy Sinfonia
From Naxos 8.553476

5. MOZART, Piano Concerto No. 17 in G, first movement (11:23)
Mátyás Antal, conductor, Concentus Hungaricus
Jenö Jandó, piano
From Naxos 8.550205

6. SCHUBERT, Quintet in C, second movement (15:00)
Ensemble Villa Musica
From Naxos 8550388

CD 2

1. VIVALDI, "Spring" from *The Four Seasons* (3:33)
Stephen Gunzenhauser, conductor, Capella Istropolitana
Takako Nishizaki, violin
From Naxos 8.553219

2. BACH, Toccata and Fugue in D Minor (10:08)
Wolfgang Rubsam, organ
From Naxos 8.550184

3. HANDEL, "Allegro" from *Water Music,* Suite 1, No. 3 (2:15)
Andrew Mogrelia, conductor, Prague Chamber Soloists
From Naxos/Amadis 7118

4. BRAHMS, Symphony No. 4 in E Minor, second movement (12:27)
    Alexander Rahbari, conductor, Belgian Radio and Television Philharmonic
    Orchestra
    From Naxos 8.550281

5. CHOPIN, Etude Op. 10, No. 12 in C Minor ("Revolutionary")
    (2:27)
    István Székely, piano
    From Naxos/Amadis 7064

6. DVORAK, Symphony No. 9 ("From the New World"), fourth
    movement (11:01)
    Stephen Gunzenhauser, conductor, Slovak Philharmonic Orchestra
    From Naxos 8.553229

7. MAHLER, "Adagietto" from Symphony No. 5 (12:05)
    Antoni Wit, conductor, Polish National Radio Symphony Orchestra
    From Naxos 8.550528

8. DEBUSSY, "La fille aux cheveux du lin," *Préludes,* Book 1, No. 8
    (2:13)
    François-Joel Thiollier, piano
    From Naxos 8.555800

9. RACHMANINOFF, Piano Concerto No. 2, first movement (11:06)
    György Lehel, conductor, Budapest Symphony Orchestra
    Jenö Jandó, piano
    From Naxos 8.550117

10. HOLST, "Jupiter, the Bringer of Jollity" from *The Planets* (7:58)
    David Lloyd-Jones, conductor, Royal Scottish National Orchestra
    From Naxos 8.555776